I0435197

2013 ANNUAL REPORT OF
THE BOARDS OF TRUSTEES OF THE
FEDERAL HOSPITAL INSURANCE AND
FEDERAL SUPPLEMENTARY MEDICAL INSURANCE
TRUST FUNDS

COMMUNICATION

From

THE BOARDS OF TRUSTEES,
FEDERAL HOSPITAL INSURANCE AND
FEDERAL SUPPLEMENTARY MEDICAL INSURANCE
TRUST FUNDS

Transmitting

THE 2013 ANNUAL REPORT OF
THE BOARDS OF TRUSTEES OF THE
FEDERAL HOSPITAL INSURANCE AND
FEDERAL SUPPLEMENTARY MEDICAL INSURANCE
TRUST FUNDS

LETTER OF TRANSMITTAL

BOARDS OF TRUSTEES OF THE
FEDERAL HOSPITAL INSURANCE AND
FEDERAL SUPPLEMENTARY MEDICAL INSURANCE TRUST FUNDS,
Washington, D.C., May 31, 2013

HONORABLE JOHN A. BOEHNER,
Speaker of the House of Representatives

HONORABLE JOSEPH R. BIDEN, JR.,
President of the Senate

GENTLEMEN:

We have the honor of transmitting to you the 2013 Annual Report of the Boards of Trustees of the Federal Hospital Insurance Trust Fund and the Federal Supplementary Medical Insurance Trust Fund, the 48th such report.

Respectfully,

/S/
JACOB J. LEW,
Secretary of the Treasury,
and Managing Trustee of the Trust Funds.

/S/
SETH D. HARRIS,
Acting Secretary of Labor, and Trustee.

/S/
KATHLEEN SEBELIUS,
Secretary of Health and Human Services,
and Trustee.

/S/
CAROLYN W. COLVIN,
Acting Commissioner of Social Security,
and Trustee.

/S/
CHARLES P. BLAHOUS III,
Trustee.

/S/
ROBERT D. REISCHAUER,
Trustee.

/S/
MARILYN B. TAVENNER,
Administrator,
Centers for Medicare & Medicaid Services,
and Secretary, Boards of Trustees.

CONTENTS

I. INTRODUCTION

The Medicare program has two components. Hospital Insurance (HI), otherwise known as Medicare Part A, helps pay for hospital, home health following hospital stays, skilled nursing facility, and hospice care for the aged and disabled. Supplementary Medical Insurance (SMI) consists of Medicare Part B and Part D. Part B helps pay for physician, outpatient hospital, home health, and other services for the aged and disabled who have voluntarily enrolled. Part D provides subsidized access to drug insurance coverage on a voluntary basis for all beneficiaries and premium and cost-sharing subsidies for low-income enrollees. Medicare also has a Part C, which serves as an alternative to traditional Part A and Part B coverage. Under this option, beneficiaries can choose to enroll in and receive care from private "Medicare Advantage" and certain other health insurance plans. Medicare Advantage and Program of All-Inclusive Care for the Elderly (PACE) plans receive prospective, capitated payments for such beneficiaries from the HI and SMI Part B trust fund accounts; the other plans are paid on the basis of their costs.

The Social Security Act established the Medicare Board of Trustees to oversee the financial operations of the HI and SMI trust funds.[1] The Board has six members. Four members serve by virtue of their positions in the Federal Government: the Secretary of the Treasury, who is the Managing Trustee; the Secretary of Labor; the Secretary of Health and Human Services; and the Commissioner of Social Security. Two other members are public representatives whom the President appoints and the Senate confirms. Charles P. Blahous III and Robert D. Reischauer began serving on September 17, 2010. The Administrator of the Centers for Medicare & Medicaid Services (CMS) serves as Secretary of the Board.

The Social Security Act requires that the Board, among other duties, report annually to the Congress on the financial and actuarial status of the HI and SMI trust funds. The 2013 report is the 48th that the Board has submitted.

The projections in this report, with one additional specification, are based on current law; that is, they assume that laws on the books will be implemented and adhered to with respect to scheduled taxes, premium revenues, and payments to providers and health plans. The additional specification is that the projections disregard payment

---

[1]The Social Security Act established separate boards for HI and SMI. Both boards have the same membership, so for convenience they are collectively referred to as the Medicare Board of Trustees in this report.

1

reductions that would result from the projected depletion of the Medicare Hospital Insurance trust fund. Under current law, payments would be reduced to levels that could be covered by incoming tax and premium revenues when the HI trust fund was depleted. If the projections reflected such payment reductions, then any imbalances between payments and revenues would be automatically eliminated, and the report would not serve its essential purpose, which is to inform policy makers and the public about the size of any trust fund deficits that would need to be resolved to avert program insolvency. To date, lawmakers have never allowed the assets of the Medicare HI trust fund to become depleted.

Projections of Medicare costs are highly uncertain, especially when looking out more than several decades. One reason for uncertainty is that scientific advances will make possible new interventions, procedures, and therapies. Some conditions that are untreatable today will be handled routinely in the future. Spurred by economic incentives, the institutions through which care is delivered will evolve, possibly becoming more efficient. While most health care technological advances to date have tended to increase expenditures, the health care landscape is shifting. No one knows whether these future developments will, on balance, increase or decrease costs.

The financial outlook for Medicare is also uncertain because some provisions of current law that are designed to reduce expenditures may be difficult to sustain. The clearest example of this issue is the sustainable growth rate (SGR) formula for physician fee schedule payment levels. The projections in this report assume that, as required by current law, CMS will implement a reduction in Medicare payment rates for physician services of almost 25 percent at the start of 2014. However, it is a virtual certainty that lawmakers, cognizant of the disruptive consequences of such a sudden, sharp reduction in payments, will override this reduction as they have every year since 2003.

The Patient Protection and Affordable Care Act, as amended by the Health Care and Education Reconciliation Act of 2010, introduced even larger policy changes and projection uncertainty. This legislation, referred to collectively as the "Affordable Care Act" or ACA, contains roughly 165 provisions affecting the Medicare program by reducing costs, increasing revenues, improving benefits, combating fraud and abuse, and initiating a major program of research and development to identify alternative provider payment mechanisms, health care delivery systems, and other changes intended to improve the quality of health care and reduce costs. The Board assumes that the various cost-reduction measures—the most important of which are the reductions in the annual payment rate updates for most categories of Medicare providers by the growth in economy-wide multifactor productivity—will occur as the Affordable Care Act requires. The Trustees believe that this outcome is achievable if health care providers are able to realize productivity improvements at a faster rate than experienced historically. However, if the health sector cannot transition to more efficient models of care delivery and achieve productivity increases commensurate with economy-wide productivity, and if the provider reimbursement rates paid by commercial insurers continue to follow the same negotiated process used to date, then the availability and quality of health care received by Medicare beneficiaries would, under current law, fall over time relative to that received by those with private health insurance.

Given these uncertainties, future Medicare costs could be substantially higher than shown in the Trustees' current-law projection. At a minimum, readers should not assume that the SGR-related payment rate reductions will take place. Figure I.1 illustrates how Medicare's costs would increase from the Trustees' current-law projections under two alternative scenarios.[2]

Figure I.1 shows the extent to which the current-law Medicare cost projections depend on the SGR reductions to physicians' payment rates and on the ACA-mandated reductions in other Medicare payment rates. The figure illustrates scenarios in which the scheduled SGR reductions are overridden so that physicians' payment rates increase at a 0.7-percent annual rate from 2014 through 2022, or roughly 1 percent more slowly than the Medicare Economic Index (MEI). This assumption reflects the average Medicare physician fee schedule payment update that occurred from 2004 through 2013, a period during which SGR reductions were consistently overridden by legislative action. From 2023 through 2037 (after the short-range valuation period has ended), the payment updates in this scenario are assumed to gradually rise so that Medicare expenditures per

---

[2]At the request of the Trustees, the Office of the Actuary at CMS has prepared these illustrative Medicare projections under hypothetical modifications to current law. A summary of the illustrative alternative projections is contained in appendix V.C of this report, and a more detailed discussion is available at http://www.cms.gov/Research-Statistics-Data-and-Systems/Statistics-Trends-and-Reports/ReportsTrustFunds/Downloads/2013TRAlternativeScenario.pdf. Readers should not infer any endorsement of the policies represented by the illustrative alternatives by the Trustees, CMS, or the Office of the Actuary. Appendix V.C also provides additional information on the uncertainties associated with the SGR provision and productivity adjustments to other provider payment updates.

beneficiary for physician services are increasing at the same rate as per capita national health expenditures by 2037.

Figure I.1.—Medicare Expenditures as a Percentage of the Gross Domestic Product under Current Law and Illustrative Alternative Projections

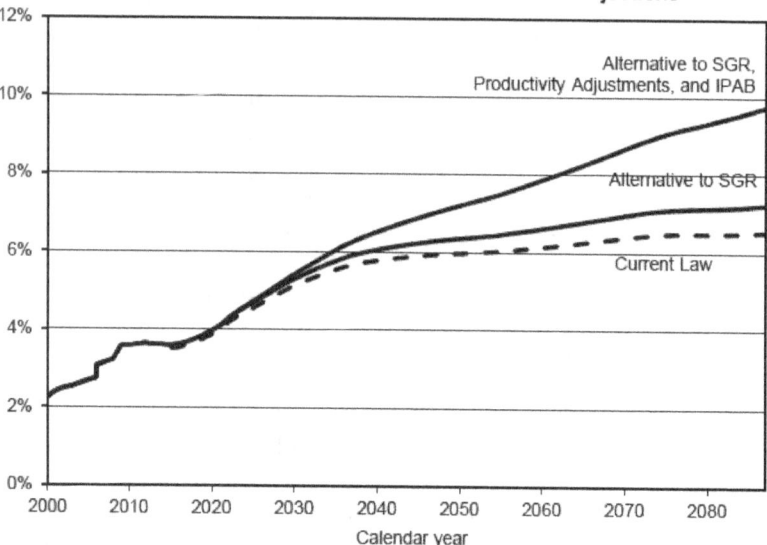

The full illustrative alternative shown in the top line in figure I.1 incorporates the aforementioned overrides of SGR physician payment rates, a partial phase-out of the ACA reductions in Medicare payment rates from 2020 through 2034, and an assumed legislative override of the cost-saving actions of the Independent Payment Advisory Board (IPAB). The middle line shows costs assuming only the overrides of the SGR physician payment rates, and the bottom line shows the current-law projections. The difference between the current-law projections and the alternative projections illustrates the potential financial consequences should these existing payment provisions not be implemented.[3]

As can be seen in figure I.1, Medicare's costs under the Trustees' current-law assumptions rise from their current level of 3.6 percent of GDP to 5.8 percent in 2040 and 6.5 percent in 2087. If the SGR restraint were overridden, as described above, projected Medicare costs would rise to 6.1 percent of GDP in 2040 and 7.2 percent in 2087. Under the full scenario, in which adherence to the ACA cost-saving measures also erodes, projected costs would rise to 6.5 percent of GDP in 2040 and 9.8 percent in 2087.

As the preceding discussion explains, and as the substantial differences between the Trustees' current-law projections and those for the alternative scenarios illustrate, Medicare's actual future costs are highly uncertain and are likely to exceed those shown by the current-law projections in this report. Therefore, the Board recommends that readers interpret the current-law projections as an illustration of the very favorable financial outcomes that would be experienced if the physician fee reductions were implemented and if the productivity adjustments and IPAB measures in the Affordable Care Act could be sustained in the long range. Readers are also strongly encouraged to review appendix V.C for further information on this important subject. Where possible, the Trustees illustrate the potential understatement of Medicare costs and other projection results by reference to these alternative projections.

---

[3]Under the ACA, Medicare's annual payment rate updates for most categories of providers would be reduced below the increase in providers' input prices by the growth in economy-wide multifactor productivity (1.1 percent over the long range). In addition, the IPAB would be charged with recommending cost savings as are necessary to hold overall per capita Medicare growth to the average of the CPI and CPI-medical increases in 2015-2019 and to the rate of per capita GDP growth plus 1 percentage point thereafter (subject to certain limits). Unless overridden by lawmakers, these recommendations would be automatically implemented. After 2036, this illustrative projection assumes that Medicare payment updates will be set at the increase in providers' input prices minus a productivity adjustment of 0.4 percent per year so that they equal the growth rates assumed by the Trustees for the private sector; this increase reflects an assumption of health sector productivity growth that is consistent with the recommendations by the 2010-2011 Medicare Technical Review Panel.

II. OVERVIEW

A. HIGHLIGHTS

The major findings of this report under the intermediate set of assumptions appear below. The balance of the "Overview" and the following "Actuarial Analysis" section describe these findings in more detail.

In 2012

In 2012, Medicare covered 50.7 million people: 42.1 million aged 65 and older, and 8.5 million disabled. About 27 percent of these beneficiaries have chosen to enroll in Part C private health plans that contract with Medicare to provide Part A and Part B health services. Total expenditures in 2012 were $574.2 billion. Total income was $536.9 billion, which consisted of $523.5 billion in non-interest income and $13.4 billion in interest earnings. Assets held in special issue U.S. Treasury securities decreased by $37.3 billion to $287.6 billion.

Short-Range Results

The estimated depletion date for the HI trust fund is 2026, 2 years later than was shown in last year's report. As in past years, the Trustees have determined that the fund is not adequately financed over the next 10 years. HI taxable earnings in 2012 were slightly lower than last year's estimate. The projected rate of growth in these earnings is lower in 2013 and 2014 but then exceeds last year's growth assumptions after 2014. HI expenditures in 2012 were slightly lower than the previous estimate, but after 2014, the projected level grows more rapidly than shown in last year's report because of assumed higher payment updates.

HI expenditures have exceeded income annually since 2008, and projected amounts continue doing so through 2014. The Trustees then project slight surpluses in 2015 thorough 2020 with a return to deficits thereafter until the fund becomes depleted in 2026. In 2012, $23.8 billion in trust fund assets were redeemed to cover the shortfall of income relative to expenditures. The Treasury also paid from the general fund $10.8 billion in interest to the HI trust fund in 2012. The assets were $244.2 billion at the beginning of 2012, representing about 92 percent of expenditures during the year, which is below the Trustees' minimum recommended level of 100 percent. The HI trust fund has not met the Trustees' formal test of short-range financial adequacy since 2003 (as discussed in section III.B). Growth in HI expenditures has averaged 5.6 percent annually over the last 5 years and is projected to average 3.7 percent over the next 5 years.

The SMI trust fund is adequately financed over the next 10 years and beyond because premium and general revenue income for Parts B and D are reset each year to cover expected costs and ensure a reserve for Part B contingencies. Part B and Part D costs have both averaged 6.1 percent annual growth over the last 5 years, as compared to 2.3 percent growth for the U.S. economy. Under current law, the Trustees project an average annual Part B growth rate of 5.1 percent for the next 5 years. This rate is unrealistically constrained due to a physician fee reduction of almost 25 percent that is called for in 2014 under current law. If lawmakers override this reduction, as they have for 2003 through 2013, the Part B growth rate would instead average 6.3 percent. For Part D, the estimated average annual increase in expenditures is 9.3 percent over the next 5 years. The projected average annual rate of growth for the U.S. economy is 5.4 percent during this period, significantly slower than for Part D and the growth rate for Part B under the illustrative alternative scenarios.

The difference between Medicare's total outlays and its "dedicated financing sources" reaches an estimated 45 percent of outlays in fiscal year 2013, the first year of the projection. Based on this result, Federal law requires that the Trustees issue a determination of projected "excess general revenue Medicare funding" in this report. This is the eighth consecutive such finding, and it again triggers a statutory "Medicare funding warning" that Federal general revenues are becoming a substantial share of total financing for Medicare. The law directs the President to submit to Congress proposed legislation to respond to the warning within 15 days after the date of the Budget submission for the succeeding year.

Long-Range Results

For the 75-year projection period, the HI actuarial deficit has decreased from 1.35 percent of taxable payroll, as shown in last year's report, to 1.11 percent of taxable payroll. The more favorable outlook is primarily due to (i) lower projected spending for most HI service categories—especially for skilled nursing facilities—to reflect lower-than-expected spending in 2012 and other recent data; (ii) lower projected Medicare Advantage program costs that reflect recent data suggesting that certain provisions of the Affordable Care Act will reduce growth in these costs by more than was previously projected; and (iii) a refinement in projection methods that reduces assumed per beneficiary cost growth during the transition period between the short-range projections and the long-range projections. Partially offsetting these favorable changes to the projections are somewhat lower projected levels of tax income that reflect lower-than-expected tax income in 2012. (Under the full illustrative alternative projections, the HI actuarial deficit would be 2.17 percent of taxable payroll, compared to 2.43 percent in last year's report.)

Part B outlays were 1.5 percent of GDP in 2012, and the Board projects that they will grow to about 2.6 percent by 2087. These outlay projections are slightly higher than those in last year's report mostly due to an administrative action[4] that increased Medicare Advantage rates beginning in 2014 to reflect assumed future legislative overrides of the physician payment reductions. (Under the full illustrative alternative projections, Part B costs would be 4.3 percent of GDP in 2087.)

The Board estimates that Part D outlays will increase from 0.4 percent of GDP in 2012 to about 1.4 percent by 2087. These outlay projections are slightly lower than those shown in last year's report primarily because the expirations of the patents for several major drugs in 2012 had a greater impact than was expected last year, and the projected trend for 2013 is lower than last year.

Transfers from the general fund are the major source of financing for the SMI trust fund and are central to the automatic financial balance of the fund's two accounts. Such transfers represent a large and growing requirement for the Federal budget. SMI general revenues currently equal 1.4 percent of GDP and would increase to an estimated 2.9 percent in 2087 under current law.

Conclusion

Total Medicare expenditures were $574 billion in 2012. The Board projects that, under current law, expenditures will increase in future years at a somewhat faster pace than either aggregate workers' earnings or the economy overall and that, as a percentage of GDP, they will increase from 3.6 percent in 2012 to 6.5 percent by 2087 (based on the Trustees' intermediate set of assumptions). If lawmakers continue to override the statutory decreases in physician fees, and if the reduced price increases for other health services under Medicare are not sustained and do not take full effect in the long range, then Medicare spending would instead represent roughly

---

[4]Additional information is available at http://www.cms.gov/Medicare/Health-Plans/MedicareAdvtgSpecRateStats/Downloads/Announcement2014.pdf.

9.8 percent of GDP in 2087. Growth of this magnitude, if realized, would substantially increase the strain on the nation's workers, the economy, Medicare beneficiaries, and the Federal budget.

The Trustees project that HI tax income and other dedicated revenues will fall short of HI expenditures in most future years under current law. The HI trust fund does not meet either the Trustees' test of short-range financial adequacy or their test of long-range close actuarial balance.

The Part B and Part D accounts in the SMI trust fund are adequately financed under current law because premium and general revenue income are reset each year to cover expected costs. Such financing, however, would have to increase faster than the economy to cover expected expenditure growth under current law.

The financial projections in this report indicate a need for additional steps to address Medicare's remaining financial challenges. Consideration of further reforms should occur in the near future. The sooner solutions are enacted, the more flexible and gradual they can be. Moreover, the early introduction of reforms increases the time available for affected individuals and organizations—including health care providers, beneficiaries, and taxpayers—to adjust their expectations. Congress and the executive branch must work closely together with a sense of urgency to address the depletion of the HI trust fund and the projected growth in HI (Part A) and SMI (Parts B and D) expenditures.

B. MEDICARE DATA FOR CALENDAR YEAR 2012

HI and SMI have separate trust funds, sources of revenue, and categories of expenditures. Table II.B1 presents Medicare data for calendar year 2012, in total and for each part of the program. The largest category of HI expenditures is inpatient hospital services, while the largest SMI expenditure categories are physician services and prescription drugs. Payments to private health plans for providing Part A and Part B services currently represent slightly more than one-fourth of total A and B benefit outlays.

Table II.B1.—Medicare Data for Calendar Year 2012

		SMI		
	HI or Part A	Part B	Part D	Total
Assets at end of 2011 (billions)	$244.2	$79.7	$1.0	$324.9
Total income	$243.0	$227.0	$66 9	$536.9
Payroll taxes	205.7	—	—	205.7
Interest	10.6	2.8	0 0	13.4
Taxation of benefits	18.6	—	—	18.6
Premiums	3.4	58.0	8 3	69.8
General revenue	0.5	163.8	50.1	214.4
Transfers from States	—	—	8.4	8.4
Other	4.1	2.4	—	6.5
Total expenditures	$266.8	$240.5	$66 9	$574.2
Benefits	262.9	236.5	66.5	565.9
Hospital	139.7	39.1	—	178.8
Skilled nursing facility	28.0	—	—	28.0
Home health care	6.8	11.8	—	18.6
Physician fee schedule services	—	69.6	—	69.6
Private health plans (Part C)	70.2	66.0	—	136.2
Prescription drugs	—	—	66.5	66.5
Other	18.1	50.1	—	68.2
Administrative expenses	$3.9	$3.9	$0.4	$8.3
Net change in assets	−$23.8	−$13.5	$0.0	−$37.3
Assets at end of 2012	$220.4	$66.2	$1.0	$287.6
Enrollment (millions)				
Aged	41.8	38.7	n/a	42.1
Disabled	8.5	7.7	n/a	8.5
Total	50.3	46.4	37.4	50.7
Average benefit per enrollee	$5,227	$5,097	$1,779	$12,103

Notes: 1. Totals do not necessarily equal the sums of rounded components.
2. "n/a" indicates data are not available.

For HI, the primary source of financing is the payroll tax on covered earnings. Employers and employees each pay 1.45 percent of wages, while self-employed workers pay 2.9 percent of their net earnings. Starting in 2013, high-income workers pay an additional 0.9 percent tax on their earnings above an unindexed threshold ($200,000 for single taxpayers and $250,000 for married couples). Other HI revenue sources include a portion of the Federal income taxes that Social Security recipients with incomes above certain thresholds pay on their benefits, as well as interest paid on the U.S. Treasury securities held in the HI trust fund.

For SMI, transfers from the general fund of the Treasury represent the largest source of income and currently cover about 70 percent of program costs.[5] Also, beneficiaries pay monthly premiums for Parts B and D that finance a portion of the total cost. As with HI, the U.S. Treasury securities held in the SMI trust fund earn interest.

---

[5]At the end of 2011, Part B account assets were above the adequate level. Therefore, the 2012 Part B financing was set to intentionally draw down some of the excess Part B account assets.

C. ECONOMIC AND DEMOGRAPHIC ASSUMPTIONS

1. General Discussion

Future Medicare expenditures will depend on a number of factors, including the size and composition of the population eligible for benefits, changes in the volume and intensity of services, and increases in the price per service. Future HI trust fund income will depend on the size of the covered work force and the level of workers' earnings, and future SMI trust fund income will depend on projected program costs. These factors will depend in turn upon future birth rates, death rates, labor force participation rates, wage increases, and many other economic and demographic circumstances affecting Medicare. To illustrate the uncertainty and sensitivity inherent in estimates of future Medicare trust fund operations under current law, the Board has prepared projections under a "low-cost" and a "high-cost" set of economic and demographic assumptions as well as under an intermediate set.

Table II.C1 summarizes the key assumptions used in this report. Many of the demographic and economic variables that determine Medicare costs and income are common to the Old-Age, Survivors, and Disability Insurance (OASDI) program, and the OASDI annual report explains these variables in detail. These variables include changes in the Consumer Price Index (CPI) and wages, real interest rates, fertility rates, mortality rates, and net immigration levels. ("Real" indicates that the effects of inflation have been removed.) The assumptions vary, in most cases, from year to year during the first 5 to 30 years before reaching their "ultimate" values for the remainder of the 75-year projection period. With the exception of the immigration assumption, the ultimate assumptions are unchanged from last year.

The Trustees expect the gap between actual and full-employment GDP to narrow so that actual GDP rises from 94 percent of full-employment GDP in 2012 to 98 percent in 2016 and 100 percent in 2020. In last year's report, projected real GDP growth was more rapid, and the economy reached full employment in 2019. This revision in the economic outlook contributes to a worsening of Medicare's short-range projected finances. The OASDI report describes the assumed impact of the 2008-2009 recession on the key economic factors in more detail.

Other assumptions are specific to Medicare. As with all of the assumptions underlying the financial projections, the Trustees review the Medicare-specific assumptions annually and update them based on the latest available data and analysis of trends. In addition, the assumptions and projection methodology are subject to periodic review by independent panels of expert actuaries and economists. The most recent review occurred with the 2010-2011 Technical Review Panel on the Medicare Trustees Report.[6]

Table II.C1.—Ultimate Assumptions

	Intermediate	Low-Cost	High-Cost
Economic:			
Annual percentage change in:			
Gross Domestic Product (GDP) per capita[1]	4.1	3 9	4 2
Average wage in covered employment	3.9	3 5	4 3
Private non-farm business multifactor productivity	1.1	1 3	0 9
Consumer Price Index (CPI)	2.8	1 8	3 8
Real-wage differential (percent)	1.1	1.7	0 5
Real interest rate (percent)	2.9	3.4	2.4
Demographic:			
Total fertility rate (children per woman)	2.00	2.30	1.70
Average annual percentage reduction in total			
age-sex adjusted death rates from 2037 to 2087	0.73	0.41	1.05
Net annual immigra ion:			
Legal	787,500	1,000,000	595,000
Other	273,000	354,000	206,000
Health cost growth:			
Annual percentage change in per beneficiary			
Medicare expenditures (excluding demographic			
impacts)[1]			
HI (Part A)	4.3[2]	[3]	[3]
SMI Part B	4.1[2]	[3]	[3]
SMI Part D	5.1[2]	[3]	[3]
Total Medicare	4.3[2]	[3]	[3]

[1]The assumed ultimate increases in per capita GDP and per beneficiary Medicare expenditures can also be expressed in real terms, adjusted to remove the impact of assumed inflation. When adjusted by the chain-weighted GDP price index, assumed real per capita GDP growth is 1.7 percent, and real per beneficiary Medicare cost growth is 1.9 percent, 1.7 percent, and 2.6 percent for Parts A, B, and D, respectively.
[2]Cost growth assumptions in the last 50 years of the projection vary year by year and follow a path determined by the "factors contributing to grow h" model. See text for the basis of these assumptions.
[3]See section III.B for further explanation.

2. Health Care Growth Assumptions

The assumed long-range rate of growth in annual Medicare expenditures per beneficiary is one of the most critical determinants of the projected cost of Medicare-covered health care services in the more distant future. Starting with the 2001 Medicare Trustees Report, the assumed average increase in expenditures per beneficiary for the 25th through 75th years of the projection has been based in whole or in part on the growth in per capita GDP plus 1 percentage

---

[6]The Panel's final report is available at http://aspe.hhs.gov/health/reports/2013/ MedicareTech/TechnicalPanelReport2010-2011.pdf.

point.[7] This assumption was recommended by the 2000 Medicare Technical Review Panel and confirmed as reasonable by the 2004 panel. Beginning with the 2006 report, the Trustees adopted a slight refinement of the long-range growth assumption that provided a more gradual transition from current health cost growth rates, which had been roughly 2 to 3 percentage points above the level of GDP growth, to the ultimate assumed level of GDP plus zero percent just after the 75th year and for the indefinite future.[8] Prior to its implementation, an independent group of experts in health economics and long-range forecasting reviewed the new methodology and advised that its use for this purpose was appropriate.

Following enactment of the Affordable Care Act, the long-range Medicare cost growth assumptions for the 2010 and 2011 Medicare Trustees Reports continued to use this same methodology to establish a pre-ACA "baseline" set of annual growth rates. The Trustees then reduced these growth rates for most categories of Medicare expenditures by the 10-year moving average increase in private, non-farm business multifactor productivity, as required under the ACA.[9]

In December 2011, the Technical Panel unanimously recommended a new approach that builds on the longstanding "GDP plus 1 percent" assumption while incorporating several key refinements.[10] Both the Office of the Actuary at CMS and the Board of Trustees supported these recommendations, and they formed the basis for the long-range cost growth assumptions used in the 2012 report. The methodology involves use of two separate means of establishing long-range growth rates:

- The first approach is a refinement to the traditional "GDP plus 1 percent" growth assumption, which better accounts for the magnitude of payment rate updates for Medicare (prior to the ACA) compared to private health insurance and other payers of health care. Under this approach, the rate of growth in Medicare

---

[7]This assumed increase in the expenditures per beneficiary excludes the impacts of the aging of the population and changes in the gender composition of the Medicare population, which are estimated and applied separately.

[8]The year-by-year growth assumptions were based on a simplified economic model and were determined in a way such that the 75-year actuarial balance for the HI trust fund was consistent with that generated by the constant "GDP plus 1 percent" assumption.

[9]"Multifactor productivity" is a measure of real output per combined unit of labor and capital, reflecting the contributions of all factors of production.

[10]For convenience, the assumed increase in Medicare expenditures per beneficiary, before consideration of demographic effects, is referred to as the "Medicare cost growth" and is often expressed in relation to the per capita increase in GDP, with the result characterized simply as "GDP plus X percent."

prices prior to the provisions of the ACA, which was assumed to be the same as the rate of private medical price growth in earlier reports, is now assumed to be 0.4 percent faster. This change results in the long-range pre-ACA "baseline" cost growth assumption being "GDP plus 1.4 percent," which equals 5.5 percent per year. One can also view this increase as a pre-ACA price update of about 3.6 percent and an increase in the volume and intensity of services per beneficiary of 1.9 percent.

- The second approach recommended by the Technical Panel is the "factors contributing to growth" model developed by the Office of the Actuary at CMS as a possible replacement for the existing process. This model also builds upon the key considerations used in establishing the earlier "GDP plus 1 percent" assumption, together with subsequent refinements in the analysis of growth factors, additional years of data on national health expenditures available since the 2000 Technical Panel's deliberations, and use of projected trends in these factors. The model is based on economic research that separates health spending growth into its major drivers—income growth, relative medical price inflation, insurance coverage, and a residual factor that primarily reflects the impact of technological development.[11]

Applied independently in the 2012 report, the "factors contributing to growth" model produces almost exactly the same long-range HI actuarial balance as did the constant "GDP plus 1.4 percent" assumption described above, after the impacts of the ACA are reflected in each case. The close similarity in results occurs principally because both approaches incorporate the more refined analysis of Medicare versus non-Medicare payment rate updates.

The Technical Panel did not specify a process for how to establish one set of growth rate assumptions from the two separate and independent techniques. For the 2012 report, the Trustees decided (i) to base the average ultimate growth rate on the updated "GDP plus 1.4 percent" baseline assumption and (ii) to use the "factors contributing to growth" model to create the specific, year-by-year declining growth rates during the last 50 years of the projection.

For this report, the Trustees have decided to use the factors model as the basis for determining the long-range Medicare cost growth assumption and to apply the "GDP plus" framework as a

---

[11]Smith, S., Newhouse, J., and Freeland, M., "Income, Insurance, and Technology: Why Does Health Spending Outpace Economic Growth?" *Health Affairs,* September/October 2009.

reasonableness check. The long-range Medicare cost growth assumptions under current law are established in three steps, as described in more detail in section IV.D. Based on the factors model, the Trustees (i) create specific, year-by-year declining national health expenditure (NHE) growth rates over the long-range period and derive the growth in the volume and intensity of NHE services; (ii) assume, consistent with Finding III-2 of the 2010-2011 Medicare Technical Review Panel's report, that the growth in the volume and intensity of Medicare services prior to the effects of the Affordable Care Act is identical to the growth in the volume and intensity of overall NHE services; and (iii) determine the Medicare payment rate updates required by the Affordable Care Act and their estimated effects on increases in the volume and intensity of services. For Medicare services for which the Affordable Care Act permanently reduces the annual increases in Medicare payment rates by the increase in economy-wide productivity, the Trustees adjust the growth rates in the volume and intensity of services by −0.1 percent annually. This assumption is consistent with Recommendation III-2 of the 2010-2011 Medicare Technical Review Panel's report.

As with the 2010-2012 Medicare Trustees Reports, the different provisions for updating payment rates under current law require the development of separate long-range cost growth assumptions for four categories of health care providers:

(i) *All HI, and some SMI Part B, services that are updated annually by provider input price increases less the increase in economy-wide productivity.*

HI services are inpatient hospital, skilled nursing facility, home health, and hospice. The primary Part B services affected are outpatient hospital, home health, and dialysis. The Trustees set the per beneficiary growth rate for these services equal to the sum of the statutory price update and the assumed growth in the volume and intensity of services per person. The first factor equals the market basket price increase (3.6 percent) minus the productivity adjustment (1.1 percent), for a statutory price update of 2.5 percent per year. The second factor equals the year-by-year increase in the volume and intensity assumption from the "factors contributing to growth" model less the ACA growth impact of 0.1 percent. Under the Trustees' intermediate economic assumptions, the resulting year-by-year increases for these provider services start at 4.5 percent in 2037, or "GDP plus 0.4 percent," declining gradually to 3.6 percent in 2087, or "GDP minus 0.5 percent." On average, the resulting ultimate cost growth rate for these provider services is 4.3 percent, or "GDP plus 0.2 percent," which is consistent with Recommendation III-4 of the 2010-2011 Medicare Technical Review Panel's report.

(ii) *Certain SMI Part B services that are updated annually by the CPI increase less the increase in productivity.*

Such services include durable medical equipment, laboratory tests, care at ambulatory surgical centers, ambulance services, and medical supplies. The Trustees set the per beneficiary growth rate equal to the sum of the statutory price update and the assumed growth in the volume and intensity of services per person. The first factor equals the CPI increase (2.8 percent) minus the productivity adjustment (1.1 percent), and the latter factor equals the increase in the volume and intensity assumption from the factors model less the ACA growth impact of 0.1 percent. The resulting year-by-year rates are 3.6 percent in 2037, or "GDP minus 0.5 percent," declining to 2.8 percent in 2087, or "GDP minus 1.3 percent." On average, the total assumed rate of growth for these services is 3.5 percent, which equates to "GDP minus 0.6 percent."

(iii) *Services payable under the physician fee schedule, as governed by the sustainable growth rate formula in current law.*

The Trustees assume that these per beneficiary expenditures will increase at approximately the rate of per capita GDP growth in every year (or 4.1 percent), consistent with the requirements of the SGR formula.

(iv) *All other Medicare services, for which payments are established based on market processes, such as prescription drugs provided through Part D and the remaining Part B services.*

These other Part B outlays constitute an estimated 11 percent of total Part B expenditures in 2022 and consist mostly of payments for physician-administered drugs and small facility services. Medicare payments to Part D plans are based on a competitive-bidding process and are not affected by the productivity adjustments. Similarly, payments for the other Part B services are based on market factors.[12] The long-range per beneficiary cost growth rate for Part D and these Part B services is assumed to equal the increase in per capita national

---

[12]For example, physician-administered Part B drugs are reimbursed at the level of the average sales price in the market plus 6 percent.

health expenditures as determined from the factors model. The corresponding year-by-year growth rates for these services are 5.3 percent in 2037, or "GDP plus 1.2 percent," declining to 4.4 percent by 2087, or "GDP plus 0.3 percent." On average, the rate of growth for these services is 5.1 percent, or "GDP plus 1 percent."

After combining the rates of growth from the four long-range assumptions, the weighted average growth rate for Part B is 4.1 percent per year for the last 50 years of the projection period, or "GDP plus 0 percent," on average. When Parts A, B, and D are combined, the weighted average growth rate for Medicare is 4.3 percent over this same period. Both rates are shown in table II.C1.

As in the past, the Trustees establish detailed growth rate assumptions for the initial 10 years (2013 through 2022) by individual type of service (for example, inpatient hospital care and physician services). These assumptions reflect recent trends and the impact of all provisions of the Affordable Care Act, Budget Control Act, and other applicable statutory provisions. For each of Parts A, B, and D, the assumed growth rates for years 11 through 25 of the projection period are set by interpolating between the rate at the end of the short-range projection period and the rate at the start of the last 50 years of the long-range period described above.

For the HI high-cost assumptions under current law, the assumed annual increase in the ratio of aggregate costs to taxable payroll (the cost rate) during the initial 25-year period is 2 percentage points greater than under the intermediate assumptions. Similarly, under the low-cost assumptions, the assumed annual rate of increase in the cost rate for the initial period is 2 percentage points less than under the current-law intermediate assumptions. After 25 years, the Trustees assume that the 2-percentage-point differentials will decline gradually to zero in 2062, after which the growth in cost rates is the same under all three sets of assumptions. The low-cost and high-cost projections shown in this report provide an indication of how Medicare expenditures could vary in the future under current law as a result of different economic and demographic trends.[13]

The basis for the Medicare cost growth rate assumptions, described above, has been chosen primarily to incorporate the productivity

---

[13]Due to the automatic financing provisions for Parts B and D, the Trustees expect that the SMI trust fund will be adequately financed in all future years and so have not conducted a long-range analysis using high-cost and low-cost assumptions.

adjustments and SGR provision in a relatively simple, straightforward manner and with the assumption that these elements of current law will operate in all future years as specified. The Trustees use this approach in part due to the uncertainty associated with these provisions and in part due to the difficulty of modeling such consequences as access to care, health status, and utilization if these provisions of current law do not operate satisfactorily. Purposely not considered at this time are the potential effects of sustained slower payment increases on provider participation, beneficiary access to care, quality of services, and other factors. Similarly, there has been no modeling of the possible effects of future changes in payment mechanisms, delivery systems, and other aspects of health care that could arise in response to the payment limitations and the ACA-directed research activities.[14]

In view of the possibility that these statutory provisions may not be sustained, the Technical Panel recommended continued presentation of projections based on illustrative alternatives to current law, in which average Medicare spending per beneficiary would increase faster than under current law. The Panel further recommended that a summary of the illustrative alternative projections be included in the annual report and that the discussion incorporate a chart showing both the potential impacts of further legislative overrides of the SGR formula and changes that would curtail the productivity adjustments to most other provider payment updates. The Trustees present this information in appendix V.C of this report.

Consistent with the practice in the 2010-2012 reports, the Trustees have asked the Office of the Actuary to develop the illustrative alternative projections. An actuarial memorandum on this subject is available on the CMS website.[15] For the short range, physician payment updates are assumed to be 0.7 percent annually, which is the average physician fee update legislated by Congress during 2004 through 2013. The 2010-2011 Medicare Technical Panel recommended that the physician payment update be based on the average physician payment increase for the last 10 years, calculated on a 10-year rolling average basis. For the long range, the illustrative alternative projection assumes that the economy-wide productivity

---

[14]The 2010-2011 Medicare Technical Review Panel considered these issues at some length. Their final report contains an extensive discussion of alternative long-term scenarios with different possible behavioral reactions by providers and with varying implications for the financial viability of providers and the availability and quality of health care services for beneficiaries.

[15]See http://www.cms.gov/Research-Statistics-Data-and-Systems/Statistics-Trends-and-Reports/ReportsTrustFunds/Downloads/2013TRAlternativeScenario.pdf.

adjustments would be gradually phased out during 2020 to 2034 and replaced with adjustments based on estimated health-specific provider productivity gains of 0.4 percent annually. Based on the factors model, the year-by-year long-range growth rate assumptions for HI and SMI Part B under the illustrative alternative projections are 5.3 percent in 2037, or "GDP plus 1.2 percent," declining to 4.4 percent by 2087, or "GDP plus 0.3 percent." (The average ultimate assumption equals the traditional "GDP + 1 percent" assumption for per capita national health expenditures, as described previously for Part D and other Medicare services for which price updates are based on market processes.) Readers should not infer any endorsement of this theoretical alternative to current law by the Trustees, CMS, or the Office of the Actuary.

While it is reasonable to expect that actual economic and demographic experience under current law will fall within the range defined by the three alternative sets of assumptions, there can be no assurances that it will do so in light of the wide variations in these factors over past decades. In general, readers can place a greater degree of confidence in the assumptions and estimates for the earlier years than for the later years. Nonetheless, even for the earlier years, the estimates are only an indication of the expected trends and the general ranges of future Medicare experience. In addition, as a result of the improbable reductions in physician payments required under the current-law SGR formula and the uncertain long-range adequacy of other payments affected by the statutory productivity adjustments, actual future Medicare expenditures are likely to exceed the intermediate projections shown in this report, possibly by quite large amounts. References to key results under the illustrative alternative projection demonstrate this potential understatement.

D. FINANCIAL OUTLOOK FOR THE MEDICARE PROGRAM

This report evaluates the financial status of the HI and SMI trust funds. For HI, the Trustees apply formal tests of financial status for both the short range and the long range; for SMI, the Trustees assess the ability of the trust fund to meet incurred costs over the period for which financing has been set.

HI and SMI are financed in very different ways. Within SMI, current law provides for the annual determination of Part B and Part D beneficiary premiums and general revenue financing to cover expected costs for the following year. In contrast, HI is subject to substantially greater variation in asset growth, since employee and employer tax rates under current law do not change or adjust to meet expenditures except through new legislation.

Despite the significant differences in benefit provisions and financing, the two components of Medicare are closely related. HI and SMI operate in an interdependent health care system. Most Medicare beneficiaries are enrolled in HI and SMI Parts B and D, and many receive services from all three. Accordingly, efforts to improve and reform either component must necessarily have repercussions for the other component. In view of the anticipated growth in Medicare expenditures, it is also important to consider the distribution among the various sources of revenues for financing Medicare and the manner in which this distribution will change over time under current law.

This section reviews the projected total expenditures for the Medicare program, along with the primary sources of financing. Figure II.D1 shows projected costs as a percentage of GDP. Medicare expenditures represented 3.6 percent of GDP in 2012. Under current law, costs would increase to about 5.6 percent of GDP by 2035, largely due to the rapid growth in the number of beneficiaries, and then to 6.5 percent of GDP in 2087, with growth in health care cost per beneficiary becoming the larger factor later in the valuation period. If the physician payment reductions are overridden and the other update constraints are modified as in the illustrative alternative projections, then Medicare expenditures would reach an estimated 9.8 percent of GDP in 2087.

**Figure II.D1.—Medicare Expenditures as a Percentage
of the Gross Domestic Product**

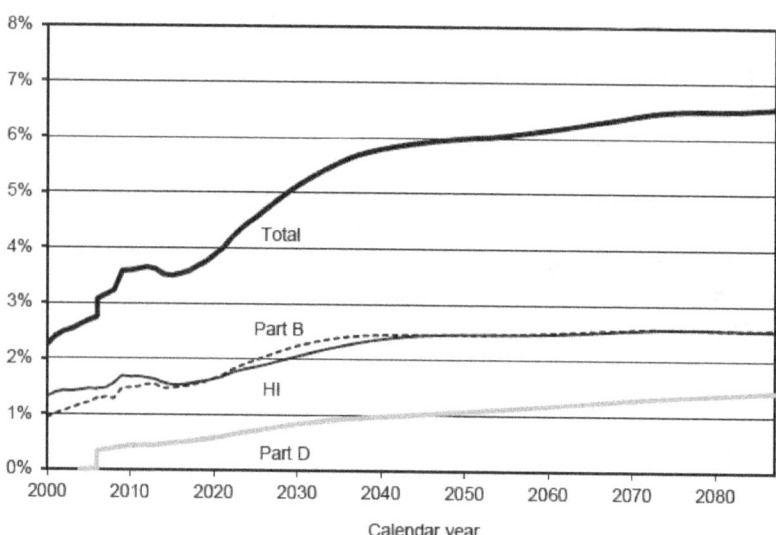

The Medicare projections reflect (i) continuing growth in the volume and intensity of services provided per beneficiary throughout the projection period; (ii) the impact of a large increase in beneficiaries, which started in 2011, as members of the 1946-1965 baby boom generation reach age 65 and become eligible to receive benefits (thereby increasing the annual growth in the number of beneficiaries from 2 percent to about 3 percent); and (iii) other key demographic trends, including future birth rates at roughly the same level as the last 2 decades and continuing improvements in life expectancy. The projections also reflect current law, which includes the Affordable Care Act, the Budget Control Act of 2011, and other applicable legislation. See appendix V.A.

Most beneficiaries have the option to enroll in private health insurance plans that contract with Medicare to provide Part A and Part B medical services. The share of Medicare beneficiaries in such plans has risen rapidly in recent years; it reached 26.8 percent in 2012 from 12.4 percent in 2004. Plan costs for the standard benefit package can be significantly lower or higher than the corresponding cost for beneficiaries in the "traditional" or "fee-for-service" Medicare program. Prior to the Affordable Care Act, private plans were generally paid a higher average amount, and they used the additional payments to reduce enrollee cost-sharing requirements, provide extra benefits, and/or reduce Part B and Part D premiums. These enhancements were valuable to enrollees but also resulted in higher Medicare costs overall and higher premiums for all Part B beneficiaries, not just those enrolled in Medicare Advantage plans. The ACA requires that payments to plans phased in during 2012-2017 be based on "benchmarks" in a range of 95 to 115 percent of local fee-for-service Medicare costs, with bonus amounts payable for plans meeting high quality-of-care standards.[16] Based on an administrative action, the Medicare Advantage rates beginning in 2014 will be set to anticipate a 0-percent legislative override of the sustainable growth rate formula. In previous years, the rates were calculated assuming the current law physician payment reductions were applied. In response to these changes, the Trustees project that the overall participation rate for private health plans will reach a high of almost 29 percent in 2014, then decline to about 23 percent in 2018, and reach an ultimate level of 25 percent by 2025, which is significantly higher than assumed in last year's report.

Figure II.D2 shows the past and projected amounts of Medicare revenues under current law, excluding interest income, which would not be a significant part of program financing in the long range. The figure compares total Medicare expenditures to Medicare revenues—from HI payroll taxes, HI income from the taxation of Social Security benefits, SMI Part D State transfers for certain Medicaid beneficiaries, HI and SMI premiums, new fees under the ACA on manufacturers and importers of brand-name prescription drugs (allocated to Part B), and HI and SMI statutory general revenues. For 2013, the Trustees expect total Medicare expenditures to exceed revenue by a significant margin due to recent decreases in HI payroll tax income caused by the weak economy. During the period 2014-2016 the deficit decreases. Projected non-interest revenues exceed overall expenditures in 2017, but after that the opposite relationship is expected as a result of the projected financial imbalance in the HI trust fund. Expenditures are reduced from April 1, 2013 through March 31, 2022 as a result of provisions of the Budget Control Act of 2011, as amended by the American Taxpayer Relief Act of 2012, that require a 2-percent sequester of Medicare payments during this period (as discussed further in sections II.E and II.F).

---

[16]Prior to the ACA, the benchmark range was generally 100 to 140 percent of fee-for-service costs.

Figure II.D2.—Medicare Sources of Non-Interest Income and Expenditures as a Percentage of the Gross Domestic Product

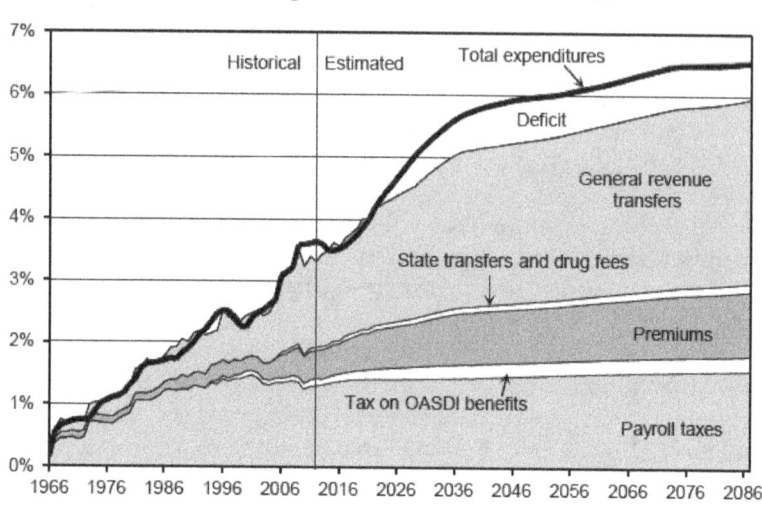

Calendar year

As shown in figure II.D2, for most of the historical period, payroll tax revenues increased steadily as a percentage of GDP due to increases in the HI payroll tax rate and in the limit on taxable earnings, the latter of which lawmakers eliminated in 1994. Under the Affordable Care Act, high-income workers pay an additional 0.9 percent of earnings to the HI trust fund.[17] The Trustees project that as this provision takes effect in 2013, payroll taxes will grow slightly faster than GDP.[18] HI revenue from income taxes on Social Security benefits will gradually increase as a share of GDP as additional beneficiaries become subject to such taxes.

The Trustees expect growth in SMI Part B and Part D premiums and general fund transfers to continue to outpace GDP growth and HI

---

[17]The ACA also specifies that individuals with incomes greater than $200,000 per year and couples above $250,000 pay an additional "Medicare contribution" of 3.8 percent on some or all of their non-work income (such as investment earnings). However, the revenues from this tax are not allocated to the Medicare trust funds.

[18]Although the Trustees expect total worker compensation to grow at the same rate as GDP, wages and salaries would increase more slowly and fringe benefits (health insurance costs in particular) more rapidly. Thus, taxable earnings would gradually decline as a percentage of GDP. Absent any change to the tax rate scheduled under current law, HI payroll tax revenue would similarly decrease as a percentage of GDP (since fringe benefits are not subject to this tax). Over time, however, a growing proportion of workers will exceed the fixed earnings thresholds specified in the ACA ($200,000 and $250,000) and will become subject to the additional 0.9-percent HI payroll tax. The net effect of these factors is an increasing trend in payroll taxes as a percentage of GDP.

payroll tax growth in the future. This phenomenon occurs primarily because, under current law, SMI revenue increases at the same rate as expenditures, whereas HI revenue does not. Accordingly, as the HI sources of revenue become increasingly inadequate to cover HI costs, SMI revenues would represent a growing share of total Medicare revenues. Beginning in 2009, as HI payroll tax receipts declined due to the recession and general revenue transfers increased, the latter income source became the largest single source of income to the Medicare program as a whole. General revenues are expected to continue growing as a share of total Medicare financing under current law—and to add significantly to the Federal budget pressures. Although a smaller share of the total, SMI premiums would grow just as rapidly as general revenue transfers, thereby also placing a growing burden on beneficiaries. For high-income enrollees, SMI premiums began to increase more rapidly in 2011 and will continue to do so as a result of ACA provisions that increase Part D premiums and freeze the income thresholds used to determine Part B and Part D income-related premiums for 2011-2019.

The interrelationship between the Medicare program and the Federal budget is an important topic—one that will become increasingly critical over time as the general revenue requirements for SMI continue to grow. While transfers from the general fund are the major source of financing for the SMI trust fund, and are central to the automatic financial balance of the fund's two accounts, they represent a large and growing requirement for the Federal budget. SMI general revenues currently equal 1.4 percent of GDP and would increase to an estimated 2.9 percent in 2087 under current law. Moreover, in the absence of legislation to address the financial imbalance, interest earnings on trust fund assets and redemption of those assets would cover the difference between HI dedicated revenues and expenditures until 2026.[19] Both of these financial resources for the HI trust fund require cash transfers from the general fund of the Treasury, placing a further obligation on the budget. In 2025, these transactions would require general fund transfers equal to 0.3 percent of GDP. Appendix F describes the interrelationship between the Federal budget and the Medicare and Social Security trust funds; it illustrates the programs' long-range financial outlook from both a "trust fund perspective" and a "budget perspective."

The Medicare Modernization Act requires the Board of Trustees to test whether the difference between program outlays and dedicated

---

[19]After asset depletion in 2026, as described in the next section, no provision exists to use general revenues or any other means to cover the HI deficit.

financing sources exceeds 45 percent of Medicare outlays.[20] If this level is attained within the first 7 fiscal years of the projection, Federal law requires a determination of projected "excess general revenue Medicare funding." The Trustees made such determinations in the 2006 through 2012 reports. If such determinations are present in two consecutive Trustees Reports, then they trigger a "Medicare funding warning." This warning was first triggered as a result of the projections in the 2007 report. In this year's report, the difference would exceed 45 percent in fiscal year 2013—the first year of the projection period. This is the eighth consecutive time that the threshold has been exceeded within the first 7 years of the projection.[21] Consequently, the Board is again issuing a finding of projected "excess general revenue Medicare funding," which triggers another "Medicare funding warning." (Section V.B contains additional details on these tests.)

This section has summarized the total financial obligation posed by Medicare and the manner in which it is financed. Under current law, however, the HI and SMI components of Medicare have separate and distinct trust funds, each with its own sources of revenues and mandated expenditures. Accordingly, it is necessary to assess the financial status of each Medicare trust fund separately. The next two sections of the overview present such assessments for the HI trust fund and the SMI trust fund, respectively.

---

[20]The dedicated financing sources are HI payroll taxes, the HI share of income taxes on Social Security benefits, Part B receipts from the new fees on manufacturers and importers of brand-name prescription drugs, Part D State transfers, and beneficiary premiums. These sources are the first four layers depicted in figure II.D2.

[21]Due to the changes made by the ACA, the ratio is projected to decline below 45 percent for 2014 through 2021 under the intermediate assumptions.

E. FINANCIAL STATUS OF THE HI TRUST FUND

1. 10-Year Actuarial Estimates (2013-2022)

Expenditures from the HI trust fund have exceeded income each year since 2008, with the fund deficit amounting to $23.8 billion in 2012. As a result of the provisions of the Affordable Care Act, the Budget Control Act of 2011, and the assumed economic recovery, however, the Trustees project that HI income will grow faster than expenditures through 2017 under the intermediate assumptions. Specifically, HI expenditure growth would average 5.5 percent per year over the next 10 years, while HI income growth would average 6.0 percent per year. In 2013, total income to the HI trust fund would again fall short of estimated expenditures by about $22 billion, primarily due to depressed levels of economic activity. Trust fund deficits would continue through 2014, but then annual surpluses would occur for the next 6 years before deficits would return for the remainder of the projection period in the absence of further corrective legislation. Payment of expenditures in full and on time will continue to require redemption of trust fund assets most years until the trust fund's depletion in 2026.

Table II.E1 presents the projected operations of the HI trust fund under the intermediate assumptions for the next decade. At the beginning of 2013, HI assets represented 81 percent of annual expenditures. This ratio has declined from 150 percent over the past 6 years. The Board has recommended an asset level at least equal to annual expenditures, to serve as an adequate contingency reserve in the event of adverse economic or other conditions.

The Trustees apply an explicit test of short-range financial adequacy, described in section III.B of this report. Based on the 10-year projection shown in table II.E1, the HI trust fund does not meet this test because estimated assets are below 100 percent of annual expenditures and are not projected to attain this level under the intermediate assumptions. This outlook indicates the need for prompt legislative action to achieve financial adequacy for the HI trust fund throughout the short-range period.

**Table II.E1.—Estimated Operations of the HI Trust Fund
under Intermediate Assumptions, Calendar Years 2012-2022**

[Dollar amounts in billions]

Calendar year	Total income[1]	Total expenditures	Change in fund	Fund at year end	Ratio of assets to expenditures[2]
2012[3]	$243.0	$266.8	−$23.8	$220.4	92
2013	248.2	270.5	−22.2	198.1	81
2014	265.1	275.2	−10.2	188.0	72
2015	286.4	283.6	2.8	190.8	66
2016	308.2	301.3	6.9	197.7	63
2017	330.4	320.5	9.9	207.6	62
2018	352.8	345.5	7.3	214.9	60
2019	374.3	367.9	6.4	221.3	58
2020	393.9	393.6	0.3	221.6	56
2021	415.1	421.8	−6.7	215.0	53
2022	434.6	457.7	−23.1	191.8	47

[1]Includes interest income.
[2]Ratio of assets in the fund at the beginning of the year to expenditures during the year.
[3]Figures for 2012 represent actual experience.

Note: Totals do not necessarily equal the sums of rounded components.

The short-range financial outlook for the HI trust fund is somewhat better than that projected in last year's annual report, and the estimated date of depletion is 2 years later. A number of factors have changed as compared to last year's report, including lower projected spending for most HI service categories—especially for skilled nursing facilities—to reflect lower-than-expected spending in 2012 and other recent data, and lower projected Medicare Advantage program costs that reflect recent data suggesting that certain provisions of the Affordable Care Act will reduce growth in these costs by more than was previously projected. Partially offsetting these favorable changes to the projections are somewhat lower projected levels of tax income that reflect lower-than-expected tax income in 2012.

Under the intermediate assumptions, the assets of the HI trust fund would continue decreasing as a percentage of annual expenditures from the beginning of 2013 through the short-range projection period and would be depleted in 2026, as illustrated in figure II.E1. If assets were depleted, Medicare could pay health plans and providers only to the extent allowed by ongoing tax revenues—and these revenues would be inadequate to fully cover costs. Beneficiary access to health care services would rapidly be curtailed. To date, Congress has never allowed the HI trust fund to become depleted.

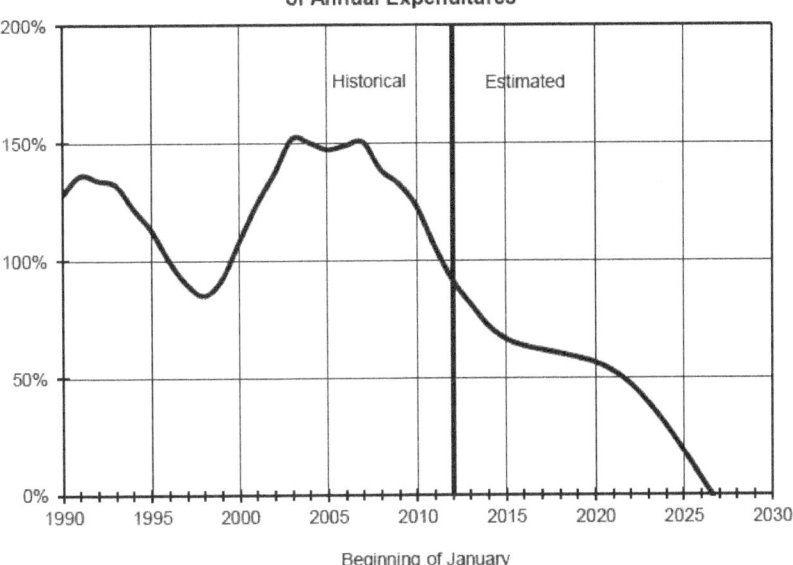

Figure II.E1.—HI Trust Fund Balance at Beginning of Year as a Percentage of Annual Expenditures

There is substantial uncertainty in the economic, demographic, and health care projection factors for HI trust fund expenditures and revenues. Accordingly, under current law the date of HI trust fund depletion could differ substantially in either direction from the 2026 intermediate estimate. Under the low-cost assumptions, trust fund assets would start to increase in 2014 and continue to increase throughout the projection period if the provisions of current law were to continue unchanged. Under the high-cost assumptions, however, asset depletion would occur in 2019.

2. 75-Year Actuarial Estimates (2013-2087)

Each year, the Board prepares 75-year estimates of the financial and actuarial status of the HI trust fund. Although financial outcomes are inherently uncertain, particularly over periods as long as 75 years, such estimates can indicate whether the trust fund—as seen from today's vantage point—is in satisfactory financial condition.

Due to the difficulty in comparing dollar values for different periods without some type of relative scale, the Trustees show income and expenditure amounts relative to the earnings in covered employment that are taxable under HI (referred to as "taxable payroll"). The ratio of HI tax income (including both payroll taxes and income from taxation of Social Security benefits, but excluding interest income) to taxable payroll is called the "income rate," and the ratio of expenditures to taxable payroll is the "cost rate."[22]

Under current law, the standard HI payroll tax rate is scheduled to remain constant at 2.90 percent (for employees and employers, combined). As noted, high-income workers pay an additional 0.9 percent of their earnings above $200,000 (for single workers) or $250,000 (for married couples filing joint income tax returns) in 2013 and later. Since current law does not index these income thresholds, over time an increasing proportion of workers and their earnings will become subject to the additional HI tax rate. Thus, HI payroll tax revenues will increase steadily as a percentage of taxable payroll. (By the end of the long-range projection period, an estimated 80 percent of workers would pay the higher tax rate.) Similarly, income from taxation of Social Security benefits will also increase as a greater proportion of Social Security beneficiaries and their benefits becomes subject to such taxation over time, since the income thresholds determining taxable benefits are not indexed for price inflation.

The cost rate declined in 2012 largely due to the economic recovery. During the expected continuation of the economic recovery, the projected cost rate continues to decline in 2013-2016, but then it escalates in the longer term primarily due to retirements of those in the baby boom generation and partly due to health services cost growth, as mentioned in the prior section. The accumulating effect of the productivity adjustments to provider price updates, which are estimated to reduce annual HI per capita cost growth by an average 0.8 percent through 2029 and 1.1 percent per year thereafter, will somewhat offset the effect of these factors under current law. After 25, 50, and 75 years, for example, the prices paid to HI providers under current law would be 21 percent, 40 percent, and 55 percent lower than under the prior law.

Figure II.E2 compares projected income and cost rates under the intermediate assumptions. As indicated, projected HI expenditures continue to exceed tax income—but by a decreasing margin—for the next several years. Thereafter, the income rate is projected to exceed the cost rate for a few years before falling below it in 2018 and later. The HI cost rate increases more rapidly than the income rate through about 2045. From a low of 0.01 percent of taxable payroll in 2018, the projected annual deficits would increase to between 1.50 and

---

[22]Includes estimated costs attributable to insured beneficiaries only, on an incurred basis. The Trustees expect benefits and administrative costs for noninsured persons to be financed through general revenue transfers and premium payments, rather than through payroll taxes.

1.70 percent after 2045. During this latter period, expenditures and tax revenues would be growing at roughly similar rates on average. The convergence of growth rates reflects the continuing effects of the slower payment rate updates under current law, assumed decelerating growth in the volume and intensity of services, and the increasing proportion of workers affected by the additional 0.9-percent payroll tax. During 2045 to 2085, tax revenues would cover between 70 and 73 percent of projected expenditures.

The shaded area in figure II.E2 represents the excess of expenditures over tax income that interest earnings and the redemption of trust fund assets could cover under current law. Both types of transactions occur through transfers from the general fund of the Treasury. Starting in 2008, the fund began using interest earnings and asset redemptions to cover the excess of expenditures over tax income. The deficits in 2008-2012 required the redemption of one-third of the assets available at the beginning of this period. In the absence of other changes, this process would continue for most years until 2026, at which time the fund would be depleted. For a few years, asset redemptions would not be needed, but interest earnings would, and for 1 year (2017), neither of these sources would be required.

Although the Trustees project that the HI trust fund would not be depleted until 2026 under current law, the demands on general revenue (to pay interest and redeem the Treasury bonds held by the trust fund) have been occurring every year since 2008. By 2025, without legislation to address the HI deficits, redemption of assets would have to cover an estimated 11 percent of HI expenditures in that year.

Figure II.E2.—Long-Range HI Income and Cost as a Percentage of Taxable Payroll, Intermediate Assumptions

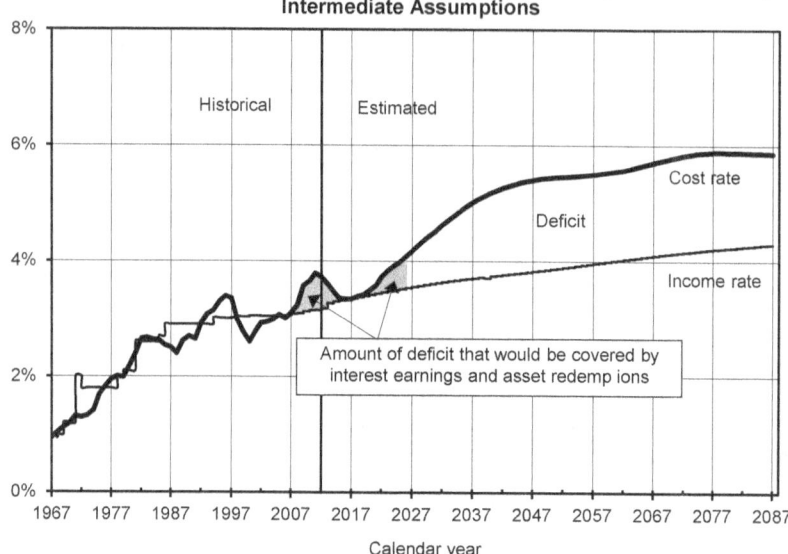

Calendar year

It is possible to summarize the year-by-year cost rates and income rates shown in figure II.E2 into single values representing, in effect, the average value over a given period. Based on the intermediate assumptions, the Trustees project an actuarial deficit of 1.11 percent of taxable payroll for the 75-year period under current law, which represents the difference between the summarized income rate of 3.83 percent and the corresponding cost rate of 4.94 percent. Based on this measure, the HI trust fund fails the Trustees' test for long-range financial balance, as it has for many years. Under the illustrative alternative projections, the long-range HI deficit would be 2.17 percent of payroll.

Lawmakers could address the long-range financial imbalance in several different ways. In theory, they could immediately increase the standard 2.90-percent payroll tax by the amount of the actuarial deficit to 4.01 percent, or they could reduce expenditures by a corresponding amount. Note, however, that these changes would require an immediate 38-percent increase in the standard tax rate or an immediate 22-percent reduction in expenditures.[23] More realistically, the tax and/or benefit changes could occur gradually but would ultimately have to reach significantly higher levels to eliminate the deficit throughout the long-range period.

The projected long-range HI cost rates shown in this report are lower than those from the 2012 report. The primary reasons are (i) lower projected spending for most HI service categories—especially for skilled nursing facilities—to reflect lower-than-expected spending in 2012 and other recent data; (ii) lower projected Medicare Advantage program costs that reflect recent data suggesting that certain provisions of the Affordable Care Act will reduce growth in these costs by more than was previously projected; and (iii) a refinement in projection methods that reduces assumed per beneficiary cost growth during the transition period between the short-range projections and the long-range projections.

---

[23]The corresponding immediate changes in the standard tax rate or expenditure levels are 75 percent and 36 percent, respectively, under the illustrative alternative projections. Under either of these two scenarios, tax income would initially be substantially greater than expenditures, and trust fund assets would accumulate rapidly. Subsequently, however, tax income would be inadequate, and assets would be drawn down to cover the difference. This example illustrates that if lawmakers designed legislative solutions only to eliminate the overall actuarial deficit, without consideration of such year-by-year patterns, then a substantial financial imbalance could still remain at the end of the period, and the long-range sustainability of the program could still be in doubt.

F. FINANCIAL STATUS OF THE SMI TRUST FUND

SMI differs fundamentally from HI in regard to the nature of its financing and the method by which its financial status is evaluated. SMI comprises two parts, Part B and Part D, each with its own separate account within the SMI trust fund. The Trustees must determine the financial status of the SMI trust fund by evaluating the financial status of each account separately, since there is no provision in the law for transferring assets or income between the Part B and Part D accounts. The nature of the financing for both parts of SMI is similar in that the law establishes a mechanism by which income from the Part B premium and the Part D premium, and the corresponding transfers from general revenues for each part, are sufficient to cover the following year's estimated expenditures. Accordingly, each account within SMI is automatically in financial balance under current law. This result contrasts with OASDI and HI, for which financing established many years earlier may prove significantly higher or lower than subsequent actual costs. Moreover, Part B and Part D are voluntary (whereas OASDI and HI are generally compulsory), and payroll taxes are not the source of income for these programs. These disparities result in a financial assessment that differs in some respects from that for OASDI or HI, as described in the following sections.

1. 10-Year Actuarial Estimates (2013-2022)

Table II.F1 shows the estimated operations of the Part B account, the Part D account, and the total SMI trust fund under the intermediate assumptions during calendar years 2012 through 2022. For Part B, expenditures grew at an average annual rate of 6.1 percent over the past 5 years, exceeding GDP growth by 3.8 percentage points annually, on average. Estimated Part B cost increases average about 5.1 percent for the 5-year period 2013 to 2017, slightly slower than the GDP growth rate of 5.4 percent for the same 5-year period.

Due to the nature of Part B financing, Part B income growth is normally quite close to expenditure growth. Assets were within the customary range at the end of 2012, and, under current law, projected assets held in the Part B account would be slightly above this range at the end of 2013 and would maintain an adequate contingency reserve thereafter.[24] Assets after 2013 would be substantially lower than projected, compared to the current-law projections, in the very likely event that lawmakers enact legislation to override a 24.7-percent reduction in physician fees that is projected for 2014.

Due to the structure of physician payment updates under current law, the projected Part B expenditure and income growth is unrealistically low. The law requires downward adjustments to future physician payment increases if cumulative past actual physician spending exceeds a statutory target. Actual physician spending exceeded the target spending level from 2000 through 2009. Legislative changes that increased the actual spending in each year since 2002, but that have not increased the target level of spending in every year, exacerbated this difference.[25] As a result, the "sustainable growth rate" formula under current law required a reduction in Medicare payment rates for physician services for each year since 2002, but these reductions were legislatively avoided. The legislative overrides that have been applied since 2006 have specified that future physician updates be determined as if the required reductions had not been legislatively avoided, resulting in an estimated 24.7-percent reduction for 2014.

It is nearly certain that lawmakers will again override the scheduled large reduction in physician payments per service. Consequently, the current-law projections for Part B, total SMI, and total Medicare shown for 2014 and thereafter are likely to significantly understate actual future costs, and readers should interpret these estimates cautiously. The Part B projections, in particular, may be understated by about 6 percent for 2022.

---

[24]The traditional measure used to evaluate the status of the Part B account of the SMI trust fund is defined as the ratio of the excess of Part B assets over Part B liabilities to the next year's Part B incurred expenditures. The customary range for this ratio is 15 to 20 percent; the CMS Office of the Actuary developed this range based on private health insurance standards and past studies indicating that this asset reserve level is sufficient to protect against adverse events. Due to the current strong likelihood of Congressional action to override the physician fee reductions required under current law, and to do so after establishment of Part B financing for a given year, it is appropriate to maintain a higher level of reserve assets to prevent fund depletion under this contingency.

[25]For additional information about the physician payment updates and the sustainable growth rate system, see section IV.B1.

Table II.F1.—Estimated Operations of the SMI Trust Fund under Intermediate Assumptions, Calendar Years 2012-2022

[Dollar amounts in billions]

Calendar year	Total income[1]	Total expenditures	Change in fund	Fund at year end
Part B account:				
2012[2]	$227 0	$240.5	−$13.5	$66.2
2013	254.7	251.3	3.5	69.7
2014	265 3	253.4	11.9	81.6
2015	299 0[3]	267.9	31.1	112.7
2016	300 8[3]	287.3	13.5	126.2
2017	335.7	308.6	27.1	153.3
2018	364 0	333.9	30.1	183.4
2019	394 0	360.0	34.1	217.5
2020	443 2[3]	390.1	53.1	270.5
2021	451.6[3]	422.2	29.4	299.9
2022	513.6	464.9	48.7	348.6
Part D account:				
2012[2]	66.9	66.9	0.0	1.0
2013	71.9	72.2	−0.3	0.7
2014	83.6	83.6	0.0	0.7
2015	89.5[3]	89.5	0.0	0.8
2016	96.3[3]	96.2	0.1	0.8
2017	105.4	105.3	0.1	0.9
2018	115.1	115.0	0.1	1.0
2019	125.6	125.5	0.1	1.0
2020	138 3[3]	138.2	0.1	1.1
2021	150.6[3]	150.5	0.1	1.2
2022	165 2	165.1	0.1	1.3
Total SMI:				
2012[2]	293 9	307.4	−13.5	67.2
2013	326.7	323.5	3.2	70.4
2014	348 9	337.0	11.9	82.3
2015	388 5[3]	357.3	31.2	113.5
2016	397.1[3]	383.5	13.6	127.1
2017	441.1	414.0	27.1	154.2
2018	479.1	448.9	30.1	184.4
2019	519.7	485.5	34.2	218.5
2020	581 5[3]	528.3	53.2	271.7
2021	602 2[3]	572.7	29.5	301.2
2022	678 8	630.0	48.8	350.0

[1]Includes interest income.

[2]Figures for 2012 represent actual experience.

[3]Section 708 of the Social Security Act modifies he provisions for the payment of Social Security benefits when the regularly designated day falls on a Saturday, Sunday, or legal public holiday. Payment of those benefits normally due January 3, 2016 is expected to occur on December 31, 2015. Consequently, the Part B and Part D premiums withheld from these benefits and the associated Part B general revenue contributions are expected to be added to the respective Part B or Part D account on December 31, 2015. Similarly, the payment date for those benefits normally due January 3, 2021 will be December 31, 2020.

The projected Part B expenditures shown in table II.F1 are substantially larger in 2013, and slightly higher thereafter than the corresponding amounts in last year's Trustees Report. This pattern is the result of lower actual 2012 expenditures, the legislative changes to the physician payment update for 2013, and an increase in Medicare Advantage expenditures starting in 2014. Based on an administrative action, the Medicare Advantage rates beginning in 2014 will be set to anticipate a 0-percent legislative override of the sustainable growth rate formula. In previous years, the rates were calculated assuming the current law physician payment reductions were applied. The Part B income and assets are somewhat lower than projected in last year's report, reflecting a slightly smaller contingency margin built into the financing than was included last year for the likely override of the scheduled physician payment reduction in 2014.

The Medicare prescription drug benefit began full operation in 2006. For the 10-year period 2013 to 2022, the Trustees project that income and expenditures for the Part D account will grow at an average annual rate of 9.5 percent, due to expected further increases in enrollment and continuing growth in per capita drug costs. As with Part B, income and outgo would remain in balance as a result of the annual adjustment of premium and general revenue income to cover costs. Because of the appropriations process for Part D general revenues, it is not necessary to maintain a contingency reserve in the account.

The projected Part D costs shown in table II.F1 and elsewhere in this report are lower than those in the 2012 report. The difference is primarily attributable to the further increase of the market penetration of generic drugs, the larger than previously projected impact from patent expiration of several major drugs in 2012, and a lower projected trend for 2013.

The primary test of financial adequacy for Parts B and D pertains to the level of the financing established for a given period (normally, through the end of the current calendar year). The financing for each part of SMI is considered satisfactory if it is sufficient to fund all services, including benefits and administrative expenses, provided through a given period. In addition, to protect against the possibility that cost increases under either part of SMI will be higher than expected, the accounts of the trust fund would normally need assets adequate to cover a reasonable degree of variation between actual and projected costs. For Part B, as stated previously, the Trustees estimate that the financing established through December 2013 will be sufficient to cover benefits and administrative costs incurred through that time period and that assets will be adequate to cover potential variations in costs as a result of new legislation or cost growth factors that exceed expectations. The estimated financing established for Part D, together with the flexible appropriation authority for this trust fund account, would be sufficient to cover benefits and administrative costs incurred through 2013.

The amount of the contingency reserve needed in Part B is normally much smaller (both in absolute dollars and as a fraction of annual costs) than in HI or OASDI. A smaller reserve is adequate because the premium rate and corresponding general revenue transfers for Part B are determined annually based on estimated future costs, while the HI and OASDI payroll tax rates are set in law and are therefore much more difficult to adjust should circumstances change. A statutory competitive bidding process establishes Part D revenues annually to cover estimated costs. Moreover, the flexible appropriation authority established by lawmakers for Part D allows additional general fund financing if costs are higher than anticipated, thereby eliminating the need for a contingency reserve.

2. 75-Year Actuarial Estimates (2013-2087)

Figure II.F1 shows past and projected total SMI expenditures and premium income as a percentage of the Gross Domestic Product (GDP). Annual SMI expenditures grew from about 1.2 percent of GDP in 2005 to 1.6 percent of GDP in 2006 with the commencement of prescription drug coverage. Under the current-law assumptions, SMI expenditures would grow to about 3.4 percent of GDP within 25 years and to more than 4.0 percent by the end of the projection period. (Total SMI expenditures in 2087 would be 4.7 percent of GDP if physician payment rates were set as assumed under the illustrative alternative projections. Such costs would represent more than 5.7 percent of GDP under the full illustration, including larger payment updates for most other categories of Part B providers.)

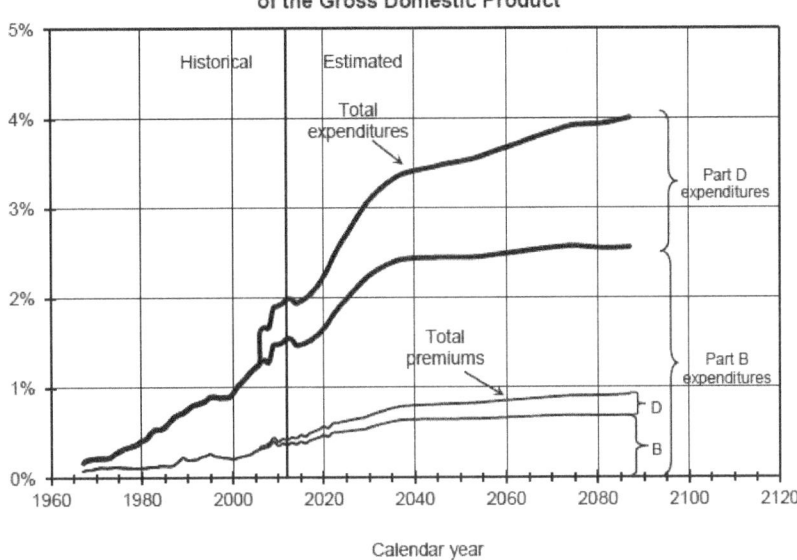

Figure II.F1.—SMI Expenditures and Premiums as a Percentage of the Gross Domestic Product

Calendar year

3. Implications of SMI Cost Growth

Financing for the SMI trust fund is adequate because beneficiary premiums and general revenue contributions, for both Part B and Part D, are established annually to cover the expected costs for the upcoming year. Should actual costs exceed those anticipated when the financing is determined, future financing rates can include adjustments to recover the shortfall. Likewise, should actual costs be less than those anticipated, the savings would result in lower future financing rates. As long as the future financing rates continue to cover the following year's estimated costs, both parts of the SMI trust fund will remain financially solvent under current law.

A critical issue for the SMI program is the impact of the rapid growth of SMI costs, which places steadily increasing demands on beneficiaries and taxpayers. This section compares the past and projected growth in SMI costs with GDP growth; it also assesses the implications of the rapid growth on beneficiaries and the budget of the Federal Government. These implications would be significantly greater if lawmakers continue to override the current-law reductions in physician payment rates or if the productivity adjustments to other Medicare price updates are not sustained.

Table II.F2 compares the growth in SMI expenditures with that of the economy as a whole. Based on the current-law estimates, SMI costs would continue to outpace growth in GDP. Compared to the last 10 years, the estimated growth differential in the future is significantly smaller in most years (and is likely understated for the reasons given above). The growth differential reflects the net effects of (i) the productivity adjustments to most Part B price updates; (ii) reduced Medicare Advantage payment "benchmarks"[26]; (iii) the increase in the SMI population as the baby boom generation turns age 65, enrolls, and is eligible to receive benefits; (iv) the faster growth trend associated with the Part D prescription drug benefit compared to other medical services; (v) the future physician payment updates; and (vi) the continuation of the 2-percent sequestration of Medicare expenditures required by the Budget Control Act of 2011, as amended by the American Taxpayer Relief Act of 2012, from April 1, 2013 through March 31, 2022. (The implementation of this reduction, and its subsequent removal, decreases the growth rate in 2013 and increases the growth rate in 2022.)

Table II.F2.—Average Annual Rates of Growth in SMI and the Economy
[In percent]

Calendar years	SMI			U.S. Economy			Growth differential[1]
	Beneficiary population	Per capita expenditures	Total expenditures	Total population	Per capita GDP	Total GDP	
Historical data:							
1968-1992	2.6%	12.6%	15.6%	1.0%	7.4%	8.5%	6.5%
1993-2002	1.2	6.9	8.1	1.0	4 3	5.3	2.7
2003-2012	2.0	8.5[2]	10.7[2]	0.8	3.1	4.0	6.5[2]
Intermediate estimates:							
2013-2022	2.9	4.3	7.3	0.9	4 3	5.2	2.1
2023-2037	1.7	5.1	6.9	0.7	3 9	4.6	2.2
2038-2062	0.5	4.4	5.0	0.5	4.1	4.6	0.4
2063-2087	0.7	4.1	4.8	0.4	4.1	4.5	0.3

[1]Excess of total SMI expenditure growth above total GDP growth, calculated as a multiplicative differential.
[2]Includes the addition of the prescription drug benefit to the SMI program in 2006. Excluding 2006, the average annual per capita expenditure increase is 5.7 percent, the total expenditure increase is 7.9 percent, and the growth differential is 4 0 percent.

If, as is generally expected, SMI per capita benefits continued to grow faster than average income or per capita GDP, the premiums and coinsurance amounts paid by beneficiaries would represent a growing share of their total income. Figure II.F2 compares past and projected growth in average benefits for SMI versus Social Security. The figure also shows amounts for the average SMI premium payments and average cost-sharing payments. To facilitate comparison across long time periods, all values are in constant 2012 dollars.

Over time, the average Social Security benefit tends to increase at about the rate of growth in average earnings. As noted previously,

---

[26]The administrative action that increased Medicare Advantage benchmark rates beginning in 2014 partially offsets the benchmark reductions required by the ACA.

health care costs generally reflect increases in the earnings of health care professionals, growth in the utilization and intensity of services, and other medical cost inflation. As indicated in figure II.F2, average SMI benefits in 1970 were only about one-twelfth the level of average Social Security benefits but had grown to more than one-third by 2005. With the introduction of the Part D prescription drug benefit in 2006, this ratio grew to almost one-half. Under the intermediate projections, SMI benefits would continue increasing at a faster rate and would represent about four-fifths of the average Social Security retired-worker benefit in 2087 under current law.

Average beneficiary premiums and cost-sharing payments for SMI will increase at about the same rate as average SMI benefits.[27] Thus, a growing proportion of most beneficiaries' Social Security and other income would be necessary over time to pay total out-of-pocket costs for SMI, including both premiums and cost-sharing amounts. Most SMI enrollees have other income in addition to Social Security benefits. Other possible sources include earnings from employment, employer-sponsored pension benefits, and investment earnings. In addition, many draw down their accumulated assets to supplement their income in retirement. For simplicity, the comparisons in figure II.F2 apply to Social Security benefits only; a comparison of average SMI premiums and cost-sharing amounts to average total beneficiary income would lead to similar conclusions. For illustration, the Trustees estimate that the average Part B plus Part D premium in 2013 would equal about 11 percent of the average Social Security benefit but would increase to an estimated 19 percent in 2087. Similarly, an average cost-sharing amount in 2013 would be equivalent to about 12 percent of the Social Security benefit, which would increase to about 21 percent in 2087.

The availability of SMI Part B and Part D benefits greatly reduces the costs that beneficiaries would otherwise pay for health care services. The introduction of the prescription drug benefit increased beneficiaries' costs for SMI premiums and cost sharing, but reduced their costs for previously uncovered services by substantially more. Figure II.F2 highlights the impact of rapid cost growth for a given SMI benefit package.

---

[27]As a result, the projected ratio of average SMI out-of-pocket payments to average SMI benefits is nearly constant over time.

Figure II.F2.—Comparison of Average Monthly SMI Benefits, Premiums, and Cost Sharing to the Average Monthly Social Security Benefit
[Amounts in constant 2012 dollars]

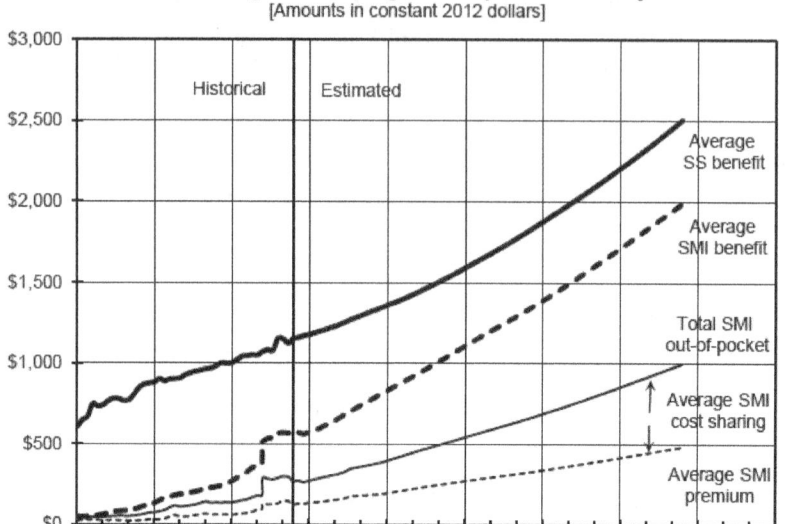

The average OASI benefit amount for all retired workers is the basis for the Social Security benefits shown in figure II.F2; individual retirees may receive significantly more or less than the average, depending on their past earnings. For purposes of illustration, figure II.F2 shows the average SMI benefit value and cost-sharing liability for all beneficiaries. The value of SMI benefits to individual enrollees, and their cost-sharing payments, varies even more substantially than OASI benefits, depending on their income, assets, and use of covered health services in a given year. In particular, Medicaid pays Part B premiums and cost-sharing amounts for beneficiaries with very low incomes, and the Medicare low-income drug subsidy pays the corresponding Part D amounts (except for nominal copayments). Moreover, Part B beneficiaries with high incomes pay a higher income-related premium beginning in 2007, and, similarly, Part D enrollees pay an income-related premium beginning in 2011. Further information on the nature of this comparison, and on the variations from the average results, is available in a memorandum by the CMS Office of the Actuary at http://www.cms.gov/Research-Statistics-Data-and-Systems/Statistics-Trends-and-Reports/ReportsTrustFunds/Beneficiaryoop.html.

Another way to evaluate the implications of rapid SMI cost growth is to compare government contributions to the SMI trust fund with total Federal income taxes (personal and corporate income taxes).

Table II.F3 indicates that SMI general revenues in fiscal year 2008 were equivalent to about 12.0 percent of total Federal income taxes collected in that year. For 2009, 2010, 2011, and 2012, the percentages were 17.7, 19.2, 17.2, and 14.5 percent, respectively, primarily as a result of lower income tax revenues caused by the recession and income tax reductions designed to stimulate the economy. Should such taxes in the future maintain their historical average level of the last 50 years relative to the national economy, then, based on the intermediate projections, SMI general revenue financing in 2087 would represent about 26 percent of total income taxes under current law and substantially more than that if Congress were to modify the physician payment system and the productivity adjustments to non-physician price updates, as indicated under the illustrative alternative projections.

Table II.F3.—SMI General Revenues as a Percentage of Personal and Corporate Federal Income Taxes

Fiscal year	Percentage of income taxes[1]
Historical data:	
1970	0.8%
1980	2.2
1990	5.9
2000	5.4
2008	12.0
2009	17.7
2010	19.2
2011	17.2
2012	14.5
Intermediate es imates:	
2013	13.4
2020	15.3
2030	19.2
2040	22.4
2050	23.0
2060	24.0
2070	25.1
2080	25.6

[1] Includes the Part D prescription drug benefit beginning in 2006.

These examples illustrate the significant impact of SMI expenditure growth on beneficiaries, taxpayers, and the Federal budget. Under current law, the projected SMI expenditure increases associated with the cost of providing health care, plus the impact of the baby boom generation reaching eligibility age, would continue to require a growing share of the economic resources available to finance these costs. Moreover, the share of beneficiaries' incomes and the overall economy would be substantially larger if there is no reduction in physician payment rates as required under current law or if the productivity adjustments to most other provider payment updates are curtailed. This outlook reinforces the Trustees' recommendation for development and enactment of further reforms to reduce the rate of growth in SMI expenditures.

G. CONCLUSION

Total Medicare expenditures were $574 billion in 2012, and under current law the Board projects them to increase in most future years at a somewhat faster pace than either aggregate workers' earnings or the economy overall. The excess increase is primarily due to growth in the number of beneficiaries, and partly due to growth in expenditures per beneficiary, which are projected to increase slightly faster than the per capita rate of growth of the economy overall. Based on the intermediate set of assumptions and current law, expenditures as a percentage of GDP would increase from the current 3.6 percent to a projected 6.5 percent by 2087.

The assets of the HI trust fund declined by $23.8 billion in 2012 and are expected to continue to decline through 2014, but then annual surpluses are expected to occur for the next 6 years, with deficits returning for the remainder of the projection period under current law. The projected trust fund depletion date is 2026, 2 years later than estimated in last year's report. Actual HI expenditures in 2012 were slightly lower than the previous estimate and remain that way throughout the projection period. Actual HI taxable earnings in 2012 were slightly lower than the level previously projected, and the projected level of real (inflation-adjusted) HI taxes is lower through 2021 than in last year's report, with the difference narrowing initially as the economy recovers from the recent economic recession and then becoming greater throughout the remainder of the projection period. The HI trust fund fails to meet the Board of Trustees' short-range test of financial adequacy.

The HI actuarial deficit in this year's report is 1.11 percent of taxable payroll, down from 1.35 percent in last year's report, due to more recent data and technical changes in projection methods. As in past reports, the HI trust fund fails to meet the Trustees' long-range test of close actuarial balance.

The financial outlook for SMI is fundamentally different than for HI due to the statutory differences in the methods of financing for these two components of Medicare. The Trustees project that both the Part B and Part D accounts of the SMI trust fund will remain in financial balance for all future years because beneficiary premiums and general revenue transfers will be set at a level to meet expected costs each year. However, projected SMI costs double as a share of GDP over the next 75 years, from 2.0 percent to 4.0 percent. This projection assumes a reduction of almost 25 percent in payment rates for physician services in 2014, as required under current law; if lawmakers act to prevent this decrease, as they have for 2003 through 2013, then actual Part B and total SMI costs will significantly exceed the projections shown in this report.

The projected Part B costs in this report are slightly higher than in the previous report due to a change in Medicare Advantage payment policy, lower productivity adjustments, and slightly higher enrollment. The Part D projections are lower than in past years' reports largely due to the further increase of the market penetration of generic drugs, the larger than previously projected impact from patent expiration of several major drugs in 2012, and a lower projected trend for 2013.

The financial projections shown for the Medicare program in this report reflect substantial, but very uncertain, cost savings deriving from provisions of the Affordable Care Act. It is important to note, however, that the improved results for HI and SMI Part B depend in part on the long-range feasibility of the various cost-saving measures in the Affordable Care Act—in particular, the lower increases in Medicare payment rates to most categories of health care providers. Without fundamental change in the current delivery system, these adjustments would probably not be viable indefinitely.

In view of these issues with physician and other provider payment rates, the Trustees note that the actual future costs for Medicare are likely to exceed those shown by the current-law projections in this report. Use of alternative projections, as provided in appendix V.C and in a memorandum from the Office of the Actuary,[28] can help illustrate the potential magnitude of this understatement. For example, the total cost of Medicare in 2087 is 9.8 percent of GDP under the alternative projections (versus 6.5 percent under current law), and the HI actuarial deficit would be 2.17 percent of taxable payroll (versus 1.11 percent). (The projected depletion date for the HI trust fund would be only slightly affected.) Readers should not interpret the projections shown in this report for current law as the Trustees' most likely expectation of actual Medicare financial operations in the future but rather as illustrations of the very favorable impact of permanently slower growth in health care costs, if such slower growth is achievable. The illustrative alternative projections underscore the uncertainty associated with these elements of current law.

---

[28]See http://www.cms.gov/Research-Statistics-Data-and-Systems/Statistics-Trends-and-Reports/ReportsTrustFunds/Downloads/2013TRAlternativeScenario.pdf.

Policy makers should determine effective solutions to the long-range HI financial imbalance. Even assuming that the current-law payment rates will be adequate, the HI program does not meet either the Trustees' short-range test of financial adequacy or long-range test of close actuarial balance. Under current law, scheduled HI tax income would cover only 87 percent of estimated expenditures in 2026 and 71 percent in 2050. By the end of the 75-year projection period, HI revenues could pay 73 percent of HI costs. Policy makers should also consider the likelihood that the price adjustments in current law may prove difficult to adhere to fully and should develop additional means to achieve financial balance.

The projections in this year's report continue to demonstrate the need for timely and effective action to address Medicare's remaining financial challenges—including the projected depletion of the HI trust fund, this fund's long-range financial imbalance, and the issue of rapid growth in Medicare expenditures. Furthermore, if the lower prices payable for health services under Medicare cannot be sustained, then these further policy reforms will have to address much larger financial challenges than implied by the current-law projections. The Board of Trustees believes that solutions can and must be found to ensure the financial integrity of HI in the short and long term and to reduce the rate of growth in Medicare costs through viable means. Consideration of such reforms should occur in the near future. The sooner the solutions are enacted, the more flexible and gradual they can be. Moreover, the early introduction of reforms increases the time available for affected individuals and organizations—including health care providers, beneficiaries, and taxpayers—to adjust their expectations. Congress and the executive branch must work closely together with a sense of urgency to address these challenges.

III. ACTUARIAL ANALYSIS

A. INTRODUCTION

The Actuarial Analysis section focuses on the costs and financing of the individual HI and SMI trust fund accounts. The Trustees perform an analysis for each trust fund individually, to determine whether each account's income and expenditures are balanced as necessary to maintain solvency. (It is also valuable to consider Medicare's total expenditures and the sources and relative magnitudes of the program's revenues. Appendix V.B presents such information for Medicare overall.)

Under current law, the HI and SMI trust funds are separate and distinct, each with its own sources of financing. There are no provisions for using HI revenues to finance SMI expenditures, or vice versa, or for lending assets between the two trust funds. Moreover, the benefit provisions, financing methods, and, to a lesser degree, eligibility rules are very different between these Medicare components. In particular, both accounts of the SMI trust fund are automatically in financial balance under current law, whereas the HI fund is not.

For these reasons, the Trustees can evaluate the financial status of the Medicare trust funds only by separately assessing the status of each fund. Sections III.B, III.C, and III.D of this report present such assessments for HI (Part A), SMI Part B, and SMI Part D, respectively.

As noted previously, the actual future costs for Parts A and B are likely to exceed those shown by the current-law projections in this report. Accordingly, readers should use the estimates shown under current law cautiously in evaluating the overall financial obligation created by Parts A and B and in assessing the financial status of the individual trust fund accounts. To help illustrate the degree to which the current-law projections potentially understate actual future costs, the Trustees also provide key results based on alternatives to current law in appendix V.C.

B. HI FINANCIAL STATUS

1. Financial Operations in Calendar Year 2012

On July 30, 1965, the Social Security Act established the Federal Hospital Insurance Trust Fund as a separate account in the U.S. Treasury. All the HI financial operations occur within this fund.

Table III.B1 presents a statement of the revenue and expenditures of the fund in calendar year 2012, and of its assets at the beginning and end of the calendar year.

The total assets of the trust fund amounted to $244.2 billion on December 31, 2011. During calendar year 2012, total revenue amounted to $243.0 billion, and total expenditures were $266.8 billion. Total assets thus decreased by $23.8 billion during the year to $220.4 billion on December 31, 2012.

Table III.B1.—Statement of Operations of the HI Trust Fund
during Calendar Year 2012
[In thousands]

Total assets of the trust fund, beginning of period	$244,189,396
Revenue:	
Payroll taxes	$205,729,562
Income from taxation of OASDI benefits	18,643,000
Interest on investments	10,615,680
Premiums collected from voluntary participants	3,441,227
Premiums collected from Medicare Advantage participants	240,947
Transfer from Railroad Retirement account	483,900
Reimbursement, transitional uninsured coverage	262,000
Reimbursement, program management general fund	226,337
Interfund interest payments[1]	1,203
Interest on reimbursements, Railroad Retirement	26,978
Other	2,689
Reimbursement, Union activity	1,122
Fraud and abuse control receipts:	
Criminal fines	1,389,127
Civil monetary penalties	16,665
Civil penalties and damages, CMS	1,494
Civil penalties and damages, Department of Justice	1,486,103
Asset forfeitures, Department of Justice	32,110
3% administrative expense reimbursement, Department of Justice	46,077
3% administrative expense reimbursement, CMS	71
General fund transfer, Small Jobs Act	100,000
General fund transfer, Discretionary	167,736
Fraud and abuse appropriation for FBI	131,872
Total revenue	$243,045,900
Expenditures:	
Net benefit payments	$262,894,240
Administrative expenses:	
Treasury administrative expenses	145,108
Salaries and expenses, SSA[2]	874,105
Salaries and expenses, CMS[3]	1,289,906
Salaries and expenses, Office of the Secretary, HHS	25,874
Medicare Payment Advisory Commission	7,067
AOA MIPPA funding	11,924
CMS program management – Patient Protection and Affordable Care Act	2,461
Transfer to PCOR trust fund	24,730
Fraud and abuse control expenses:	
HHS Medicare integrity program	750,642
HHS Office of Inspector General[4]	340,699
Department of Justice	46,956
FBI	126,258
HCFAC DOJ Discretionary, CMS	35,462
HCFAC OIG Discretionary, CMS	17,406
HCFAC Other HHS Discretionary, CMS	12,666
HCFAC Discre ionary, CMS	235,360
Total administrative expenses	3,946,624
Total expenditures	$266,840,864
Net addition to the trust fund	-23,794,964
Total assets of the trust fund, end of period	$220,394,432

[1]Reflects interest adjustments on the reallocation of administrative expenses between the Medicare trust funds, the OASDI trust funds, and the general fund of the Treasury. Estimated payments are made from he trust funds and then are reconciled, with interest, the next year when the actual costs are known. A positive figure represents a transfer to the HI trust fund from the other trust funds. A negative figure represents a transfer from the HI trust fund to the other funds.

[2]For facilities, goods, and services provided by SSA.

[3]Includes administrative expenses of the intermediaries.

[4]A positive figure represents a transfer from the HI trust fund. A negative figure represents a transfer to he HI trust fund.

Note: Totals do not necessarily equal the sums of rounded components.

a. Revenues

The trust fund's primary source of income consists of amounts appropriated to it, under permanent authority, on the basis of taxes paid by workers, their employers, and individuals with self-employment income, in work covered by HI. Included in HI are workers covered under the OASDI program, those covered under the Railroad Retirement program, and certain Federal, State, and local employees not otherwise covered under the OASDI program.

HI taxes are payable without limit on a covered individual's total wages and self-employment income. For calendar years prior to 1994, taxes were computed on a person's annual earnings up to a specified maximum annual amount called the maximum tax base. Table III.B2 presents the maximum tax bases for 1966-1993. Legislation enacted in 1993 removed the limit on taxable income beginning in calendar year 1994.

Table III.B2 also shows the HI tax rates applicable in each of the calendar years 1966 and later. For 2014 and thereafter, the tax rates shown are the rates scheduled in current law. As indicated in the footnote to the table, in 2013 and later employees and self-employed individuals with earnings above certain thresholds pay an additional HI tax of 0.9 percent on their earnings above the thresholds.

Table III.B2.—Tax Rates and Maximum Tax Bases

Calendar years	Maximum tax base	Tax rate (Percentage of taxable earnings) Employees and employers, each	Self-employed
Past experience:			
1966	$6,600	0.35%	0.35%
1967	6,600	0.50	0.50
1968-71	7,800	0.60	0.60
1972	9,000	0.60	0.60
1973	10,800	1.00	1.00
1974	13,200	0.90	0.90
1975	14,100	0.90	0.90
1976	15,300	0.90	0.90
1977	16,500	0.90	0.90
1978	17,700	1.00	1.00
1979	22,900	1.05	1.05
1980	25,900	1.05	1.05
1981	29,700	1.30	1.30
1982	32,400	1.30	1.30
1983	35,700	1.30	1.30
1984	37,800	1.30	2.60
1985	39,600	1.35	2.70
1986	42,000	1.45	2.90
1987	43,800	1.45	2.90
1988	45,000	1.45	2.90
1989	48,000	1.45	2.90
1990	51,300	1.45	2.90
1991	125,000	1.45	2.90
1992	130,200	1.45	2.90
1993	135,000	1.45	2.90
1994-2012	no limit	1.45	2.90
2013	no limit	1.45[1]	2.90[1]
Scheduled in current law:			
2014 & later	no limit	1.45[1]	2.90[1]

[1]Beginning in 2013, workers pay an additional 0.9 percent of their earnings above $200,000 (for those who file an individual tax return) or $250,000 (for those who file a joint income tax return).

Total HI payroll tax income in calendar year 2012 amounted to $205.7 billion—an increase of 5.2 percent over the amount of $195.6 billion for the preceding 12-month period. This increase in tax income resulted primarily from increases in the number of workers and in their average earnings.

Up to 85 percent of an individual's or couple's OASDI benefits may be subject to Federal income taxation if their income exceeds certain thresholds. The income tax revenue attributable to the first 50 percent of OASDI benefits is allocated to the OASI and DI trust funds. The revenue associated with the amount between 50 and 85 percent of benefits is allocated to the HI trust fund. Income from the taxation of OASDI benefits amounted to $18.6 billion in calendar year 2012.

Another substantial source of trust fund income is interest credited from investments in government securities held by the fund. In calendar year 2012, the fund received $10.6 billion in such interest. A description of the trust fund's investment procedures appears later in this section.

Section 1818 of the Social Security Act provides that certain persons not otherwise eligible for HI protection may obtain coverage by enrolling in HI and paying a monthly premium. In 2012, premiums collected from such voluntary participants (or paid on their behalf by Medicaid) amounted to about $3.4 billion.

The Railroad Retirement Act provides for a system of coordination and financial interchange between the Railroad Retirement program and the HI trust fund. This financial interchange requires a transfer that would place the HI trust fund in the same position in which it would have been if the Social Security Act had always covered railroad employment. In accordance with these provisions, a transfer of $484 million in principal and about $17 million in interest from the Railroad Retirement program's Social Security Equivalent Benefit Account to the HI trust fund balanced the two systems as of September 30, 2011. The trust fund received this transfer, together with interest to the date of transfer totaling about $10 million, in June 2012.

Legislation in 1982 added transitional entitlement for those Federal employees who retire before having had a chance to earn sufficient quarters of Medicare-qualified Federal employment. The general fund of the Treasury provides reimbursement for the costs of this coverage, including administrative expenses. In calendar year 2012, such reimbursement amounted to $262 million, all for estimated benefit payments and all for such beneficiaries.

The Health Insurance Portability and Accountability Act of 1996 established a health care fraud and abuse control account within the HI trust fund. Monies derived from the fraud and abuse control program are transferred from the general fund of the Treasury to the HI trust fund. During calendar year 2012, the trust fund received about $3,371 million from this program, significantly more than the $1,704 million received in 2011, due to increased program integrity activities.

b. Expenditures

The HI trust fund pays expenditures for HI benefit payments and administrative expenses. All HI administrative expenses incurred by the Department of Health and Human Services, the Social Security Administration, the Department of the Treasury (including the

Internal Revenue Service), and the Department of Justice in administering HI are charged to the trust fund. Such administrative duties include payment of benefits, the collection of taxes, fraud and abuse control activities, and experiments and demonstration projects designed to determine various methods of increasing efficiency and economy in providing health care services, while maintaining the quality of such services, under HI and SMI.

In addition, Congress has authorized expenditures from the trust funds for construction, rental and lease, or purchase contracts of office buildings and related facilities for use in connection with the administration of HI. Although trust fund expenditures include these costs, the statement of trust fund assets presented in this report does not carry the net worth of facilities and other fixed capital assets because the proceeds of sales of such assets revert to the General Services Administration. Since the value of fixed capital assets does not represent funds available for benefit or administrative expenditures, the Trustees do not consider it in assessing the actuarial status of the funds.

Of the $266.8 billion in total HI expenditures, $262.9 billion represented net benefits paid from the trust fund for health services.[29] Net benefit payments increased 4.0 percent in calendar year 2012 over the corresponding amount of $252.9 billion paid during the preceding calendar year. This increase was small due to the implementation of certain provisions of the Affordable Care Act and a downward adjustment for inpatient hospital payment rates to offset differences in claims coding under the new Medicare Severity-Diagnosis Related Groups (MS-DRG) basis for categorizing hospital stays. Further information on HI benefits by type of service is available in section IV.A.

The remaining $3.9 billion in expenditures was for net HI administrative expenses, after adjustments to the preliminary allocation of administrative costs among the Social Security and Medicare trust funds and the general fund of the Treasury. This amount included $1.6 billion for the health care fraud and abuse control program.

---

[29]Net benefits equal the total gross amounts initially paid from the trust fund during the year, less recoveries of overpayments identified through fraud and abuse control activities.

c. Actual experience versus prior estimates

Table III.B3 compares the actual experience in calendar year 2012 with the estimates presented in the 2011 and 2012 annual reports. A number of factors can contribute to differences between estimates and subsequent actual experience. In particular, actual values for key economic and other variables can differ from assumed levels, and legislative and regulatory changes may occur after a report's preparation. The comparison in table III.B3 indicates that actual HI tax income in 2012 was slightly lower than estimated in the 2012 and 2011 reports; this difference occurred primarily because actual wage growth was lower than the earlier estimates due to the recent economic recession. Actual HI benefit payments in calendar year 2012 were lower than the amounts projected in the 2011 and 2012 reports largely as a result of lower payment updates due to lower wage and price growth in the hospital sector.

Table III.B3.—Comparison of Actual and Estimated Operations of the HI Trust Fund, Calendar Year 2012

[Dollar amounts in millions]

| | | Comparison of actual experience with estimates for calendar year 2012 published in— | | | |
| | | 2012 report | | 2011 report | |
Item	Actual amount	Estimated amount[1]	Actual as percentage of estimate	Estimated amount[1]	Actual as percentage of estimate
Payroll taxes	$205,730	$207,641	99%	$210,952	98%
Benefit payments	262,500	266,383	99	271,291	97

[1]Under the intermediate assumptions.

d. Assets

The Department of Treasury invests, on a daily basis, the portion of the trust fund not needed to meet current expenditures for benefits and administration in interest-bearing obligations of the U.S. Government. The Social Security Act authorizes the issuance of special public-debt obligations for purchase exclusively by the trust fund. The law requires that these special public-debt obligations bear interest at a rate based on the average market yield (computed on the basis of market quotations as of the end of the calendar month immediately preceding the date of such issue) for all marketable interest-bearing obligations of the United States forming a part of the public debt that are not due or callable until after 4 years from the end of that month. Currently, all invested assets of the HI trust fund are in the form of such special-issue securities.[30] Table V.H9,

---

[30]The Department of Treasury may also make investments in obligations guaranteed as to both principal and interest by the United States, including certain federally sponsored agency obligations.

presented in appendix H, shows the assets of the HI trust fund at the end of fiscal years 2011 and 2012.

2. 10-Year Actuarial Estimates (2013-2022)

While the previous section addressed the transactions of the HI trust fund during the preceding calendar year, this section presents estimates of the trust fund's operations and financial status for the next 10 years. The next section discusses the long-range actuarial status of the trust fund. In both this and the following section, the projections shown under current law assume that no changes will occur in the present statutory provisions and regulations under which HI operates.

The estimates shown in this section provide detailed information concerning the short-range financial status of the trust fund, including the estimated levels of future income and outgo, annual differences between income and outgo, and annual trust fund balances. This section also discusses two particularly important indicators of solvency for the HI trust fund—the estimated year of depletion and the test of short-range financial adequacy.

To illustrate the sensitivity of future costs to different economic and demographic factors and to portray a reasonable range of possible future trends, the Trustees show estimates for current law under three alternative sets of economic and demographic assumptions. Due to the uncertainty inherent in such projections, however, the actual operations of the HI trust fund in the future could differ significantly from these estimates.

Figure III.B1 shows past and projected income and expenditures for the HI trust fund under the Trustees' intermediate assumptions. Following the Balanced Budget Act of 1997, the fund experienced annual surpluses in the range of $21 billion to $36 billion through 2003. This difference decreased to between $13 billion and $16 billion in 2004 and 2005, but then reached about $20 billion in 2006 and 2007—in large part as a result of a misallocation of certain hospice benefit costs to the Part B trust fund account. The Centers for Medicare & Medicaid Services corrected this accounting error in 2008. Beginning in 2008, expenditures exceeded income, and the Trustees expect this situation to continue through 2014. Annual surpluses are expected from 2015 through 2020, and annual deficits are expected to return in 2021 and continue throughout the remainder of the projection period.

Figure III.B1.—HI Expenditures and Income
[In billions]

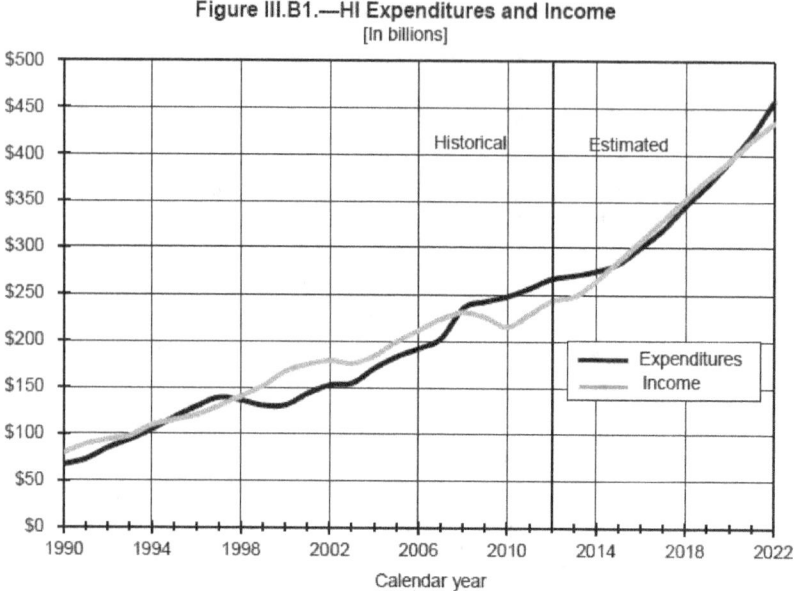

The impact of the recent serious economic recession on HI payroll tax income is apparent in figure III.B1. In 2009 and 2010, payroll taxes decreased substantially as a result of higher unemployment and slow growth in wages along with collection lags; these factors contributed to the $32.3-billion trust fund deficit in 2010. In 2011 and 2012, revenues rebounded somewhat but not enough to reach the level of expenditures, which continue growing due to increased utilization of services and the regular updating of the payment rates. Together these factors resulted in trust fund deficits of $27.7 billion in 2011 and $23.8 billion in 2012.

The provisions of the Affordable Care Act and the Budget Control Act, and an assumed strengthening economic recovery, sharply reduce the magnitude of, and for some years eliminate, trust fund deficits in the short-range period. A downward adjustment to price updates for all HI providers by the growth in economy-wide productivity will slow expenditure growth rates by 0.5 to 1.0 percentage point from 2013 through 2022. The reductions in Medicare Advantage payment benchmarks under the ACA will also significantly reduce the level of expenditures, and the additional 0.9-percent tax rate for high-income workers in 2013 and later will increase HI payroll tax revenues.

HI expenditures are further affected by the sequestration of non-salary Medicare expenditures, which applies from April 1, 2013 to March 31, 2022, as required by the Budget Control Act of 2011 as amended by the American Taxpayer Relief Act of 2012. Under the sequestration, Medicare benefit payments will be reduced by an assumed 2 percent, and administrative expenses will be reduced by an assumed 5 percent. The reduction in benefit payments will end on March 31, 2022, and the administrative expense reductions will end on September 30, 2021. Together, the statutory and economic factors would eliminate the trust fund deficits in 2015-2020, and small surpluses would result. After 2020, annual deficits would occur.

As figure III.B1 illustrates, estimated HI income increases at a faster rate during 2011-2017 than projected HI expenditures, in contrast to the situation that has prevailed during most of the program's history. The projected recovery from the economic recession (which ended in 2009) accelerates income growth during this period, as does the additional 0.9-percent HI payroll tax rate, which began in 2013 and will result in an increasing proportion of workers paying this tax over time. At the same time, the other ACA provisions mentioned previously will slow expenditure growth significantly.

Table III.B4 shows the expected operations of the HI trust fund during calendar years 2013 to 2022 based on the intermediate set of assumptions, together with the past experience. Section IV.A of this report presents the detailed assumptions underlying the intermediate projections.

Table III.B4.—Operations of the HI Trust Fund during Calendar Years 1970-2022

[In billions]

				Income						Expenditures			Trust fund	
Calendar year	Payroll taxes	Income from taxation of benefits	Railroad Retirement account transfers	Reimbursement for uninsured persons	Premiums from voluntary enrollees	Payments for military wage credits	Interest and other[1,2]	Total	Benefit payments[2,3]	Adminis-trative expenses[4]	Total	Net change	Fund at end of year
Historical data:													
1970	$4.9	—	$0.1	$0.9	—	$0.0	$0.2	$6.0	$5.1	$0.2	$5.3	$0.7	$3.2
1975	11.5	—	0.1	0.6	$0.0	0.0	0.7	13.0	11.3	0.3	11.6	1.4	10.5
1980	23.8	—	0.2	0.7	0.0	0.1	1.1	26.1	25.1	0.5	25.6	0.5	13.7
1985	47.6	—	0.4	0.8	0.0	-0.7[5]	3.4	51.4	47.6	0.8	48.4	4.8[6]	20.5
1990	72.0	—	0.4	0.4	0.1	-1.0[7]	8.5	80.4	66.2	0.8	67.0	13.4	98.9
1995	98.4	$3.9	0.4	0.5	1.0	0.1	10.8	115.0	116.4	1.2	117.6	-2.6	130.3
2000	144.4	8.8	0.5	0.5	1.4	0.0	11.7	167.2	128.5[8]	2.6	131.1	36.1	177.5
2005	171.4	8.8	0.4	0.3	2.4	0.0	16.1	199.4	180.0	2.9	182.9	16.4	285.8
2006	181.3	10.3	0.5	0.4	2.6	0.0	16.4	211.5	189.0	2.9	191.9	19.6	305.4
2007	191.9	10.6	0.5	0.5	2.8	0.0	17.5	223.7	200.2	2.9	203.1	20.7	326.0
2008	198.7	11.7	0.5	0.5	2.9	0.0	16.4	230.8	232.3[9]	3.3	235.6	-4.7	321.3
2009	190.9	12.4	0.5	0.6	2.9	1.0[10]	17.1	225.4	239.3	3.2	242.5	-17.1	304.2
2010	182.0	13.8	0.5	-0.1	3.3	0.0	16.1	215.6	244.5	3.5	247.9	-32.3	271.9
2011	195.6	15.1	0.5	0.3	3.3	0.0	14.2	228.9	252.9	3.8	256.7	-27.7	244.2
2012	205.7	18.6	0.5	0.3	3.4	0.0	14.5	243.0	262.9	3.9	266.8	-23.8	220.4
Intermediate estimates:													
2013	216.5	14.7	0.5	0.2	3.5	0.0	12.9	248.2	266.6	3.9	270.5	-22.2	198.1
2014	230.4	18.2	0.5	0.2	3.4	0.0	12.3	265.1	271.1	4.2	275.2	-10.2	188.0
2015	248.4	21.0	0.6	0.2	3.5	0.0	12.7	286.4	279.0	4.6	283.6	2.8	190.8
2016	266.5	23.6	0.6	0.2	3.7	0.0	13.6	308.2	296.2	5.1	301.3	6.9	197.7
2017	284.9	26.1	0.6	0.2	3.9	0.0	14.7	330.4	314.8	5.7	320.5	9.9	207.6
2018	303.2	28.7	0.6	0.2	4.2	0.0	15.9	352.8	339.3	6.2	345.5	7.3	214.9
2019	319.7	32.4	0.7	0.2	4.4	0.0	17.0	374.3	361.2	6.7	367.9	6.4	221.3
2020	335.5	35.1	0.7	0.2	4.7	0.0	17.8	393.9	386.4	7.2	393.6	0.3	221.6
2021	352.0	39.2	0.7	0.2	5.0	0.0	18.1	415.1	414.0	7.7	421.8	-6.7	215.0
2022	368.4	42.4	0.7	0.1	5.4	0.0	17.6	434.6	449.2	8.5	457.7	-23.1	191.8

[1]Other income includes recoveries of amounts reimbursed from the trust fund that are not obligations of the trust fund, receipts from the fraud and abuse control program, and a small amount of miscellaneous income. These receipts amount to $1 8-$4.0 billion each year for the 10-year projection period. In 2008, other income includes an adjustment of −$0.9 billion for interest earned as a result of Part A hospice costs that were misallocated to the Part B trust fund account.

[2]Values after 2005 include additional premiums for Medicare Advantage plans that are deducted from beneficiaries' Social Security benefits. These additional premiums are beneficiary obligations and occur when a beneficiary chooses an MA plan whose monthly plan payment exceeds the benchmark amount. Beneficiaries subject to such premiums may choose to either reimburse the plans direc ly or have the premiums deducted from heir Social Security benefits. The premiums deducted from the Social Security benefits are transferred to the HI and SMI trust funds and then transferred from the trust funds to the plans.

[3]Includes costs of Peer Review Organizations from 1983 through 2001 (beginning with the implementation of the prospective payment system on October 1, 1983) and costs of Quality Improvement Organizations beginning in 2002.

[4]Includes costs of experiments and demonstration projects. Beginning in 1997, includes fraud and abuse control expenses, as provided for by Public Law 104-191.

[5]Includes the lump-sum general revenue adjustment of −$0.8 billion, as provided for by section 151 of Public Law 98-21.

[6]Includes repayment of loan principal, from the OASI trust fund, of $1.8 billion.

[7]Includes the lump-sum general revenue adjustment of −$1.1 billion, as provided for by section 151 of Public Law 98-21.

[8]For 1998 to 2003, includes monies transferred to the SMI trust fund for home health agency costs, as provided for by Public Law 105-33.

[9]Includes the $8.5 billion transferred to the general fund of the Treasury for Part A hospice costs that were previously misallocated to the Part B trust fund account.

[10]Includes the lump-sum general revenue adjustment of $1.0 billion, as provided for by section 151 of Public Law 98-21.

Note: Totals do not necessarily equal the sums of rounded components.

The increases in estimated income shown in table III.B4 primarily reflect increases in payroll tax income to the trust fund since such taxes are the main source of HI financing. As noted, payroll tax revenues increase in 2013 and later as a result of the additional 0.9-percent tax rate on earnings for high-income workers. For all other workers, while the payroll tax rate will remain constant under current law, covered earnings would increase every year after 2010 under the intermediate assumptions due to projected increases in both the number of HI workers covered and the average earnings of these workers.

The Trustees project that over the next 10 years most of the smaller sources of financing for the HI trust fund will increase as well. More detailed descriptions of these sources of income were discussed earlier in this section.

Interest earnings have been a significant source of income to the trust fund for many years, surpassed only by payroll taxes. As the trust fund balance declines over time (as income falls short of expenditures), in the absence of corrective legislation, interest earnings would follow the same pattern.

Since future economic, demographic, and health care usage and cost experience may differ considerably from the intermediate assumptions on which the cost estimates shown in table III.B4 were based, the Trustees have also prepared projections on the basis of "low-cost" and "high-cost" assumptions. These three sets of assumptions illustrate the sensitivity of costs to different economic and demographic trends and provide an indication of the uncertainty associated with HI financial projections under current law. The low-cost and high-cost alternatives provide for a fairly wide range of possible experience. While actual experience may fall within the range, other outcomes are possible, particularly in light of the wide variations in experience that have occurred in the past and the likelihood of further legislation affecting HI. Section IV.A of this report discusses more fully the assumptions used in preparing projections under the low-cost and high-cost alternatives, as well as under the intermediate assumptions.

Table III.B5 summarizes the estimated operations of the HI trust fund during calendar years 2012 to 2022, under all three alternatives. The trust fund ratio, defined as the ratio of assets at the beginning of the year to expenditures during the year, was 92 percent for 2012, below the Trustees' recommended minimum level of 100 percent during the year. Under the intermediate assumptions and current law, the trust fund ratio would decline further to a level of 47 percent at the beginning of 2022. Without legislation to correct the financial imbalance, the fund would continue decreasing and use up all its remaining assets in 2026, and would thus become depleted under the intermediate assumptions.

Under the low-cost alternative, the trust fund would continue to grow indefinitely after the first few years, while under the high-cost alternative depletion would occur in 2019. Without corrective legislation, therefore, the assets of the HI trust fund would be depleted within the next 6 to 13 years under the high-cost and intermediate assumptions. The fact that depletion would occur under a fairly broad range of future economic conditions indicates the importance of promptly addressing the HI trust fund's remaining financial imbalance. Moreover, early corrections—that is, those made while HI trust fund assets are still at or near an adequate level— would require addressing only the underlying financial imbalance. If lawmakers were to delay corrections until there was a significant depletion of HI assets, then more substantial changes would be required.

**Table III.B5.—Estimated Operations of the HI Trust Fund
during Calendar Years 2012-2022, under Alternative Sets of Assumptions**
[Dollar amounts in billions]

Calendar year	Total income	Total expenditures	Net increase in fund	Fund at end of year	Ratio of assets to expenditures[1] (percent)
Intermediate:					
2012[2]	$243.0	$266.8	−$23.8	$220.4	92%
2013	248.2	270.5	−22.2	198.1	81
2014	265.1	275.2	−10.2	188.0	72
2015	286.4	283.6	2.8	190.8	66
2016	308.2	301.3	6.9	197.7	63
2017	330.4	320.5	9.9	207.6	62
2018	352.8	345.5	7.3	214.9	60
2019	374.3	367.9	6.4	221.3	58
2020	393.9	393.6	0.3	221.6	56
2021	415.1	421.8	−6.7	215.0	53
2022	434.6	457.7	−23.1	191.8	47
Low-cost:					
2012[2]	243.0	266.8	−23.8	220.4	92
2013	250.1	267.0	−16.9	203.5	83
2014	273.4	268.8	4.6	208.1	76
2015	295.1	272.7	22.4	230.5	76
2016	316.7	283.9	32.7	263.2	81
2017	338.9	295.1	43.8	307.0	89
2018	360.2	309.8	50.4	357.4	99
2019	379.9	321.3	58.6	416.1	111
2020	400.2	335.5	64.7	480.8	124
2021	422.8	351.6	71.2	552.0	137
2022	444.6	373.7	71.0	622.9	148
High-cost:					
2012[2]	243.0	266.8	−23.8	220.4	92
2013	245.0	276.6	−31.6	188.8	80
2014	254.2	284.5	−30.3	158.5	66
2015	271.6	295.8	−24.2	134.3	54
2016	289.6	319.2	−29.6	104.8	42
2017	310.3	347.8	−37.5	67.2	30
2018	332.9	385.8	−52.9	14.3	17
2019[3]	354.5	424.0	−69.5	−55.1	3
2020[3]	375.8	468.5	−92.7	−147.8	−12
2021[3]	394.3	516.8	−122.5	−270.3	−29
2022[3]	410.6	575.3	−164.8	−435.1	−47

[1]Ratio of assets in the fund at the beginning of the year to expenditures during the year.
[2]Figures for 2012 represent actual experience.
[3]Estimates for 2019 and later are hypothetical, since he HI trust fund would be depleted in those years.

Note: Totals do not necessarily equal the sums of rounded components.

The Board of Trustees has established an explicit test of short-range financial adequacy. The requirements of this test are as follows: (i) if the HI trust fund ratio is at least 100 percent at the beginning of the projection period, then it must remain at or above 100 percent throughout the 10-year projection period; (ii) alternatively, if the fund ratio is initially less than 100 percent, it must reach a level of at least 100 percent within 5 years (with no depletion of the trust fund at any time during this period), and then remain at or above 100 percent throughout the rest of the 10-year period. The Trustees apply this test based on the intermediate projections.

Failure of the trust fund to meet this test is an indication that HI solvency over the next 10 years is in question and that action is necessary to improve the short-range financial adequacy of the fund. As table III.B5 shows, the HI trust fund does not meet this short-range test. The Trustees project that the trust fund ratio, which was below the 100-percent level at the beginning of 2013, will decrease steadily through 2022. Accordingly, the financing for HI is not considered adequate in the short-range projection period (2013-2022).

Table III.B6 shows the ratios of assets in the HI trust fund at the beginning of a calendar year to total expenditures during that year for selected historical years.

Table III.B6.—Ratio of Assets at the Beginning of the Year to Expenditures during the Year for the HI Trust Fund

Calendar year	Ratio
1967	28%
1970	47
1975	79
1980	52
1985	32
1990	128
1995	113
2000	108
2005	147
2006	149
2007	150
2008	138
2009	132
2010	123
2011	106
2012	92

Figure III.B2 shows the historical trust fund ratios and the projected ratios under the three sets of assumptions. The labels "I," "II," and "III" indicate projections under the low-cost, intermediate, and high-cost alternatives, respectively. Figure III.B2 shows the declining level of assets (as a percentage of expenditures) in the immediate future under all three sets of assumptions, reflecting the current financial imbalance, as exacerbated by the recent economic recession. The fund ratio would continue declining under the intermediate and high-cost assumptions. Only under conditions of robust economic growth and extremely low health care cost increases, as assumed in the low-cost alternative, would HI assets grow significantly relative to expenditures, absent legislative changes.

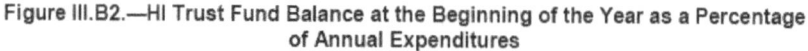

Figure III.B2.—HI Trust Fund Balance at the Beginning of the Year as a Percentage of Annual Expenditures

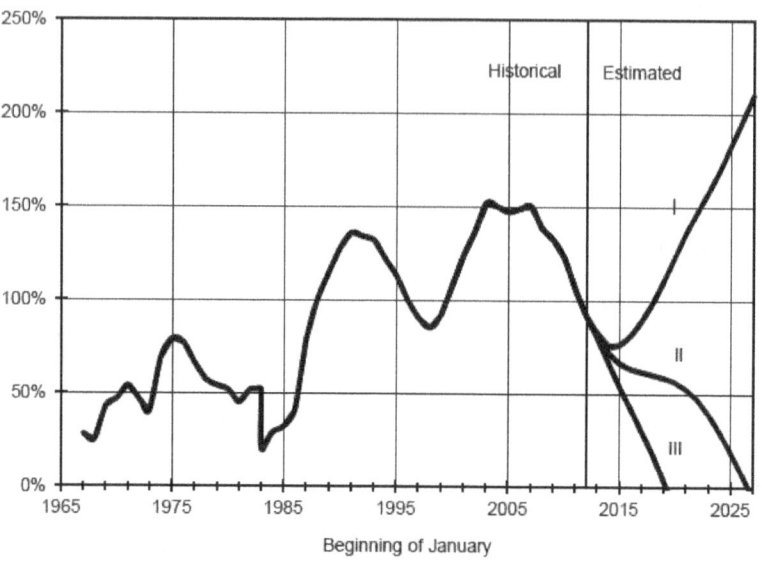

Beginning of January

The Trustees have recommended maintenance of HI trust fund assets at a level of at least 100 percent of annual expenditures. Such a level would provide a cushion of several years in the event that income falls short of expenditures, thereby allowing time for policy makers to implement legislative corrections. While the short-range test is stringent, its purpose is to ensure that health care benefits continue to be available without interruption to the millions of aged and disabled Americans who rely on such coverage.

3. Long-Range Estimates

This section examines the long-range actuarial status of the trust fund under the three alternative sets of economic and demographic assumptions, while section IV.A summarizes the assumptions used in preparing projections. Since the vast majority of total HI costs are related to insured beneficiaries, and since the Trustees expect general revenue appropriations and premium payments to support the uninsured segments (those paying the HI premium and those receiving HI coverage through special statutes requiring general revenue transfers to cover their costs), the remainder of this section will focus on the financing for insured beneficiaries only.

The Trustees measure the long-range actuarial status of the HI trust fund by comparing, on a year-by-year basis, the income (from payroll taxes and from taxation of OASDI benefits) with the corresponding incurred costs, expressed as percentages of taxable payroll.[31] These percentages are referred to as "income rates" and "cost rates," respectively. Incurred amounts include the costs for the misallocated hospice benefit payments (described earlier in this report) in the years in which the HI trust fund should have paid these costs rather than the year in which the HI fund reimbursed the SMI fund.

Table III.B7 shows historical and projected current-law HI costs and income under the intermediate assumptions, expressed as percentages of taxable payroll. The ratio of expenditures to taxable payroll has generally increased over time; it has risen from 0.94 percent in 1967 to 3.39 percent in 1996, an increase that reflects rapid growth in HI expenditures, growth in average earnings per worker, and increases in (and eventual elimination of) the maximum taxable wage base for HI. Cost rates declined significantly between 1996 and 2000 to 2.61 percent due to favorable economic performance, the impact of the Balanced Budget Act of 1997, and efforts to curb fraud and abuse in the Medicare program. The cost rate increased to 3.12 percent by 2005 as a result of legislation and, after remaining about level through 2007, increased rapidly to 3.67 percent in 2009, reflecting the impact of the recession, which lowered taxable payroll. Cost rates then increased slightly in 2010 and 2011 due to the lower taxable payroll, which was not offset by lower spending. The resulting deficit in 2011 as a percentage of taxable payroll was the largest since the program began (0.56 percent). In 2012, the cost rate decreased to 3.67 percent due to a lower increase in spending.

---

[31]Taxable payroll is the total amount of wages, salaries, tips, self-employment income, and other earnings subject to the HI payroll tax.

Table III.B7.—HI Cost and Income Rates[1]

Calendar year	Cost rates[2]	Income rates	Difference[3]
Historical data:			
1967	0.94%	1 00%	+0.06%
1970	1.20	1 20	0.00
1975	1.69	1 80	+0.11
1980	2.19	2.10	−0.09
1985	2.62	2.70	+0.08
1990	2.70	2 90	+0.20
1995	3.30	3 01	−0.29
2000	2.61	3 07	+0.46
2005	3.12	3 07	−0.05
2006	3.11	3 07	−0.04
2007	3.12	3 09	−0.03
2008	3.30	3 06	−0.24
2009	3.67	3.12	−0.55
2010	3.69	3.15	−0.54
2011	3.71	3.15	−0.56
2012	3.67	3.18	−0.49
Intermediate estimates:			
2013	3.62	3 27	−0.35
2014	3.48	3 30	−0.18
2015	3.37	3 32	−0.05
2016	3.34	3 34	−0.00
2017	3.34	3 36	+0.02
2018	3.39	3 38	−0.01
2019	3.43	3.40	−0.03
2020	3.50	3.42	−0.08
2021	3.58	3.44	−0.14
2022	3.73	3.46	−0.26
2025	3.99	3 52	−0.47
2030	4.45	3.61	−0.84
2035	4.86	3.68	−1.18
2040	5.18	3.74	−1.44
2045	5.36	3 80	−1.56
2050	5.44	3 86	−1.58
2055	5.48	3 94	−1.54
2060	5.54	4 01	−1.53
2065	5.65	4 07	−1.58
2070	5.78	4.14	−1.64
2075	5.88	4.19	−1.69
2080	5.89	4 24	−1.65
2085	5.87	4 28	−1.59

[1]Based on the Trustees intermediate assumptions, and expressed as a percentage of taxable payroll.
[2]Estimated costs attributable to insured beneficiaries only, on an incurred basis. The Trustees expect benefits and administrative costs for noninsured persons to be financed through general revenue transfers and premium payments, rather than through payroll taxes. Taxable payroll includes statutory wage credits for military service for 1957-2001.
[3]Difference between the income rates and cost rates. Negative values represent deficits.

The Trustees expect the recovery from the recession and the provisions of the Affordable Care Act to generate a small surplus in 2017. Then the impact of demographic shifts causes the annual deficits to increase rapidly through about 2045. After 2050, the income rates are still insufficient, but the size of the projected deficit largely levels off at roughly 1.6 percent of taxable payroll. Projected HI expenditures are 5.44 and 5.87 percent of taxable payroll in 2050 and 2085, respectively. (Under the illustrative alternative projections, the corresponding HI cost rates would equal 6.55 and 9.22 percent, respectively.)

Figure III.B3 shows the year-by-year costs as a percentage of taxable payroll for each of the three sets of assumptions. The labels "I," "II," and "III" indicate projections under the low-cost, intermediate, and high-cost alternatives, respectively. Figure III.B3 also shows the income rates, but only for the intermediate assumptions in order to simplify the presentation—and because the variation in the income rates by alternative is very small (by 2087, the annual income rates under the low-cost and high-cost alternatives differ by less than 0.6 percent of taxable payroll).

Figure III.B3.—Estimated HI Cost and Income Rates as a Percentage of Taxable Payroll

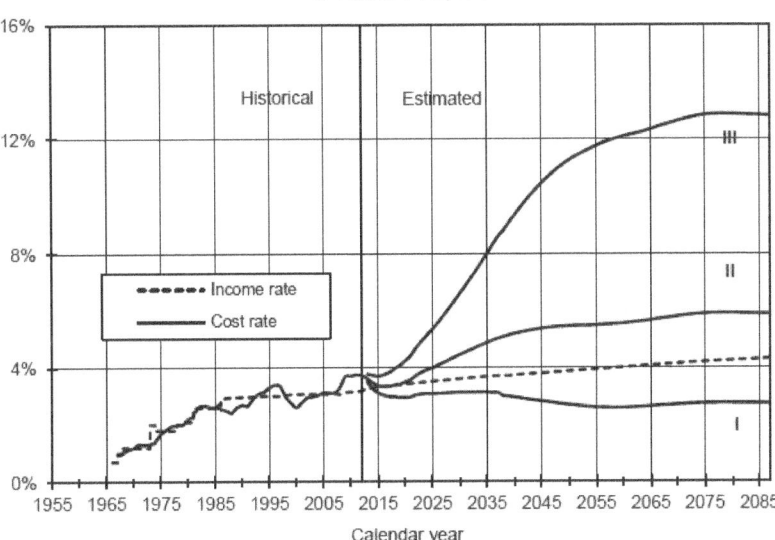

Figure III.B3 shows the remaining financial imbalance projected under current law, based on the intermediate assumptions. The Trustees project that cost rates will continue to exceed income rates by a decreasing margin for the next few years, eventually causing small surpluses for a couple of years before the deficits begin to increase until about 2050. This deficit reaches a peak of about 1.6 percent of taxable payroll in 2050 and decreases gradually for the next several years until 2060. After this point, the deficits increase slightly through 2075 before beginning to decline again. By the end of the 75-year period, this differential would be about 1.6 percent of taxable payroll and would continue to decline thereafter under current law.

Under the more favorable economic and demographic conditions assumed in the low-cost assumptions, HI costs would continue to exceed scheduled income through 2014. After that, the Trustees project steadily growing surpluses for the remainder of the projection period. This very favorable result is due in large part to HI expenditure growth rates that would average only about 4 percent per year, reflecting the combined effects of slower growth in utilization and intensity of services, the price reductions from the Affordable Care Act, and slower improvement in beneficiary life expectancies.

The high-cost projections illustrate the large financial imbalance that could occur if future economic conditions resemble those of the 1973-95 period, if HI expenditure growth accelerates toward pre-1997 levels, and if fertility rates decline to the levels currently experienced in comparable European countries.[32]

The Trustees project costs beyond the initial 25-year period for the intermediate estimate based on the assumption that average HI expenditures per beneficiary will increase at a rate determined by the economic model described in sections II.C and IV.D, less the price update adjustments based on economy-wide multifactor productivity gains. This net rate is about 0.4 percent faster than the increase in Gross Domestic Product (GDP) per capita in 2037 and declines to about 0.5 percent *slower* than GDP by 2087. Accordingly, changes in the next 75 years of the projection period reflect both the impact of the changing demographic composition of the population and average benefits that initially increase somewhat more rapidly than average wages but more slowly after about 2064. Beyond the initial 25-year projection period, the low-cost and high-cost alternatives assume that HI cost increases, relative to taxable payroll increases, are initially 2 percentage points less rapid and 2 percentage points more rapid, respectively, than the results under the intermediate assumptions. The assumed initial 2-percentage-point differentials decrease gradually until the year 2062, when HI cost increases (relative to taxable payroll) are assumed to be the same as under the intermediate assumptions.

Figure III.B3 shows the cost rates and income rates over a 75-year valuation period in order to present fully the future economic and demographic developments that one may reasonably expect to occur, such as the impact of the large increase in the number of people over

---

[32]Actual experience during these periods was similar on average to the high-cost economic and programmatic assumptions for the future.

age 65 that began to take place in 2011. Growth occurs in part because the ratio of workers to beneficiaries will decrease as persons born during the period between the end of World War II and the mid-1960s (known as the baby boom generation) will reach eligibility age and begin to receive benefits.

For the most part, current workers pay for current benefits. Figure III.B4 shows the projected ratio of workers per HI beneficiary from 1980 to 2087.

Figure III.B4.—Workers per HI Beneficiary
[Based on intermediate assumptions]

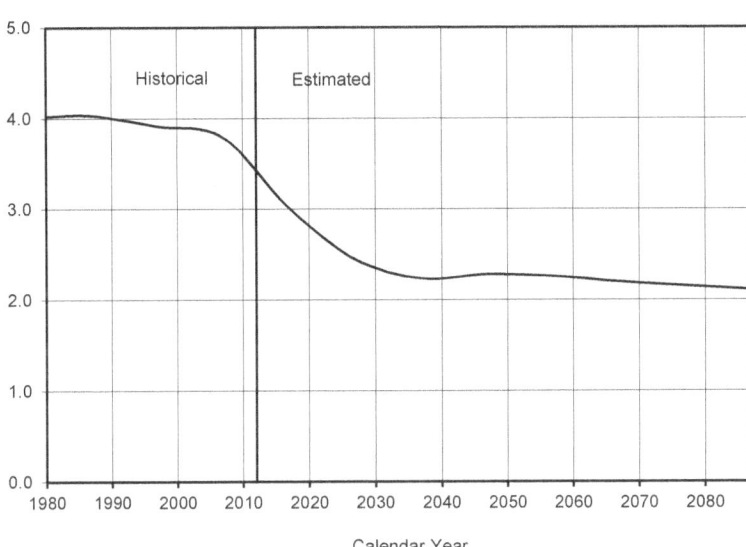

Calendar Year

As figure III.B4 indicates, the ratio of workers to beneficiaries was relatively stable at about 4 percent from 1980 through 2008. It began to decline initially due to the recession but then declined further due to the retirement of the baby boom generation. While every beneficiary in 2012 had about 3.3 workers to pay for his or her HI benefit, in 2030 under the intermediate demographic assumptions there would be only about 2.3 workers for each beneficiary. This ratio would then continue to decline until there are only 2.1 workers per beneficiary in 2087. This reduction implies an increase in the HI cost rate of about 70 percent in 2087, relative to its current level, solely due to demographic factors.[33]

While year-by-year comparisons of revenues and costs are necessary to measure the adequacy of HI financing, the financial status of the trust fund is often summarized, over a specific valuation period, by a single measure known as the actuarial balance. The actuarial balance of the HI trust fund is defined as the difference between the summarized income rate for the valuation period and the summarized cost rate for the same period.

The summarized income rates, cost rates, and actuarial balance are based upon the present values of future income, costs, and taxable payroll. The Trustees calculate the present values, as of the beginning of the valuation period, by discounting the future annual amounts of income and outgo at the assumed rates of interest credited to the HI trust fund, and then obtain the summarized income and cost rates over the projection period by dividing the present value of income and cost, respectively, by the present value of taxable payroll. The difference between the summarized income rate and cost rate over the long-range projection period, after an adjustment to take into account the fund balance at the valuation date and a target trust fund balance at the end of the valuation period, is the actuarial balance.

In keeping with a decision by the Board of Trustees that it is advisable to maintain a balance in the trust fund equal to a minimum of 1 year's expenditures, the target trust fund balance is equal to the following year's estimated costs at the end of the 75-year projection period. While a zero or positive actuarial balance implies that the end-of-period trust fund balance is at least as large as the target trust fund balance, there is no such implication for the trust fund balance at other times during the projection period.

Table III.B8 shows the actuarial balances under current law and based on the Trustees' three sets of economic and demographic assumptions, for the next 25, 50, and 75 years. Based on the intermediate set of assumptions, the summarized income rate for the entire 75-year period is 3.83 percent of taxable payroll. Based on the intermediate assumptions, the summarized HI cost rate under

---

[33]In addition to this factor, the projected increase in the HI cost rate reflects greater use of health care services as the beneficiary population ages and higher average costs per service due to medical price inflation and technological advances in care. The slower growth in Medicare payment rates to HI providers under the Affordable Care Act substantially offsets these increases under current law.

current law for the entire 75-year period is 4.94 percent. As a result, the actuarial balance is −1.11 percent, and the HI trust fund fails to meet the Trustees' long-range test of close actuarial balance.[34]

One can interpret the actuarial balance as the percentage that could be added to the current-law income rates and/or subtracted from the current-law cost rates immediately and throughout the entire valuation period in order for the financing to support HI costs and provide for the targeted trust fund balance at the end of the projection period. The income rate increase according to this method is 1.11 percent of taxable payroll. However, if no such changes occurred until 2026, when the trust fund would be depleted under current law, then the required increase would be 1.44 percent of taxable payroll under the intermediate assumptions. If changes instead occurred year by year, as needed to balance each year's costs and tax revenues, the changes would be minor over the next 10 years and then would grow rapidly to roughly 1.6 percent of taxable payroll in 2045, remaining at that level through the end of the projection period.

Table III.B8.—HI Actuarial Balances under Three Sets of Assumptions

| | Intermediate assumptions | Alternative | |
		Low-Cost	High-Cost
Valuation periods:[1]			
25 years, 2013-2037:			
Summarized income rate	3.62	3 57	3.68
Summarized cost rate	4.20	3 21	5.82
Actuarial balance	−0.58	0 36	−2.14
50 years, 2013-2062:			
Summarized income rate	3.73	3.64	3.81
Summarized cost rate	4.69	2 99	7.91
Actuarial balance	−0.97	0.66	−4.09
75 years, 2013-2087:			
Summarized income rate	3.83	3.73	3.94
Summarized cost rate	4.94	2 91	8.87
Actuarial balance	−1.11	0 82	−4.93

[1]Income rates include beginning trust fund balances, and cost rates include the cost of attaining a trust fund balance at the end of the period equal to 100 percent of the following year's estimated expenditures.

Notes: Totals do not necessarily equal the sums of rounded components.

The divergence in outcomes among the three sets of assumptions is apparent both in the estimated operations of the trust fund on a cash basis (as discussed in section III.B2) and in the 75-year summarized costs. Under the low-cost economic and demographic assumptions, the summarized cost rate for the 75-year valuation period is 2.91 percent of taxable payroll, and the summarized income rate is 3.73 percent of taxable payroll; accordingly, HI income rates would be

---

[34]This test is complex; it is defined in section V.I.

adequate under the highly favorable conditions assumed in the low-cost alternative. Under the high-cost assumptions, the summarized cost rate for the 75-year projection period is 8.87 percent of taxable payroll, which is more than twice the summarized income rate of 3.94 percent of taxable payroll.

As suggested earlier, past experience has indicated that economic and demographic conditions that are as financially adverse as those assumed under the high-cost alternative can, in fact, occur. Readers should view all of the alternative sets of economic and demographic assumptions as plausible. The wide range of results under the three sets of assumptions is indicative of the uncertainty of HI's future cost under current law and its sensitivity to future economic and demographic conditions. Accordingly, it is important to maintain an adequate balance in the HI trust fund as a reserve for contingencies and to promptly address financial imbalances through corrective legislation.

Table III.B9 shows the long-range actuarial balance under the intermediate projections with its component parts—the present values of tax income, expenditures, and asset requirement of the HI program over the next 75 years.

Table III.B9.—Components of 75-Year HI Actuarial Balance under Intermediate Assumptions (2013-2087)

Present value as of January 1, 2013 (in billions):	
a. Payroll tax income	$13,931
b. Taxation of benefits income	1,969
c. Fraud and abuse control receipts	291
d. Total income (a + b + c)	16,192
e. Expenditures	20,963
f. Expenditures minus income (e − d)	4,772
g. Trust fund assets at start of period	220
h. Open-group unfunded obligation (f − g)	4,552
i. Ending target trust fund[1]	206
j. Present value of actuarial balance (d − e + g − i)	−4,758
k. Taxable payroll	428,225
Percent of taxable payroll:	
Actuarial balance (j ÷ k)	−1.11%

[1]The calculation of the actuarial balance includes the cost of accumulating a target trust fund balance equal to 100 percent of annual expenditures by the end of the period.

Note: Totals do not necessarily equal the sums of rounded components.

The present value of future expenditures less future tax income, decreased by the amount of HI trust fund assets on hand at the beginning of the projection, amounts to $4.6 trillion. This value is referred to as the 75-year "unfunded obligation" for the HI trust fund, and it is lower than last year's value of $5.3 trillion. The actuarial balance is like the unfunded obligation except that (i) it is a measure of the degree to which the program is funded rather than unfunded and so is opposite in sign; (ii) it includes the trust fund balance at the end of 75 years as a cost; and (iii) it is expressed as a percent of taxable payroll. Specifically, the actuarial balance is −1.11 percent of taxable payroll and is calculated as the trust fund balance plus the present value of revenues less the present value of costs (−$4.6 trillion), less the present value of the target trust fund balance ($206 billion), all divided by the present value of future taxable payroll ($428.2 trillion).

Figure III.B5 shows the present values, as of January 1, 2013, of cumulative HI taxes less expenditures (plus the 2013 trust fund) through each of the next 75 years. The Trustees estimate these values under current-law expenditures and tax rates.

Figure III.B5.—Present Value of Cumulative HI Taxes Less Expenditures through Year Shown, Evaluated under Current-Law Tax Rates and Legislated Expenditures

[Present value as of January 1, 2013; in trillions]

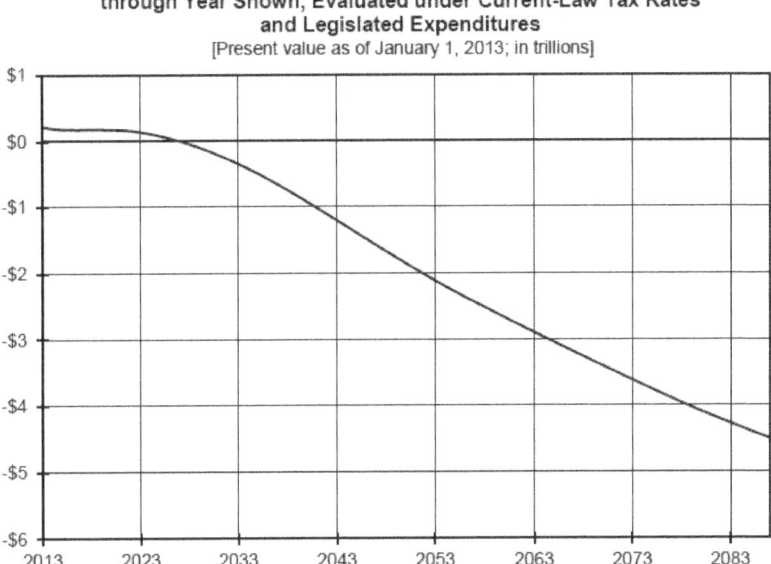

Ending year of valuation period

The cumulative annual balance of the trust fund is highest at the beginning of 2013 with beginning trust fund assets of about $0.2 trillion. The cumulative present value trends steadily downward over the projection period due to the anticipated shortfall of tax revenues, relative to expenditures, in most years from 2013 and later. The projected depletion date of the trust fund is 2026, at which time cumulative expenditures would have exceeded cumulative tax revenues by enough to equal the initial fund assets accumulated with interest. The continuing downward slope in the line thereafter further illustrates the unsustainable difference between the HI expenditures promised under current law and the financing currently scheduled to support these expenditures. As noted previously, over the full 75-year period, the fund has a projected present value unfunded obligation of $4.6 trillion. This unfunded obligation indicates that if $4.6 trillion were added to the trust fund at the beginning of 2013, the program would meet the projected cost of current-law expenditures over the next 75 years. More realistically, additional annual revenues and/or reductions in expenditures, with a present value totaling $4.6 trillion, would be necessary to reach financial balance (but with zero trust fund assets at the end of 2087).

The estimated unfunded obligation of $4.6 trillion and the closely associated present value of the actuarial deficit ($4.8 trillion) are useful indicators of the sizable financial burden facing the American public. In other words, increases in revenues and/or reductions in benefit expenditures—equivalent to a lump-sum amount today of about $5 trillion—would be necessary to bring the HI trust fund into long-range financial balance. At the same time, long-range measures expressed in dollar amounts can be difficult to interpret, even when calculated as present values, which are sensitive to the underlying discount rate assumptions. For this reason, the Board of Trustees has customarily emphasized relative measures, such as the income rate and cost rate comparisons shown earlier in this section, and comparisons to the present value of future taxable payroll or GDP.

Figure III.B6 compares the year-by-year HI cost and income rates for the current annual report with the corresponding projections from the 2012 report.

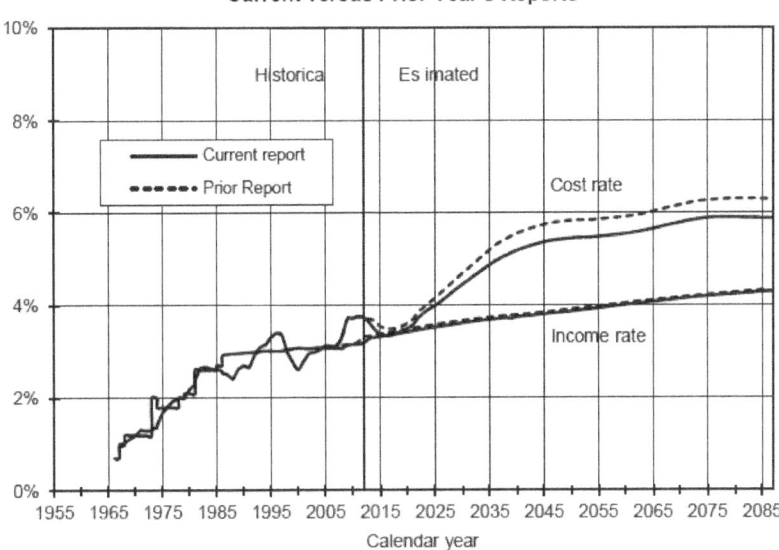

Figure III.B6.—Comparison of HI Cost and Income Rate Projections: Current versus Prior Year's Reports

As figure III.B6 indicates, the intermediate HI cost rate projections in this year's report are slightly lower than those in the 2012 report for the entire projection period. The projected income rates are very slightly lower.

Both of the HI expenditure projections described above are based on the same set of projected long-range rates of increase in average HI costs per beneficiary. For both the 2012 and 2013 reports, the long-range growth rates are drawn from a "factors contributing to growth" economic model developed by the Office of the Actuary at CMS. In both reports these assumptions reflect the price update reductions in the ACA which lower HI prices by the productivity adjustments. In addition, both sets of income rates include the impact of the higher tax rate required of high-income workers by the ACA, together with the growing proportion of workers who will be required to pay the higher tax over time, since the income thresholds are not indexed.

The Trustees' estimate of the 75-year HI actuarial balance under the intermediate assumptions, −1.11 percent of taxable payroll, is 0.24 percentage point larger (more favorable) than estimated in the 2012 annual report. The reasons for this change, which are listed in table III.B10, are explained below:

(1) Change in valuation period: Updating the valuation period from 2012-2086 to 2013-2087 adds a larger deficit year to

the calculation of the actuarial balance. The effect on the actuarial balance is −0.03 percent of taxable payroll.

(2) Updating the projection base: Actual 2012 incurred HI expenditures were lower than previously estimated, and taxable payroll was slightly lower. The result is a slightly lower cost as a percentage of taxable payroll for 2012 than estimated previously. These base-year differences change the actuarial balance by +0.05 percent of taxable payroll.

(3) Private health plan assumptions: In this year's report, the Medicare Advantage plan bid assumptions were lowered to reflect recent data suggesting that certain provisions of the Affordable Care Act will reduce growth in these costs by more than was previously projected. The impact on the actuarial balance of this assumption change and other minor changes is +0.07 percent of taxable payroll.

(4) Hospital assumptions: The primary changes in hospital assumptions in this report are (i) a revised methodology for inpatient rehabilitation facilities, long-term care hospitals, and psychiatric hospitals to more accurately reflect their costs, and (ii) a longer transition period for the non-labor differential in the market basket. The combined impact of these and other minor changes results in a +0.02-percent change in the actuarial balance.

(5) Other provider assumptions: The Trustees assume lower skilled nursing facility utilization and case mix increases for the next several years in this year's report mainly due to recent expenditure data indicating that the base estimate used in last year's projection was abnormally high. In addition, an improvement to the methodology of determining the fee for service utilization increases resulted in smaller projected increases. The effect of these changes, along with other minor factors, is a +0.11-percent difference in the actuarial balance.

(6) Economic and demographic assumptions: The net effect of several adjustments to the economic and demographic assumptions is a +0.02-percent change in the actuarial balance. The major changes in these assumptions in this year's report are the much lower increases in productivity and refinements in the methodology used to transition from the short-range projections to the long-range projections, resulting in smaller increases during this transition period. In addition, the new larger increases in taxable payroll improve the actuarial balance. As indicated, the combined

effect of these changes has only a minor impact on the balance.

Table III.B10.—Change in the 75-Year Actuarial Balance since the 2012 Report

1. Actuarial balance, intermediate assumptions, 2012 report	−1.35%
2. Changes:	
a. Valuation period	−0.03
b. Base estimate	0.05
c. Private health plan assumptions	0.07
d. Hospital assumptions	0.02
e. Other provider assumptions	0.11
f. Economic and demographic assumptions	0.02
Net effect, above changes	+0.24
3. Actuarial balance, intermediate assumptions, 2013 report	−1.11

4. Long-Range Sensitivity Analysis

This section presents estimates that illustrate the sensitivity of the long-range HI cost rate, income rate, and actuarial balance of HI to changes in selected individual assumptions. The estimates based on the three alternative sets of assumptions (intermediate, low-cost, and high-cost) demonstrate the effects of varying all of the principal assumptions simultaneously in order to portray a generally more optimistic or pessimistic future for the projected financial status of the HI trust fund. In the sensitivity analysis presented in this section, the intermediate set of assumptions is the reference point, and one assumption at a time varies within that alternative. In each case, the Trustees assume that the provisions of current law remain unchanged throughout the 75-year projection period.

Each table that follows shows the effects of changing a particular assumption on the HI summarized income rates, summarized cost rates, and actuarial balances for 25-year, 50-year, and 75-year valuation periods. The discussion of the tables generally does not include the income rate, since it varies only slightly with changes in assumptions. The change in each of the actuarial balances is approximately equal to the change in the corresponding cost rate, but in the opposite direction. For example, a lower projected cost rate would result in an improvement or increase in the corresponding projected actuarial balance.

a. Real-Wage Differential

Table III.B11 shows the estimated HI income rates, cost rates, and actuarial balances on the basis of the intermediate assumptions, with various assumptions about the real-wage differential. These assumptions are that the ultimate real-wage differential will be

0.5 percentage point (as assumed for the high-cost alternative), 1.1 percentage points (as assumed for the intermediate assumptions), and 1.7 percentage points (as assumed for the low-cost alternative). In each case, the assumed ultimate annual increase in the Consumer Price Index (CPI) is 2.8 percent (as assumed for the intermediate assumptions), yielding ultimate percentage increases in nominal average annual wages in covered employment of 3.3, 3.9, and 4.5 percent under the three illustrations, respectively.

Past increases in real earnings have exhibited substantial variation. During 1951-1970, real earnings grew by an average of 2.2 percent per year. During 1972-1996, however, the average annual increase in real earnings amounted to only 0.53 percent.[35] Poor performance in real-wage growth would have substantial consequences for the HI trust fund; as shown in table III.B11, projected HI cost rates are fairly sensitive to the assumed growth rates in real wages. For the 75-year period 2013-2087, the summarized cost rate decreases from 5.30 percent (for a real-wage differential of 0.5 percentage point) to 4.58 percent (for a differential of 1.7 percentage points). The HI actuarial balance over this period shows a corresponding improvement for faster rates of growth in real wages.

Table III.B11—Estimated HI Income Rates, Cost Rates, and Actuarial Balances, Based on Intermediate Estimates with Various Real-Wage Assumptions
[As a percentage of taxable payroll]

Valuation period	Ultimate percentage increase in wages-CPI[1]		
	3.3-2.8	3.9-2.8	4.5-2.8
Summarized income rate:			
25-year: 2013-2037	3.64	3.62	3.61
50-year: 2013-2062	3.73	3.73	3.73
75-year: 2013-2087	3.82	3.83	3.85
Summarized cost rate:			
25-year: 2013-2037	4.36	4.20	4.06
50-year: 2013-2062	4.96	4.69	4.44
75-year: 2013-2087	5.30	4.94	4.58
Actuarial balance:			
25-year: 2013-2037	-0.72	-0.58	-0.46
50-year: 2013-2062	-1.22	-0.97	-0.71
75-year: 2013-2087	-1.48	-1.11	-0.73

[1]The first value in each pair is the assumed ultimate annual percentage increase in average wages in covered employment. The second value is the assumed ultimate annual percentage increase in the CPI. The difference between the two values is the real-wage differential.

The sensitivity of the HI actuarial balance to different real-wage assumptions is significant, but not as substantial as one might intuitively expect. Higher real-wage differentials immediately increase both HI expenditures for health care and wages for all

---

[35]The Trustees chose this period because it begins and ends with years in which the economy reached full employment. The period thus allows measurement of trend growth over complete economic cycles.

workers. Though there is a full effect on wages and payroll taxes, the effect on benefits is only partial, since not all health care costs are wage-related. The HI cost rate decreases with increasing real-wage differentials because the higher real-wage levels increase the taxable payroll to a greater extent than they increase HI benefits. In particular, each 0.5-percentage-point increase in the assumed real-wage differential increases the long-range HI actuarial balance, on average, by about 0.31 percent of taxable payroll.

b. Consumer Price Index

Table III.B12 shows the estimated HI income rates, cost rates, and actuarial balances on the basis of the intermediate alternative, with various assumptions about the rate of increase for the CPI. These assumptions are that the ultimate annual increase in the CPI will be 1.8 percent (as assumed for the low-cost alternative), 2.8 percent (as assumed for the intermediate assumptions), and 3.8 percent (as assumed for the high-cost alternative). In each case, the assumed ultimate real-wage differential is 1.1 percent (as assumed for the intermediate assumptions), which yields ultimate percentage increases in average annual wages in covered employment of 2.9, 3.9, and 4.9 percent under the three illustrations.

Table III.B12.—Estimated HI Income Rates, Cost Rates, and Actuarial Balances, Based on Intermediate Estimates with Various CPI-Increase Assumptions

[As a percentage of taxable payroll]

	Ultimate percentage increase in wages-CPI[1]		
Valuation period	2 9-1.8	3.9-2.8	4.9-3.8
Summarized income rate:			
25-year: 2013-2037	3.61	3.62	3.64
50-year: 2013-2062	3.69	3.73	3.77
75-year: 2013-2087	3.78	3.83	3.88
Summarized cost rate:			
25-year: 2013-2037	4.21	4.20	4.20
50-year: 2013-2062	4.70	4.69	4.69
75-year: 2013-2087	4.95	4.94	4.94
Actuarial balance:			
25-year: 2013-2037	−0.60	−0.58	−0.56
50-year: 2013-2062	−1.01	−0.97	−0.92
75-year: 2013-2087	−1.16	−1.11	−1.05

[1]The first value in each pair is the assumed ultimate annual percentage increase in average wages in covered employment. The second value is the assumed ultimate annual percentage increase in the CPI.

Faster assumed growth in the CPI results in a somewhat larger HI income rate because current law does not index the income thresholds for the taxation of Social Security benefits and the application of the additional 0.9-percent payroll tax rate. Over time, consequently, these provisions affect an increasing proportion of beneficiaries and workers as their incomes exceed the fixed thresholds, and this impact accelerates under conditions of faster CPI growth. In contrast, the cost rate remains about the same with greater assumed rates of increase in the CPI. The relative insensitivity of projected HI cost rates to different levels of general inflation occurs because of the assumption that inflation affects both the taxable payroll of workers and medical care costs about equally.[36] In practice, differing rates of inflation could occur between the economy in general and the medical-care sector. Readers can judge the effect of such a difference from the sensitivity analysis shown in the subsequent section on miscellaneous health care cost factors. Overall, variation in the rate of change assumed for the CPI has only a modest effect on the long-range actuarial balance.

c. Real-Interest Rate

Table III.B13 shows the estimated HI income rates, cost rates, and actuarial balances under the intermediate alternative, with various assumptions about the annual real-interest rate for special public-debt obligations issuable to the trust fund. These assumptions are that the ultimate annual real-interest rate will be 2.4 percent (as assumed for the high-cost alternative), 2.9 percent (as assumed for the intermediate assumptions), and 3.4 percent (as assumed for the low-cost alternative). In each case, the assumed ultimate annual increase in the CPI is 2.8 percent (as assumed for the intermediate assumptions), which results in ultimate annual yields of 5.2, 5.7, and 6.2 percent under the three illustrations.

Table III.B13.—Estimated HI Income Rates, Cost Rates, and Actuarial Balances, Based on Intermediate Estimates with Various Real-Interest Assumptions
[As a percentage of taxable payroll]

Valuation period	Ultimate annual real-interest rate		
	2.4 percent	2 9 percent	3.4 percent
Summarized income rate:			
25-year: 2013-2037	3.62	3.62	3.62
50-year: 2013-2062	3.73	3.73	3.72
75-year: 2013-2087	3.85	3.83	3.81
Summarized cost rate:			
25-year: 2013-2037	4.23	4.20	4.18
50-year: 2013-2062	4.75	4.69	4.63
75-year: 2013-2087	5.03	4.94	4.86
Actuarial balance:			
25-year: 2013-2037	−0.61	−0.58	−0.55
50-year: 2013-2062	−1.02	−0.97	−0.92
75-year: 2013-2087	−1.18	−1.11	−1.04

For all periods, the cost rate decreases slightly with increasing real-interest rates. Over 2013-2087, for example, the summarized HI cost rate would decline from 5.03 percent (for an ultimate real-interest

---

[36]The slight sensitivity shown in the table results primarily from the fact that the fiscal year 2013 payment rates for all providers have already been set before publication of the actual CPI.

rate of 2.4 percent) to 4.86 percent (for an ultimate real-interest rate of 3.4 percent). Accordingly, each 1.0-percentage-point increase in the assumed real-interest rate increases the long-range actuarial balance, on average, by about 0.14 percent of taxable payroll.

d. Health Care Cost Factors

Table III.B14 shows the estimated HI income rates, cost rates, and actuarial balances on the basis of the intermediate set of assumptions, with two variations on the relative annual growth rate in the aggregate cost of providing covered health care services to HI beneficiaries. These assumptions are that starting in 2013 the ratio of costs to taxable payroll will grow 1 percentage point slower than in the intermediate assumption, the same as the intermediate assumption, and 1 percentage point faster than the intermediate assumption. In each case, the taxable payroll will be the same as assumed for the intermediate assumptions.[37]

As noted previously, factors such as wage and price increases may simultaneously affect HI tax income and the costs incurred by hospitals and other providers of medical care to HI beneficiaries. (Sections III.B4a and III.B4b evaluate the sensitivity of the trust fund's financial status to these factors.) Other factors, such as the utilization of services by beneficiaries or the relative complexity of the services provided, can have an impact on provider costs without affecting HI tax income. The sensitivity analysis shown in table III.B14 illustrates the financial effect of any combination of these factors that results in the ratio of cost to payroll taxes increasing by 1 percentage point faster or slower than the intermediate assumptions.

---

[37]These variations in HI cost growth rates are not equivalent to the high- and low-cost alternative assumptions, which use a different level and pattern of growth differentials and also vary other assumptions in addition to the cost growth factors.

Table III.B14.—Estimated HI Income Rates, Cost Rates, and Actuarial Balances,
Based on Intermediate Estimates
with Various Health Care Cost Growth Rate Assumptions

[As a percentage of taxable payroll]

Valuation period	Annual cost/payroll rela ive growth rate		
	−1 percentage point	0 percentage point	+1 percentage point
Summarized income rate:			
25-year: 2013-2037	3.62	3.62	3.62
50-year: 2013-2062	3.73	3.73	3.73
75-year: 2013-2087	3.83	3.83	3.83
Summarized cost rate:			
25-year: 2013-2037	3.66	4.20	4.85
50-year: 2013-2062	3.65	4.69	6.13
75-year: 2013-2087	3.51	4.94	7.24
Actuarial balance:			
25-year: 2013-2037	−0.04	−0.58	−1.22
50-year: 2013-2062	0.07	−0.97	−2.41
75-year: 2013-2087	0.32	−1.11	−3.40

As illustrated in table III.B14, the financial status of the HI trust fund is extremely sensitive to the relative growth rates for health care service costs versus taxable payroll. For the 75-year period, the cost rate increases from 3.51 percent (for an annual cost/payroll growth rate of 1 percentage point less than the intermediate assumptions) to 7.24 percent (for an annual cost/payroll growth rate of 1 percentage point more than the intermediate assumptions). Each 1.0-percentage-point increase in the assumed cost/payroll relative growth rate decreases the long-range actuarial balance, on average, by about 1.86 percent of taxable payroll.

C. PART B FINANCIAL STATUS

1. Financial Operations in Calendar Year 2012

Table III.C1 presents a statement of the revenue and expenditures of the Part B account of the SMI trust fund in calendar year 2012, and of its assets at the beginning and end of the year.

Table III.C1.—Statement of Operations of the Part B Account in the SMI Trust Fund during Calendar Year 2012
[In thousands]

Total assets of the Part B account in the trust fund, beginning of period		$79,692,953
Revenue:		
Premiums from enrollees:		
Enrollees aged 65 and over..................................	$48,495,035	
Disabled enrollees under age 65	9,528,652	
Total premiums		58,023,687
Premiums collected from Medicare Advantage participants		213,670
Government contributions:		
Enrollees aged 65 and over.................................	136,726,203	
Disabled enrollees under age 65	27,101,109	
Total government contributions		163,827,312
Other		2,276
Interest on investments		2,766,465
Interfund interest payments[1]........................		−1,516
Annual fees – branded Rx manufacturers and importers		2,183,532
Total revenue..........................		$227,015,425
Expenditures:		
Net Part B benefit payments............................		$236,535,315
Administrative expenses:		
Transfer to Medicaid[2]...............................	602,303	
Treasury administrative expenses	504	
Salaries and expenses, CMS[3]	2,300,679	
Salaries and expenses, Office of the Secretary, HHS..............	26,400	
Salaries and expenses, SSA	960,468	
Medicare Payment Advisory Commission	4,711	
AOA MIPPA funding	10,507	
Railroad Retirement administrative expenses........................	10,303	
Transfer to PCOR trust fund	27,265	
CMS program management – ACA	3,849	
Total administrative expenses...........................		3,946,989
Total expenditures		$240,482,305
Net addition to the trust fund		−13,466,879
Total assets of the Part B account in the trust fund, end of period		$66,226,074

[1]Reflects interest adjustments on the reallocation of administrative expenses between the Medicare trust funds, the OASDI trust funds, and the general fund of the Treasury. Estimated payments are made from he trust funds and then are reconciled, with interest, the next year when the actual costs are known. A positive figure represents a transfer to the Part B account in the SMI trust fund from the other trust funds. A negative figure represents a transfer from the Part B account in the SMI trust fund to the other funds.
[2]Represents amount transferred from the Part B account in the SMI trust fund to Medicaid to pay the Part B premium for certain qualified individuals, as legislated by the Balanced Budget Act of 1997.
[3]Includes administrative expenses of the carriers and intermediaries.

Note: Totals do not necessarily equal the sums of rounded components.

The total assets of the account amounted to $79.7 billion on December 31, 2011. During calendar year 2012, total revenue amounted to $227.0 billion, and total expenditures were $240.5 billion. Total assets thus decreased $13.5 billion during the year, to $66.2 billion as of December 31, 2012. The decrease in assets occurred primarily because the Part B financing was established to intentionally reduce the Part B assets during 2012.

a. Revenues

The major sources of revenue for the Part B account are (i) contributions of the Federal Government that the law authorizes to be appropriated and transferred from the general fund of the Treasury; and (ii) premiums paid by eligible persons who voluntarily enroll. A new source of revenues, which began in 2011 as specified by the Affordable Care Act, is the annual fees assessed on manufacturers and importers of brand-name prescription drugs. The ACA directs that these fees be allocated to the Part B trust fund account, where they will serve to slightly reduce the need for premium revenues and Federal general revenues. Eligible persons aged 65 and over have been able to enroll in Part B since its inception in July 1966. Since July 1973, disabled persons who are under age 65 and who have met certain eligibility requirements have also been able to enroll.

Of the total Part B revenue, $58.0 billion represented premium payments by (or on behalf of) aged and disabled enrollees—an increase of 0.9 percent over the amount of $57.5 billion for the preceding year.

Government contributions matched the premiums paid for fiscal years 1967 through 1973 dollar for dollar. Beginning July 1973, the amount of government contributions corresponding to premiums paid by each of the two groups of enrollees is determined by applying a "matching ratio," prescribed in the law for each group, to the amount of premiums received from that group. This ratio is equal to twice the monthly actuarial rate applicable to the particular group of enrollees, minus the standard monthly premium rate, divided by the standard monthly premium rate.

The Secretary of Health and Human Services promulgates standard monthly premium rates and actuarial rates each year. Table III.C2 shows past monthly premium rates and actuarial rates together with the corresponding percentages of Part B costs covered by the premium rate. Estimated future premium amounts under the intermediate set of assumptions appear in section V.E.

Table III.C2.—Standard Part B Monthly Premium Rates, Actuarial Rates,
and Premium Rates as a Percentage of Part B Cost

	Standard monthly premium rate[1]	Monthly actuarial rate		Premium rates as a percentage of Part B cost	
		Enrollees aged 65 and over	Disabled enrollees under age 65	Enrollees aged 65 and over	Disabled enrollees under age 65
July 1966-March 1968	$3.00	—	—	50.0%	—
April 1968-June 1970	4.00	—	—	50.0	—
12-month period ending June 30 of					
1975	6.70	6.70	18.00	50.0	18.6
1980	8.70	13.40	25.00	32.5	17.4
Calendar year					
1985	15.50	31.00	52.70	25.0	14.7
1990	28.60	57.20	44.10	25.0	32.4
1991	29.90	62.60	56.00	23.9	26.7
1992	31.80	60.80	80.80	26.2	19.7
1993	36.60	70.50	82.90	26.0	22.1
1994	41.10	61.80	76.10	33.3	27.0
1995	46.10	73.10	105 80	31.5	21.8
1996	42.50	84.90	105.10	25.0	20.2
1997	43.80	87.60	110.40	25.0	19.8
1998	43.80	87.90	97.10	24.9	22.6
1999	45.50	92.30	103 00	24.6	22.1
2000	45.50	91.90	121.10	24.8	18.8
2001	50.00	101.00	132 20	24.8	18.9
2002	54.00	109.30	123.10	24.7	21.9
2003	58.70	118.70	141 00	24.7	20.8
2004	66.60	133.20	175 50	25.0	19.0
2005	78.20	156.40	191 80	25.0	20.4
2006	88.50	176.90	203.70	25.0	21.7
2007	93.50	187.00	197 30	25.0	23.7
2008	96.40	192.70	209.70	25.0	23.0
2009	96.40	192.70	224 20	25.0	21.5
2010	110.50	221.00	270.40	25.0	20.4
2011	115.40	230.70	266 30	25.0	21.7
2012	99.90	199.80	192 50	25.0	25.9
2013	104.90	209.80	235 50	25.0	22.3

[1]The amount shown for each year represents the standard Part B premium paid by, or on behalf of, most Part B enrollees. It does not reflect other amounts that certain beneficiaries must pay, such as the income-related monthly adjustment amount for beneficiaries with high incomes and the premium surcharge for beneficiaries who enroll late. In addition, it does not reflect a reduction in premium for beneficiaries covered by the hold-harmless provision. As a result of his provision, most Part B beneficiaries had heir 2010 and 2011 monthly premium held to the 2009 rate of $96.40. Section V.E describes these amounts in more detail.

Figure III.C1 is a graph of the monthly per capita financing rates in all financing periods after 1983 for enrollees aged 65 and over and for disabled individuals under age 65. The graph shows the portion of the financing contributed by the beneficiaries and by general revenues. As indicated, general revenue financing is the largest income source for Part B.

Figure III.C1.—Part B Aged and Disabled Monthly Per Capita Trust Fund Income

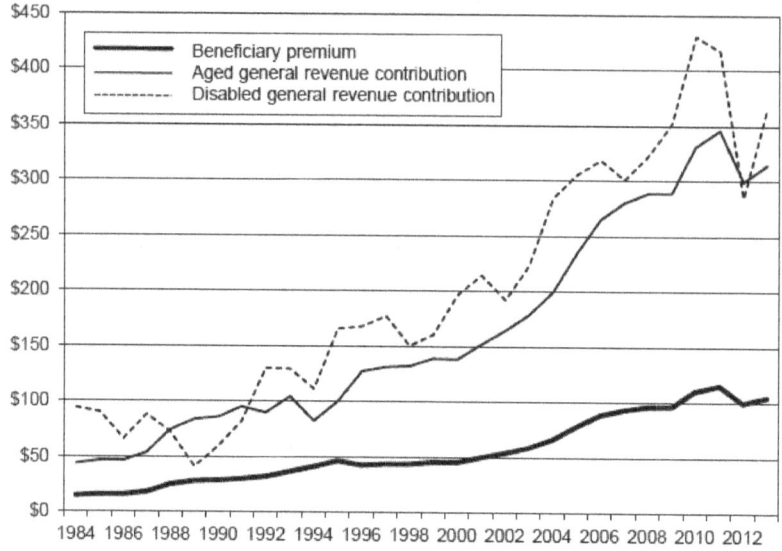

Financing period

Note: The amounts shown do not include the catastrophic coverage monthly premium rate for 1989.

In calendar year 2012, contributions received from the general fund of the Treasury amounted to $163.8 billion, which accounted for 72.2 percent of total revenue. The annual fees assessed on manufacturers and importers of brand-name prescription drugs amounted to $2.2 billion in revenue.

Another source of Part B revenue is interest received on investments held by the Part B account. A description of the investment procedures of the Part B account appears later in this section. In calendar year 2012, $2.8 billion of revenue was from interest on the investments of the account.

The Department of Treasury may accept and deposit in the Part B account unconditional money gifts or bequests made for the benefit of the fund. The Part B account received contributions in the amount of $2 million in calendar year 2012.

b. Expenditures

The account pays expenditures for Part B benefit payments and administrative expenses. All expenses incurred by the Department of Health and Human Services, the Social Security Administration, and the Department of the Treasury in administering Part B are charged to the account. Such administrative duties include payment of benefits, fraud and abuse control activities, and experiments and demonstration projects designed to determine various methods of increasing efficiency and economy in providing health care services while maintaining the quality of these services.

In addition, Congress has authorized expenditures from the trust funds for construction, rental and lease, or purchase contracts of office buildings and related facilities for use in connection with the administration of Part B. The account expenditures include such costs. The net worth of facilities and other fixed capital assets, however, does not appear in the statement of Part B assets presented in this report, since the value of fixed capital assets does not represent funds available for benefit or administrative expenditures and is not, therefore, pertinent in assessing the actuarial status of the funds.

Of total Part B expenditures, $236.5 billion represented net benefits paid from the account for health services.[38] Net benefits increased 6.7 percent over the corresponding amount of $221.7 billion paid during the preceding calendar year. This spending growth reflects increases both in the number of beneficiaries and in the price, volume, and intensity of services. Additional information on Part B benefits by type of service is available in section IV.B1.

The remaining $3.9 billion of expenditures was for administrative expenses and represented 1.7 percent of total Part B expenditures in 2012.[39] Administrative expenses are shown on a net basis, after adjustments to the preliminary allocation of such costs among the Social Security and Medicare trust funds and the general fund of the Treasury.

c. Actual experience versus prior estimates

Table III.C3 compares the actual experience in calendar year 2012 with the estimates presented in the 2011 and 2012 annual reports. A number of factors can contribute to differences between estimates and subsequent actual experience. In particular, actual values for key economic and other variables can differ from assumed

[38]Net benefits equal the total gross amounts initially paid from the trust fund during the year less recoveries of overpayments identified through fraud and abuse control activities.
[39]In 2012, the Part B salaries and expenses for the Centers for Medicare & Medicaid Services, including the administrative expenses of the carriers and intermediaries, amounted to $2.3 billion, or 1.0 percent of total Part B expenditures.

levels, and lawmakers may adopt legislative and regulatory changes after a report's preparation. Table III.C3 indicates that actual Part B benefit payments were lower than those estimated in the 2012 report and, because legislation increased physician payments for 2012 after the release of the 2011 report, were significantly higher than those estimated in the 2011 report. Actual premiums and government contributions were close to those estimated in the 2012 report, as the financing rates were determined in the fall of 2011 and were included in the 2012 report, but were lower than those estimated in the 2011 report. The estimated financing rates in the 2011 report were based on estimated benefit payments plus a margin for the likely legislative increase in physician payments in 2012. However, actual benefit payments, which reflect the legislative increase in physician payments, were lower than the estimated benefit payments plus the margin used for estimating the financing in the 2011 report.

Table III.C3.—Comparison of Actual and Estimated Operations of the Part B Account in the SMI Trust Fund, Calendar Year 2012
[Dollar amounts in millions]

Item	Actual amount	Comparison of actual experience with estimates for calendar year 2012 published in:			
		2012 report		2011 report	
		Estimated amount[1]	Actual as a percentage of estimate	Es imated amount[1]	Actual as a percentage of estimate
Premiums from enrollees	$58,024	$58,518	99%	$61,479	94%
Government contributions	163,827	165,690	99	173,527	94
Benefit payments	236,446	243,782	97	217,494	109

[1]Under the intermediate assumptions.

d. Assets

The Department of Treasury invests the portion of the Part B account not needed to meet current expenditures for benefits and administration in interest-bearing obligations of the U.S. Government.

The Social Security Act authorizes the issuance of special public-debt obligations for purchase exclusively by the account. The law requires that these special public-debt obligations shall bear interest at a rate based on the average market yield (computed on the basis of market quotations as of the end of the calendar month immediately preceding the date of such issue) for all marketable interest-bearing obligations of the United States forming a part of the public debt that are not due or callable until after 4 years from the end of that month. Since the inception of the SMI trust fund, the Department of Treasury has always invested the assets in special public-debt obligations.[40] Table V.H10, presented in appendix H, shows the assets of the SMI trust fund (Parts B and D) at the end of fiscal years 2011 and 2012.

2. 10-Year Actuarial Estimates (2013-2022)

The bases of the projected future operations of the Part B account are the Trustees' economic and demographic assumptions, as detailed in the OASDI Trustees Report, as well as other assumptions unique to Part B. Section IV.B1 presents an explanation of the effects of these assumptions on the estimates in this report. The Trustees also assume that financing for future periods will be determined according to the statutory provisions described in section III.C1a, although Part B financing rates have been set only through December 31, 2013.

In 2013 the monthly Part B premium rate increased to $104.90 from $99.90 in 2012. Under the intermediate economic assumptions, the estimated monthly premium for 2014 is again $104.90. This premium, paid by affected enrollees and Medicaid, and matched by general revenue transfers, would maintain a contingency reserve at the level necessary to accommodate normal financial variation plus the likelihood of legislative action that would raise costs after the establishment of financing rates.[41]

As noted, the Part B expenditure projections are very likely to be substantially understated in both the short range and long range because the sustainable growth rate system would unrealistically reduce current-law physician payment rates by an estimated 24.7 percent in 2014. In practice, lawmakers are nearly certain to prevent this scheduled reduction through new legislation, as they have for 2003 through 2013. Depending on the specific legislated changes, Part B costs could be about 6 percent higher in 2022 than shown here under current law.

---

[40]The Department of Treasury may also make investments in obligations guaranteed as to both principal and interest by the United States, including certain federally sponsored agency obligations.

[41]In the highly unlikely event that lawmakers allow the current-law negative physician payment updates to occur without legislative intervention, the projected Part B financing levels required to maintain an adequate level of assets in the Part B account would be substantially lower. However, the Department of Health and Human Services sets Part B financing rates prospectively, and the rates must include a margin that accounts for the probability of legislative changes that would significantly increase Part B costs after the financing had been determined. For 2003 through 2013, Congress legislatively overrode the negative updates that the sustainable growth rate formula would otherwise have required.

Projected Part B expenditures are further affected by the sequestration of Medicare expenditures required by the Budget Control Act of 2011, as modified by the American Taxpayer Relief Act of 2012, which applies from April 1, 2013 through March 31, 2022. Under the sequestration, Medicare benefit payments are reduced by up to 2 percent, and non-salary administrative expenses are reduced by an estimated 5 percent.

Table III.C4 shows the estimated operations of the Part B account under the intermediate assumptions on a calendar-year basis through 2022. As mentioned previously, readers should interpret the estimates for 2014 and later cautiously, given the near certainty of further legislation addressing physician payments. Also, the estimates include only the direct impacts of the negative payment updates on physician expenditures and do not incorporate potential secondary effects on other Medicare outlays.

Table III.C4.—Operations of the Part B Account in the SMI Trust Fund (Cash Basis) during Calendar Years 1970-2022
[In billions]

Calendar year	Premium income	General revenue[1]	Interest and other[2,3]	Total	Benefit payments[3,4]	Adminis- trative expenses	Total	Net change	Balance at end of year[5]
		Income				Expenditures		Account	
Historical data:									
1970	$1.1	$1.1	$0.0	$2.2	$2.0	$0.2	$2.2	-$0.0	$0.2
1975	1.9	2.6	0.1	4.7	4.3	0.5	4.7	-0.1	1.4
1980	3.0	7.5	0.4	10.9	10.6	0.6	11.2	-0.4	4.5
1985	5.6	18.3	1.2	25.1	22.9	0.9	23.9	1.2	10.9
1990	11.3	33.0	1.6	45.9	42.5	1.5	44.0	1.9	15.5
1995	19.7	39.0	1.6	60.3	65.0	1.6	66.6	-6.3	13.1
2000	20.6	65.9	3.4	89.9	88.9[6]	1.8	90.7	-0.8	44.0
2005	37.5	118.1	1.4	157.0	149.2	3.2	152.4	4.6	24.0
2006	42.9	132.7	1.8	177.3	165.9	3.1	169 0	8.3	32.3
2007	46.8	139.6	2.2	188.7	176.4	2.5	178 9	9.7	42.1
2008	50.2	146.8	3.6	200.6	180.3[7]	3.0	183 3	17.3	59.4
2009	56.0[8]	162.8[8]	3.1	221.9	202.6	3.1	205.7	16.2	75.5
2010	52.0[8]	153.5[8]	3.3	208.8	209.7	3.2	212 9	-4.1	71.4
2011	57.5	170.2	5.9	233.6	221.7	3.6	225 3	8.3	79.7
2012	58.0	163.8	5.2	227.0	236.5	3.9	240 5	-13.5	66.2
Intermediate es imates:									
2013	63.6	185.6	5.5	254.7	248.0	3.3	251 3	3.5	69.7
2014	64.6	194.6	6.0	265.3	249.9	3.5	253.4	11.9	81.6
2015	73.0[8]	219.1[8]	6.9	299.0	264.0	3.9	267 9	31.1	112.7
2016	74.5[8]	218.0[8]	8.3	300.8	282.9	4.3	287 3	13.5	126.2
2017	85.2	239.8	10.8	335.7	303.8	4.8	308.6	27.1	153.3
2018	93.7	257.7	12.7	364.0	328.6	5.3	333 9	30.1	183.4
2019	102.3	278.4	13.3	394.0	354.3	5.6	360 0	34.1	217.5
2020	112.4[8]	315.3[8]	15.5	443.2	384.1	6.0	390.1	53.1	270.5
2021	114.2[8]	319.4[8]	18.0	451.6	415.8	6.5	422 2	29.4	299.9
2022	130.1	362.8	20.7	513.6	457.7	7.2	464 9	48.7	348.6

[1] General fund matching payments, plus certain interest-adjustment items.
[2] Other income includes recoveries of amounts reimbursed from the trust fund that are not obliga ions of he trust fund and other miscellaneous income. In 2008, includes an adjustment of $0.8 billion for interest earned as a result of Part A hospice costs that were misallocated to the Part B trust fund account.
[3] See footnote 2 of table III.B4.

[4]Includes costs of Peer Review Organizations from 1983 through 2001 and costs of Quality Improvement Organizations beginning in 2002.
[5]The financial status of Part B depends on both the assets and the liabilities of the trust fund (see table III.C8).
[6]Benefit payments less monies transferred from the HI trust fund for home health agency costs, as provided for by the Balanced Budget Act of 1997.
[7]Benefits shown for 2008 are lower by the $8.5 billion transferred from the general fund of the Treasury to reimburse Part B for Part A hospice costs hat were previously misallocated to the Part B trust fund account.
[8]Section 708 of the Social Security Act modifies he provisions for the payment of Social Security benefits when the regularly designated day falls on a Saturday, Sunday, or legal public holiday. Payment of those benefits normally due January 3, 2010 actually occurred on December 31, 2009. Consequently, he Part B premiums withheld from these benefits and the associated general revenue contributions were added to the SMI trust fund on December 31, 2009. Similarly, the payment date for those benefits normally due on January 3, 2016 will be December 31, 2015, and he payment date for those benefits normally due on January 3, 3021 will be December 31, 2020.
Note: Totals do not necessarily equal the sums of rounded components.

As shown in table III.C4, the Part B account would increase during 2013 to an estimated $69.7 billion by the end of the year. Legislation enacted in January 2013 raised Part B physician expenditures substantially compared to the law in effect in the fall of 2012 when the 2013 financing was established. Maintenance of an asset reserve that is sufficient to handle this type of contingency is an important element in ensuring solvency for the Part B trust fund account.

Starting in 2014, the scheduled physician payment reduction of nearly 25 percent for 2014 heavily influences the Part B projections estimated under current law. The Trustees project that Part B financing margins will be set for 2014 and thereafter so that account assets would be adequate to cover a much higher level of benefits in the likely event that Congress continues to prevent reductions in Part B physician payment rates. Accordingly, table III.C4 shows rapidly increasing Part B asset levels, since expenditures reflect the current-law physician reduction but income reflects current-law expenditures plus a large margin based on the reasonable expectation that the current-law reduction will not occur.[42]

The Part B expenditures shown in this report for 2013 are significantly higher than estimated in last year's report as a result of subsequent legislation to prevent a 26.5-percent reduction in physician payment rates. The expenditure projections for 2014-2022 are slightly higher than those shown in last year's report because of two largely offsetting factors. The first is that based on an administrative action, the Medicare Advantage rates beginning in 2014 will be set to anticipate a 0-percent legislative override of the

---

[42]This rise in assets is unlikely to occur. Each year as the current-law physician payment reductions are either implemented or legislatively overridden, the Department of Health and Human Services will determine the Part B financing in a way that balances stability in the premium increases with financial soundness.

sustainable growth rate formula. The second is that actual experience for 2012 was lower than expected. In previous years, the rates were calculated assuming the current law physician payment reductions were applied.

The statutory provisions governing Part B financing have changed over time. Most recently, the Balanced Budget Act of 1997 provided for the permanent establishment of the standard Part B premium at the level of about 25 percent of average expenditures for beneficiaries age 65 and over. Figure III.C2 shows historical and projected ratios of premium income to Part B expenditures.

Figure III.C2.—Premium Income as a Percentage of Part B Expenditures

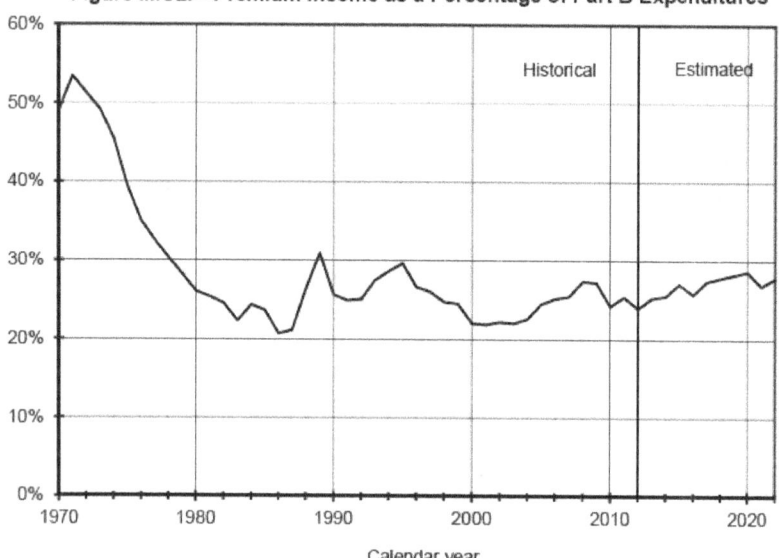

Calendar year

Beneficiary premiums are also affected by a provision of the Affordable Care Act that imposes fees on the manufacturers and importers of brand-name prescription drugs and allocates the fees to the Part B account of the SMI trust fund. The new legislation does not modify the determination of the Part B actuarial rates, premiums, or general revenue matching contributions; consequently, the normal financing, plus the new fees, would result in an excessive level of program financing without other action. Thus, there will be a reduction in the premium margin for maintaining an appropriate level of trust fund assets such that total revenues from premiums, matching general revenues, and the earmarked fees relating to brand-name prescription drugs will equal the appropriate level needed for program financing.

The amount and rate of growth of benefit payments have caused concern for many years. Table III.C5 shows payment amounts in the aggregate, on a per capita basis, and relative to the Gross Domestic Product (GDP). Rates of growth appear historically and for the next 10 years based on the intermediate estimates under current law, which is likely to change to prevent scheduled substantial reductions in physician fees.

Part B benefit growth has averaged 6.1 percent annually over the past 5 years following many years of much faster growth. The inadvertent payment of certain Part A hospice benefits by Part B from 2005 to October 2007 contributed to the large increases in benefits in the beginning of this period. The lower growth in 2008 and subsequent higher growth in 2009 are due to a one-time hospice payment correction in 2008. During 2012, Part B benefits grew 6.6 percent on an aggregate basis and increased to 1.51 percent of GDP.

Table III.C5.—Growth in Part B Benefits (Cash Basis) through December 31, 2022

Calendar year	Aggregate benefits [billions]	Percent change	Per capita benefits	Percent change	Part B benefits as a percentage of GDP
Historical data:					
1970	$2.0	5.9%	$101	3.5%	0.19%
1975	4.3	28.8	180	24.6	0.26
1980	10.6	22.1	390	19.3	0.38
1985	22.9	16.7	768	14.5	0.54
1990	42.5	10.9	1,304	9.1	0.73
1995	65.0	10.8	1,823	9.2	0.88
2000	88.9[1]	10.1	2,381	9.2	0.89
2005	149.2	10.6	3,754	8.8	1.18
2006	165.9	11.2	4,111	9.5	1.24
2007	176.4	6.3	4,293	4.4	1.26
2008	180.3[2]	2.2	4,296	0.1	1.26
2009	202.6	12.4	4,721	9.9	1.45
2010	209.7	3.5	4,779	1.2	1.45
2011	221.7	5.7	4,938	3.3	1.47
2012	236.3	6.6	5,093	3.1	1.51
Intermediate estimates:					
2013	250.3	12.9	5,216	5.6	1.53
2014	254.1	1.5	5,138	-1.5	1.48
2015	268.7	5.7	5,276	2.7	1.47
2016	288.0	7.2	5,498	4.2	1.49
2017	309.5	7.5	5,745	4.5	1.51
2018	335.0	8.2	6,047	5.3	1.55
2019	362.1	8.1	6,357	5.1	1.60
2020	392.3	8.3	6,694	5.3	1.65
2021	425.2	8.4	7,057	5.4	1.71
2022	460.9	8.4	7,444	5.5	1.77

[1]See footnote 6 of table III.C4.
[2]See footnote 7 of table III.C4.

The reduction in Part B per capita benefits shown for 2014 reflects the estimated physician payment update of −24.7 percent under the sustainable growth rate system (SGR). The SGR requires an adjustment of future physician payment increases for past actual physician spending relative to a target spending level.[43] The SGR provision was enacted in 1997, and by 2002 actual cumulative physician spending exceeded the target levels. Further significant growth in the volume and intensity of physician services subsequently widened the gap between actual and target spending. In addition, amendments enacted in 2003 through 2013 to override scheduled reductions in physician payment rates all raised (or will raise) actual payment levels, but not all raised (or will raise) the target spending levels. As noted, to address the accumulated difference between actual and allowed spending levels, the current SGR mechanism will require a fee schedule reduction in 2014 of an estimated 24.7 percent.

The Affordable Care Act also affects Part B expenditure growth rates in 2013-2022. The slower Medicare price updates for most non-physician services and the reduced payment "benchmarks" for private Medicare Advantage health plans generate significant savings during this period. As noted previously, the 2014 Part B growth rate is higher due to the increase in Medicare Advantage rates to reflect a 0-percent physician update, anticipating that the cuts required under current law by the SGR system will be legislatively overridden. The Part B expenditure growth rates in 2013-2022 are also affected by the 2-percent sequester of Medicare benefits required by the Budget Control Act of 2011, as amended by the American Taxpayer Relief Act of 2012.

Despite the statutory constraints on physician payments under the sustainable growth rate system, projected Part B costs in the 2013 annual report continue to increase faster than GDP in most years, as indicated in table III.C5.

Since future economic, demographic, and health care usage and cost experience may vary considerably from the intermediate assumptions on which the preceding cost estimates were based, the Trustees also prepared estimates under current law using two alternative sets of assumptions: low-cost and high-cost. Table III.C6 summarizes the estimated operations of the Part B account for all three alternatives. Section IV.B1 presents in substantial detail the assumptions underlying the intermediate assumptions, as well as the assumptions used in preparing estimates under the low-cost and high-cost alternatives.

---

[43]Additional information about the SGR system and the physician spending targets, including the original target levels, is available at http://www.cms.gov/Medicare/Medicare-Fee-for-Service-Payment/SustainableGRatesConFact/index.html.

Table III.C6.—Estimated Operations of the Part B Account in the SMI Trust Fund during Calendar Years 2012-2022, under Alternative Sets of Assumptions

[Dollar amounts in billions]

Calendar year	Premiums from enrollees	Other income[1]	Total income	Total expenditures	Balance in fund at end of year
Intermediate:					
2012[2]	$58 0	$169.0	$227.0	$240 5	$66.2
2013	63.6	191.2	254.7	251.3	69.7
2014	64.6	200.6	265.3	253.4	81.6
2015	73.0[3]	226.0[3]	299.0	267.9	112.7
2016	74.5[3]	226.3[3]	300.8	287.3	126.2
2017	85.2	250.6	335.7	308.6	153.3
2018	93.7	270.3	364.0	333.9	183.4
2019	102 3	291.7	394.0	360.0	217.5
2020	112.4[3]	330.8[3]	443.2	390.1	270.5
2021	114 2[3]	337.4[3]	451.6	422.2	299.9
2022	130.1	383.5	513.6	464.9	348.6
Low-cost:					
2012[2]	58.0	169.0	227.0	240.5	66.2
2013	63.6	191.2	254.8	250.1	70.9
2014	64.6	199.6	264.2	250.0	85.0
2015	69.2[3]	215.3[3]	284.5	259.2	110.3
2016	69.7[3]	212.1[3]	281.8	272.0	120.1
2017	78.2	230.2	308.4	285.2	143.3
2018	83.7	241.5	325.1	300.2	168.2
2019	89.2	253.9	343.1	315.3	196.0
2020	95.5[3]	280.7[3]	376.3	333.5	238.8
2021	94.9[3]	280.0[3]	374.9	352.5	261.2
2022	105 5	310.6	416.1	378.9	298.4
High-cost:					
2012[2]	58.0	169.0	227.0	240.5	66.2
2013	63.6	191.1	254.7	251.9	69.1
2014	65.3	202.8	268.1	255.1	82.0
2015	74.8[3]	231.2[3]	306.0	272.6	115.4
2016	77.5[3]	235.2[3]	312.7	297.0	131.1
2017	90.7	266.9	357.5	326.5	162.0
2018	102.4	295.7	398.1	362.6	197.5
2019	115 2	328.6	443.8	401.9	239.3
2020	130 5[3]	384.4[3]	514.9	449.0	305.2
2021	136 0[3]	402.3[3]	538.3	499.3	344.2
2022	158 5	467.7	626.2	563.6	406.8

[1] Other income contains government contributions, fees on manufacturers and importers of brand-name prescription drugs, and interest.
[2] Figures for 2012 represent actual experience.
[3] See footnote 8 of table III.C4.

Note: Totals do not necessarily equal the sums of rounded components.

The Trustees selected the three sets of assumptions to indicate the general range in which one might reasonably expect the cost to fall under current law. The low- and high-cost alternatives provide for a fairly wide projected range. One would expect actual experience, if current law were to continue, to fall within the range, but there can be no assurance that this would be the case in light of the wide variations in experience that have occurred since Part B began and because the potential secondary effects of the current-law physician payment updates are not included in this report. Although the SGR system would substantially reduce physician fees under current law, actual changes in utilization and/or intensity of physician and other

Part B services could readily result in current-law costs as high or low as the alternative projections shown in table III.C6. In practice, new legislation will likely affect actual costs, particularly in light of the near certainty that lawmakers will override the current-law physician payment updates.

Estimated Part B expenditures grow faster than GDP in most years under the intermediate and high-cost assumptions. Based on the low-cost assumptions, expenditures would increase more slowly than GDP in 2013 through 2017.

The alternative projections shown in table III.C6 illustrate two important aspects of the financial operations of the Part B account:

- Despite the widely differing assumptions underlying the three alternatives, the balance between Part B income and expenditures remains relatively stable. Under the low-cost assumptions, for example, by 2022 both income and expenditures would be around 19 percent lower than projected under the intermediate assumptions. The corresponding amounts under the high-cost assumptions would be about 22 percent higher than the intermediate estimates.

  This result occurs because the Department of Health and Human Services annually reestablishes the premiums and general revenue contributions underlying Part B financing to cover each year's anticipated incurred benefit costs and other expenditures and then increases these amounts by a margin that reflects the uncertainty of the projection. Thus, Part B income will automatically track Part B expenditures fairly closely, regardless of the specific economic and other conditions.

- As a result of the close matching of income and expenditures described above, projected account assets show similar, stable patterns of change under all three sets of assumptions. The annual adjustment of premiums and general revenue contributions permits the maintenance of a Part B account balance that, while typically relatively small, is sufficient to guard against chance fluctuations.

  It is important to note, however, that continued enactment of legislation to prevent a reduction in physician fees, after financing for a year has been set, requires larger than usual margins in the financing and, therefore, larger than usual projected Part B account balances.

Past legislative actions to override scheduled physician fee reductions contributed to a substantial decline in Part B assets, which, minus corresponding liabilities, in 2004 reached their lowest level relative to annual expenditures in nearly 30 years. Restoration of assets to the 2008 adequate level required substantial premium and general revenue increases over several years.

Adequacy of Part B Financing Established for Calendar Year 2013

The traditional concept of financial adequacy, as it applies to Part B, is closely related to the concept as it applies to many private group insurance plans. Part B is somewhat similar to private "yearly renewable term" insurance, with financing established each year based on estimated costs for the year. For Part B, premium income paid by the enrollees and general revenues contributed by the Federal Government provide financing. As with private plans, the income during a 12-month period for which financing is being established should be sufficient to cover the costs of services expected to be rendered during that period (including associated administrative costs), even though payment for some of these services will not occur until after the period closes. The portion of income required to cover those benefits not paid until after the end of the year is added to the account; thus assets in the account at any time should not be less than the costs of the benefits and the administrative expenses incurred but not yet paid.

Since the Department of Health and Human Services establishes the income per enrollee (premium plus government contribution) prospectively each year, it is subject to projection error. Additionally, legislation enacted after the financing has been established, but effective for the period for which financing has been set, may affect costs. Account assets, therefore, should be maintained at a level that is adequate to cover not only the value of incurred-but-unpaid expenses but also a reasonable degree of variation between actual and projected costs (in case actual costs exceed projected).

The Trustees traditionally evaluate the actuarial status or financial adequacy of the Part B account over the period for which the enrollee premium rates and level of general revenue financing have been established. The primary tests are that (i) the assets and income for years for which financing has been established should be sufficient to meet the projected benefits and associated administrative expenses incurred for that period; and (ii) the assets should be sufficient to cover projected liabilities for benefits that have not yet been paid as of the end of the period. If Part B does not meet these adequacy tests, it can still continue to operate if the account remains at a level adequate to permit the payment of claims as presented. However, to protect against the possibility that costs will be higher than assumed, assets should be sufficient to include contingency levels that cover a reasonable degree of variation between actual and projected costs.

As noted above, the tests of financial adequacy for Part B rely on the incurred experience of the account, including a liability for the costs of services performed in a year but not yet paid. Table III.C7 shows the estimated transactions of the account on an incurred basis. Readers should view the incurred experience as an estimate, even for historical years.[44]

Table III.C7.—Estimated Part B Income and Expenditures (Incurred Basis) for Financing Periods through December 31, 2013

[In millions]

Financing period	Income				Expenditures			Net operations in year
	Premium income	General revenue	Interest and other	Total	Benefit payments	Adminis- trative expenses	Total	
Historical data:								
12-month period ending June 30,								
1970	$936	$936	$12	$1,884	$1,928	$213	$2,141	−$257
1975	1,887	2,396	105	4,388	3,957	438	4,395	−7
1980	2,823	6,627	421	9,871	9,840	645	10,485	−614
Calendar year								
1985	5,613	18,243	1,248	25,104	22,750	986	23,736	1,368
1990	11,320	33,035	1,558	45,913	42,577	1,541	44,118	1,795
1995	19,717	45,743	1,739	67,199	64,918	1,607	66,525	674
2000	20,555	65,898	3,450	89,903	89,757[1]	1,770	91,526	−1,623
2005	37,535	118,091	1,365	156,992	149,515	3,185	152,700	4,291
2006	42,853	132,673	1,791	177,317	167,244	3,062	170,306	7,012
2007	46,773	148,717[2]	2,238	197,728	177,515	2,492	180,007	17,721
2008	50,232	137,731[2]	3,591	191,554	180,417	2,990	183,407	8,147
2009	52,376	151,944	3,084	207,403	202,686	3,135	205,821	1,582
2010	55,649	164,302	3,281	223,232	212,047	3,153	215,199	8,032
2011	57,514	170,224	5,867	233,605	222,181	3,623	225,805	7,801
2012	60,435	161,416	5,164	227,015	238,231	3,947	242,177	−15,162
Intermediate es imates:								
2013	63,594	185,646	5,507	254,746	248,147	3,257	251,405	3,341

[1]See footnote 7 of table III.C4.
[2]A July 1, 2008 general revenue transfer was made in the amount of $9.3 billion to restore the Part B account assets for hospice benefit accoun ing errors that occurred from 2005 through September 2007. An estimated $9.1 billion was due but unpaid by the end of 2007 when the error was discovered, and an additional estimated $0.2 billion in interest accrued un il July 1, 2008 when he corrective payment was made.

---

[44]Part B experience is substantially more difficult to determine on an incurred basis than on a cash basis. For some services, reporting of payment occurs only on a cash basis, and it is necessary to infer the incurred experience from the cash payment information. Moreover, for recent time periods the tabulations of bills are incomplete due to normal processing time lags.

Estimates of the liability amounts for benefits incurred but unpaid as of the end of each financing period, and of the administrative expenses related to processing these benefits, appear in table III.C8. In some years, account assets have not been as large as liabilities. Nonetheless, the fund has remained positive, which has allowed payment of all claims.

Table III.C8.—Summary of Estimated Part B Assets and Liabilities as of the End of the Financing Period, for Periods through December 31, 2013
[Dollar amounts in millions]

	Balance in trust fund	General revenue due but unpaid	Total assets	Benefits incurred but unpaid	Administrative costs incurred but unpaid	Total liabilities	Excess of assets over liabilities	Ratio[1]
Historical data:								
As of June 30,								
1970	$57	$15	$72	$567	—	$567	−$495	−0.21
1975	1,424	67	1,491	1,257	$14	1,271	—	0.04
1980	4,657	—	4,657	2,621	188	2,809	1,848	0.15
As of December 31,								
1985	10,924	—	10,924	3,142	−38	3,104	7,820	0.28
1990	15,482	—	15,482	4,060	20	4,080	11,402	0.24
1995	13,130	6,893[2]	20,023	4,282	−214	4,068	15,954	0.23
2000	44,027	—	44,027	7,176	−285	6,891	37,136	0.36
2001	41,269	—	41,269	7,799	—	7,799	33,471	0.29
2002	34,301	—	34,301	9,053	—	9,053	25,248	0.20
2003	23,953	—	23,953	7,322	—	7,322	16,631	0.12
2004	19,430	—	19,430	9,337	—	9,337	10,093	0.07
2005	24,008	—	24,008	9,624	—	9,624	14,384	0.08
2006	32,325	—	32,325	10,929	—	10,929	21,396	0.12
2007	42,062	9,296[3]	51,358	12,015	—	12,015	39,343	0.21
2008	59,382	—	59,382	12,119	—	12,119	47,263	0.23
2009	75,545	—	75,545	12,220	—	12,220	63,325	0.29
2010	71,435	—	71,435	14,558	—	14,558	56,877	0.25
2011	79,693	—	79,693	15,015	—	15,015	64,678	0.27
2012	66,226	—	66,226	16,710	—	16,710	49,516	0.20
Intermediate estimates:								
2013	69,710	—	69,710	16,853	—	16,853	52,857	0.21

[1]Ratio of the excess of assets over liabilities to the following year's total incurred expenditures.
[2]This amount includes both the principal of $6,736 million and the accumulated interest through December 31, 1995 for the shortfall in the fiscal year 1995 appropriation for government contributions. Normally, this transfer would have occurred on December 31, 1995, and, therefore, the trust fund balance would have reflected it. However, due to absence of funding, there was a delay in the transfer of he principal and the appropriate interest until March 1, 1996.
[3]Part B erroneously paid certain Part A benefits from 2005 through September 2007. Therefore, on July 1, 2008 the Part B account of the SMI trust fund received a general revenue transfer of $9,296 million to restore the Part B account. Beginning in 2007, the year in which the errors were discovered, the table shows these amounts to be repaid to the Part B account. The 2007 amount shown includes both the estimated principal of $8,484 million and the estimated accumulated interest through December 31, 2007.

The amount of assets minus liabilities, compared with the estimated incurred expenditures for the following calendar year, forms a relative measure of the Part B account's financial status. The last column in table III.C8 shows such ratios for past years and the estimated ratio at the end of 2013. Past studies have indicated that a ratio of roughly 15-20 percent is sufficient to protect against unforeseen contingencies, such as unusually large increases in Part B expenditures.

The Department of Health and Human Services established Part B financing through December 31, 2013. Estimated income exceeds estimated incurred expenditures in 2013, as shown in table III.C7. The excess of assets over liabilities increases by an estimated $3.3 billion by the end of December 2013, as indicated in table III.C8. This increase occurs because estimated expenditures are now lower than projected when the 2013 Part B financing was determined.

Since the financing rates are set prospectively, variations between assumed cost increases and subsequent actual experience could affect the actuarial status of the Part B account. To test the status of the account under varying assumptions, the Trustees prepared a lower growth range projection and an upper growth range projection by varying the key assumptions for 2012 and 2013. These two alternative sets of assumptions provide a range of financial outcomes within which one might reasonably expect the actual experience of Part B to fall under current law. The values for the lower and upper growth range assumptions were determined from a statistical analysis of the historical variation in the respective increase factors.

This sensitivity analysis differs from the low-cost and high-cost projections discussed previously in this section in that this analysis examines the variation in the projection factors in the period for which the financing has been established (2013 for this report). The low-cost and high-cost projections, on the other hand, illustrate the financial impact of slower or faster growth trends throughout the short-range projection period.

Table III.C9 indicates that, under the lower-growth-range scenario, account assets would exceed liabilities at the end of December 2013 by a margin equivalent to 29.2 percent of the following year's incurred expenditures. Under the upper-growth-range scenario, account assets would still exceed liabilities, but by a margin of 14.1 percent of incurred expenditures in 2013. Under either scenario, assets would be sufficient to cover outstanding liabilities. Figure III.C3 shows the reserve ratio for historical years and for 2013 under the three cost growth scenarios.

Table III.C9.—Actuarial Status of the Part B Account in the SMI Trust Fund
under Three Cost Sensitivity Scenarios for Financing Periods
through December 31, 2013

As of December 31,	2011	2012	2013
Intermediate scenario:			
Actuarial status (in millions)			
Assets	$79,693	$66,226	$69,710
Liabilities	15,015	16,710	16,853
Assets less liabilities	64,678	49,516	52,857
Ratio[1]	26.9%	19.8%	21.0%
Low-range scenario:			
Actuarial status (in millions)			
Assets	$79,693	$66,226	$81,771
Liabilities	15,015	16,227	15,543
Assets less liabilities	64,678	49,999	66,228
Ratio[1]	27.4%	21.5%	29.2%
Upper-range scenario:			
Actuarial status (in millions)			
Assets	$79,693	$66,226	$57,902
Liabilities	15,015	17,505	18,112
Assets less liabilities	64,678	48,721	39,790
Ratio[1]	26.0%	18.0%	14.1%

[1]Ratio of assets less liabilities at the end of the year to the total incurred expenditures during the following year, expressed as a percent.

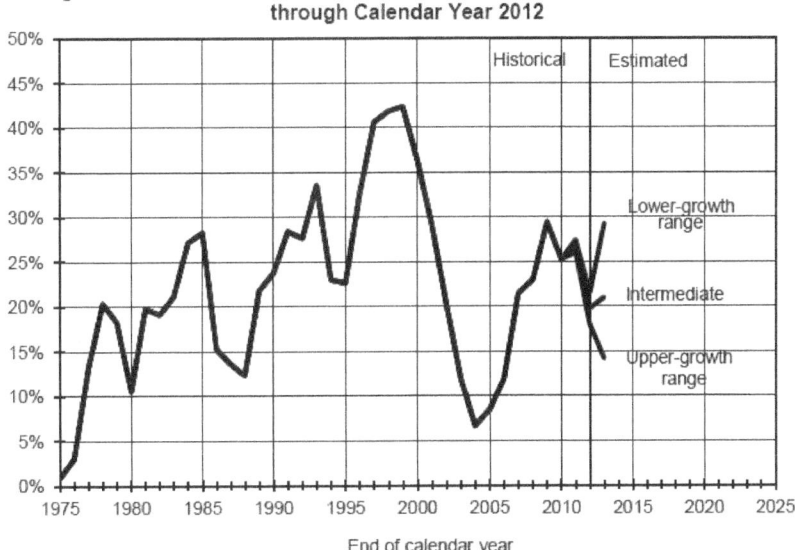

Figure III.C3.—Actuarial Status of the Part B Account in the SMI Trust Fund
through Calendar Year 2012

Note: The Trustees measure the actuarial status of the Part B account in he SMI trust fund by the ratio of (i) assets minus liabilities at the end of the year to (ii) he following year's incurred expenditures.

Based on the tests described above, the Trustees conclude that the financing established for the Part B account for calendar year 2013 is adequate to cover 2013 expected expenditures and to maintain the financial status of the Part B account in 2013 at a satisfactory level under current law.

3. Long-Range Estimates

The prior section presented the expected operations of the Part B account over the next 10 years. This section examines the long-range expenditures of the account under the intermediate assumptions. Part B expenditures after 2013 are almost certainly understated to a substantial degree, and thus of limited usefulness, due to the large current-law physician payment reduction for 2014. The significant likelihood that productivity adjustments to other Medicare price updates will not be feasible in the long term compounds this problem.[45] Due to its automatic financing provisions, the Trustees expect the Part B account to be adequately financed into the indefinite future and so have not conducted a long-range analysis using high-cost and low-cost assumptions.

Table III.C10 shows the estimated Part B incurred expenditures under the intermediate assumptions expressed as a percentage of GDP for selected years over the calendar-year period 2012-2087.[46] The 75-year projection period fully allows for the presentation of future trends that one may reasonably expect to occur, such as the impact of the large increase in enrollees as the baby boom generation begins to receive benefits.

---

[45]The projections in this report do not include any potential secondary impacts resulting from these two types of large current-law payment reductions.

[46]These estimated incurred expenditures are for benefit payments and administrative expenses combined, unlike the values in table III.C5, which express only benefit payments on a cash basis as a percentage of GDP.

Table III.C10.—Part B Expenditures (Incurred Basis) as a Percentage of the Gross Domestic Product[1]

Calendar year	Part B expenditures as a percentage of GDP
2012	1.54%
2013	1.54
2014	1.47
2015	1.48
2016	1.50
2017	1.52
2018	1.56
2019	1.60
2020	1.65
2021	1.71
2022	1.80
2025	1.98
2030	2.25
2035	2.39
2040	2.45
2045	2.45
2050	2.45
2055	2.46
2060	2.50
2065	2.53
2070	2.56
2075	2.58
2080	2.56
2085	2.56

[1]Expenditures are the sum of benefit payments and administrative expenses.

The Trustees assume that Part B costs per enrollee after the initial 10-year period will increase at rates consistent with the current-law SGR payment system for physicians, the slower price updates under the ACA for most other categories of Part B providers, and the full price updates for services not affected by the update adjustments (for example, payments for physician-administered prescription drugs). Sections II.C and IV.D describe the basis for these assumptions. Based on these assumptions and the projected demographic changes, incurred Part B expenditures as a percentage of GDP would increase from 1.54 percent in 2012 to 2.56 percent in 2087. Under the full illustrative alternative analysis, Part B expenditures would instead increase to 4.27 percent in 2087.

Figure III.C4 compares the year-by-year Part B expenditures as a percentage of GDP for the 2013 report with the corresponding projections from 2012. As indicated, the Trustees now estimate that current-law costs will be generally somewhat higher than those in the 2012 annual report.

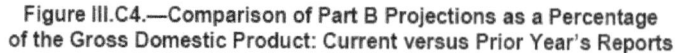

Figure III.C4.—Comparison of Part B Projections as a Percentage of the Gross Domestic Product: Current versus Prior Year's Reports

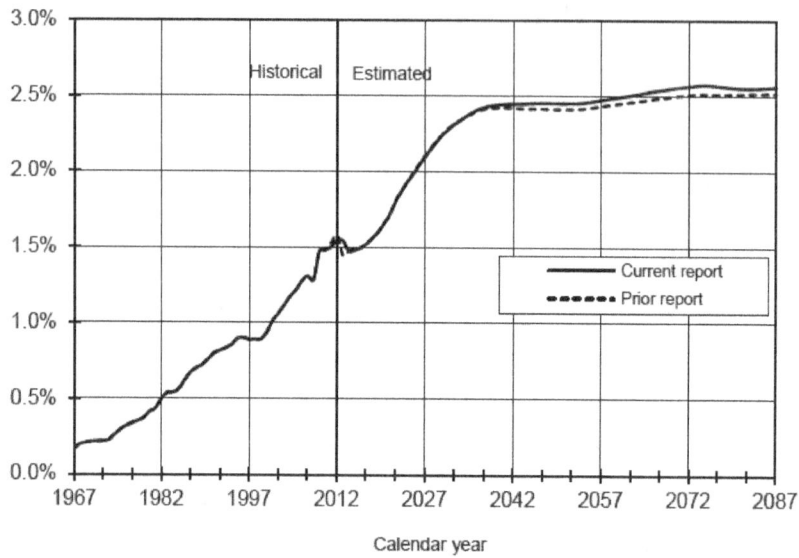

Calendar year

D. PART D FINANCIAL STATUS

The Medicare Modernization Act, enacted on December 8, 2003, established within SMI two Part D accounts related to prescription drug benefits: the Medicare Prescription Drug Account and the Transitional Assistance Account. The Medicare Prescription Drug Account handles the financial transactions for the prescription drug benefits that commenced in 2006. The purpose of the Transitional Assistance Account was to provide transitional assistance benefits, beginning in 2004 and extending through 2005, for certain low-income beneficiaries prior to the start of the new prescription drug benefit. For simplicity, this report combines both accounts and refers to them as the "Part D account."

The Medicare prescription drug benefit is significantly different from the usual HI and SMI Part B fee-for-service benefits. Beneficiaries obtain the drug benefit by voluntarily purchasing insurance policies from private stand-alone drug plans or private Medicare Advantage health plans. Medicare heavily subsidizes the premiums established by these plans. In addition, Medicare pays some or all of the remaining beneficiary drug premiums and cost-sharing liabilities for low-income beneficiaries. Medicare also pays special subsidies on behalf of beneficiaries retaining primary drug coverage through qualifying employer-sponsored retiree health plans. General revenues primarily finance the various Medicare drug subsidies. In addition, special payments from State governments finance a declining portion of the subsidy costs associated with beneficiaries who also qualify for full Medicaid benefits. Beneficiaries may have their drug insurance premiums withheld from their Social Security benefits, if they wish, and then forwarded to the drug plans on their behalf. In 2012, around 34 percent of the non-low-income enrollees in Part D drug plans exercised this option.

1. Financial Operations in Calendar Year 2012

The total assets of the account amounted to $1.0 billion on December 31, 2011. During calendar year 2012, total Part D expenditures were approximately $66.9 billion. General revenue was provided on an as-needed basis to cover the portion of these expenditures supported through Medicare subsidies. Total Part D receipts were $66.9 billion. As a result, total assets in the Part D account remained at $1.0 billion as of December 31, 2012.

Table III.D1 presents a statement of the revenue and expenditures of the Part D account of the SMI trust fund in calendar year 2012, and of its assets at the beginning and end of the calendar year.

Table III.D1—Statement of Operations of the Part D Account in the SMI Trust Fund during Calendar Year 2012
[In thousands]

Total assets of the Part D account in the trust fund, beginning of period ..		$996,514
Revenue:		
Premiums from enrollees:		
Premiums deducted from Social Security benefits......................	$3,100,460	
Premiums paid direc ly to plans[1]	5,215,288	
Total premiums...		8,315,748
Government contributions:		
Prescription drug benefits...	49,721,740	
Prescription drug administra ive expenses....................................	406,382	
Total government contributions		50,128,122
Payments from States		8,433,051
Interest on investments		5,967
Total revenue		$66,882,888
Expenditures:		
Part D benefit payments[1]..		$66,472,984
Part D administrative expenses...		406,560
Total expenditures..		$66,879,544
Net addition to he trust fund..		3,344
Total assets of the Part D account in the trust fund, end of period		$999,858

[1]Premiums paid directly to plans are not displayed on Treasury statements and are estimated. These premiums have been added to the benefit payments reported on the Treasury statement to obtain an estimate of total Part D benefits. Direct data on such benefit amounts are not yet available.

Note: Totals do not necessarily equal the sums of rounded components.

a. Revenues

The major sources of revenue for the Part D account are (i) contributions of the Federal Government authorized to be apportioned and transferred from the general fund of the Treasury; (ii) premiums paid by eligible persons who voluntarily enroll; and (iii) contributions from the States.

Of the total Part D revenue, $3.1 billion represented premium amounts withheld from Social Security benefits or other Federal benefit payments. Total premium payments, including those paid directly to the Part D plans, amount to an estimated $8.3 billion or 12.4 percent of total revenue.

In calendar year 2012, contributions received from the general fund of the Treasury amounted to $50.1 billion, which accounted for 74.9 percent of total revenue.

With the availability of Part D drug coverage and low-income subsidies beginning in 2006, Medicaid is no longer the primary payer of drug costs for full-benefit dual eligibles. States are subject to a contribution requirement and must pay the Part D account in the SMI trust fund a portion of their estimated forgone drug costs for this population. Starting in 2006, States must pay 90 percent of the estimated costs; this percentage phases down over a 10-year period to 75 percent in 2015. For calendar year 2012, these State payments amounted to $8.4 billion. Payments from States in 2010 were significantly lower than in previous years primarily because the American Recovery and Reinvestment Act of 2009 (ARRA) stipulated that Federal matching rates for Medicaid costs be temporarily increased until the end of 2010. Public Law 111-226 extended the Federal matching rate for another 6 months. Since the higher Federal rates reduced the States' obligations for Part D payments in 2011, the amount of these State payments in 2012 is noticeably higher than in 2011.

Another source of Part D revenue is interest received on investments held by the Part D account. Since this account holds only a very low amount of assets, and only for brief periods of time, the interest on the investments of the account in calendar year 2012 was negligible ($6 million).

b. Expenditures

Part D expenditures include both the costs of prescription drug benefits provided by Part D plans to enrollees and Medicare payments to employer-sponsored retiree health plans on behalf of beneficiaries who obtain their primary drug coverage through such plans. Unlike Parts A and B of Medicare, the Part D account in the SMI trust fund does not directly make or support all Part D expenditures. In particular, enrollee premiums that are paid directly to Part D plans, and thus do not flow through the Part D account, finance a portion of these expenditures. However, these premium amounts are included in the Part D account operations (both income and expenditures) presented in this report. Total expenditures are characterized as either "benefits" (representing the gross cost of enrollees' prescription drug coverage plus employer subsidy payments) or Federal administrative expenses.

All expenses incurred by the Department of Health and Human Services, the Social Security Administration, and the Department of the Treasury in administering Part D are charged to the account. Such administrative duties include making payments to Part D plans, the fraud and abuse control activities, and experiments and demonstration projects designed to improve the quality, efficiency, and economy of health care services.

In addition, Congress has authorized expenditures from the trust funds for construction, rental and lease, or purchase contracts of office buildings and related facilities for use in connection with the administration of Part D. The account expenditures include such costs. However, the statement of Part D assets presented in this report does not carry the net worth of facilities and other fixed capital assets, because the value of fixed capital assets does not represent funds available for benefit or administrative expenditures and is not, therefore, pertinent in assessing the actuarial status of the funds.

Of the $66.9 billion in total Part D expenditures, $66.5 billion represented benefits, as defined above, and the remaining $0.4 billion was for Federal administrative expenses. (The Medicare direct premium subsidy and reinsurance subsidy, together with enrollee premiums, implicitly cover administrative expenses incurred by Part D plans.)

c. Actual experience versus prior estimates

Table III.D2 compares the actual experience in calendar year 2012 with the estimates presented in the 2011 and 2012 annual reports. A number of factors can contribute to differences between estimates and subsequent actual experience. In particular, actual values for key economic and other variables can differ from assumed levels, and lawmakers may adopt legislative and regulatory changes after a report's preparation. Actual Part D benefit costs in calendar year 2012 were somewhat lower than those projected last year and about 13 percent lower than the projection from the 2011 report. Premium revenues were 5 percent lower than estimated in 2012 and about 14 percent lower than estimated in 2011. The lower actual experience as compared with prior estimates reflected the larger-than-expected impact from the patent expiration for some high-cost drugs and the continual shift from brand-name to generic drugs. Part D revenue from State transfers in 2012 was 1 percent above the projection from last year and about 3 percent higher than estimated in the 2011 Trustees Report.

Table III.D2.—Comparison of Actual and Estimated Operations of the Part D Account in the SMI Trust Fund, Calendar Year 2012
[Dollar amounts in millions]

| | | Comparison of actual experience with estimates for calendar year 2012 published in: | | | |
| | | 2012 report | | 2011 report | |
Item	Actual amount	Estimated amount[1]	Actual as a percentage of estimate	Estimated amount[1]	Actual as a percentage of estimate
Premiums from enrollees	$8,316	$8,732	95%	$9,641	86%
State transfers	8,433	8,387	101	8,197	103
Government contributions	50,128	51,396	98	58,529	86
Benefit payments	66,473	68,396	97	76,051	87

[1]Under the intermediate assumptions.

d. Assets

The Department of Treasury invests the portion of the Part D account not needed to meet current expenditures for benefits and administration in interest-bearing obligations of the U.S. Government.

The Social Security Act authorizes the issuance of special public-debt obligations for purchase exclusively by the account. The law requires that these special public-debt obligations shall bear interest at a rate based on the average market yield (computed on the basis of market quotations as of the end of the calendar month immediately preceding the date of such issue) for all marketable interest-bearing obligations of the United States forming a part of the public debt that are not due or callable until after 4 years from the end of that month. Since the inception of the SMI trust fund, the Department of Treasury has always invested the assets in special public-debt obligations.[47] Table V.H10, presented in appendix H, shows the assets of the SMI trust fund (Parts B and D) at the end of fiscal years 2011 and 2012.

As explained in the following section, the flexible apportionment of general revenues for Part D eliminates the need to maintain a normal contingency reserve. As a result, Part D assets are very low and are held only briefly in anticipation of immediate expenditures.

2. 10-Year Actuarial Estimates (2013-2022)

The projected future operations of the Part D account are based on the Trustees' economic and demographic assumptions, as detailed in the OASDI Trustees Report, as well as other assumptions unique to Part D. Section IV.B2 presents an explanation of the effects of the Trustees' intermediate assumptions, and of the other assumptions unique to Part D, on the estimates in this report.

Generally, the income to the Medicare Prescription Drug Account includes the beneficiary premiums described above and transfers from the general fund of the Treasury to cover each year's incurred benefit costs and other expenditures on an as-needed basis. The transfers from the Treasury are based on the direct premium subsidy, amounts of reinsurance payments, employer subsidies, low-income subsidies, net risk-sharing payments, administrative expenses, and advanced discount payments. This income requirement is reduced by the anticipated State transfers for the dually eligible beneficiaries who used to be covered under Medicaid. The beneficiary premiums and direct subsidy rate are calculated based on the national average bid amounts and defined prior to each year's operations, with the average premium amounting to 25.5 percent of the expected total plan costs for basic coverage. Beginning in 2011, beneficiaries with modified adjusted gross incomes exceeding a specified threshold pay "income-related" premiums in addition to the premiums charged by the plans in which the individuals have enrolled. The extra premiums are credited to the Part D trust fund account and reduce the general fund financing amounts. Also starting in 2011, the drug manufacturers provide a 50-percent ingredient cost discount for brand-name drugs in the coverage gap that reduces beneficiary out-of-pocket expenses. Medicare Part D pays advanced discount

---

[47]The Department of Treasury may also make investments in obligations guaranteed for both principal and interest by the United States, including certain federally sponsored agency obligations.

payments prospectively to the non-employer Part D plan sponsors and will be reimbursed for these amounts once the plan sponsors receive the discounts from the drug manufacturers.

The appropriation language provides, without further Congressional action, resources for benefit payments under the Part D drug benefit program on an as-needed basis. As a result of this authority there is no need for a Medicare Part D contingency reserve.[48]

Expenditures from the account include the premiums withheld from beneficiaries' Social Security or other Federal benefit payments and transferred to the private drug plans, the direct premium subsidy payments, reinsurance payments, employer subsidy amounts, low-income subsidy payments, risk-sharing payments, administrative expenses, and advanced discount payments. As noted previously, the Trustees adjust these direct expenditures to include the amount of enrollee premiums paid directly to Part D plans, thereby providing an estimate of total Part D benefit payments and other expenditures.

Table III.D3 shows the estimated operations of the Part D account under the intermediate assumptions on a calendar-year basis through 2022.

---

[48]The private Part D drug insurance plans maintain contingency reserves for incurred-but-unpaid claims and for the possibility that actual costs will exceed plan estimates. The statutory risk-sharing arrangement between Part D and the drug insurance plans mitigates this latter financial risk.

Table III.D3.—Operations of the Part D Account in the SMI Trust Fund (Cash Basis) during Calendar Years 2004-2022

[In billions]

	Income					Expenditures			Account	
Calendar year	Premium income[1]	General revenue[2]	Transfers from States[3]	Interest and other	Total	Benefit payments[4]	Adminis-trative expense	Total	Net change	Balance at end of year[5]
Historical data:										
2004	—	$0.4	—	—	$0.4	$0.4	—	$0.4	—	—
2005	—	1.1	—	—	1.1	1.1	—	1.1	0	0
2006	$3.5	39.2	$5.5	$0.0	48.2	47.1	$0.3	47.4	$0.8	$0.8
2007	4.1	38.8	6.9	0.0	49.7	48.8	0.9	49.7	0.0	0.8
2008	5.0	37.3	7.1	0.0	49.4	49.0	0.3	49.3	0.1	0.9
2009	6.3[6]	47.1	7.6	0.0	61.0	60.5	0.3	60.8	0.1	1.1
2010	6.5[6]	51.1	4.0	0.0	61.7	61.7	0.4	62.1	-0.4	0.7
2011	7.7	52.6	7.1	0.0	67.4	66.7	0.4	67.1	0.3	1.0
2012	8.3	50.1	8.4	0.0	66.9	66.5	0.4	66.9	0.0	1.0
Intermediate es imates:										
2013	9.9	53.4	8.6	0.0	71.9	71.8	0.4	72.2	-0.3	0.7
2014	11.6	63.3	8.7	0.0	83.6	83.2	0.4	83.6	0.0	0.7
2015	13.5[6]	67.0	9.0	0.0	89.5	89.1	0.4	89.5	0.0	0.8
2016	14.6[6]	72.1	9.6	0.0	96.3	95.8	0.4	96.3	0.1	0.8
2017	16.5	78.6	10.3	0.0	105.4	104.9	0.5	105.3	0.1	0.9
2018	18.3	85.7	11.1	0.0	115.1	114.6	0.5	115.0	0.1	0.9
2019	20.3	93.4	11.9	0.0	125.6	125.0	0.5	125.5	0.1	1.0
2020	22.5[6]	102 8	13.0	0.0	138.3	137.7	0.5	138.2	0.1	1.1
2021	23.8[6]	112 5	14.2	0.0	150.6	149.9	0.6	150.5	0.1	1.2
2022	26.6	123 2	15.5	0.0	165.2	164.5	0.6	165.1	0.1	1.3

[1]Premiums include bo h amounts withheld from Social Security benefits or other Federal payments and hose paid directly to Part D plans.

[2]Includes all government transfers including amounts for the general subsidy, reinsurance, low-income subsidy, administrative expenses, risk sharing, and State expenses for making low-income eligibility determinations. Includes amounts for the Transitional Assistance program of $0.4, $1.0, and $0.1 billion in 2004-2006, respec ively.

[3]Payments from the States with respect to the phased-in Federal assumption of Medicaid responsibility for premium and cost-sharing subsidies for dually eligible individuals.

[4]Includes subsidies to employer retiree prescription drug plans and payments to States for making low-income eligibility determinations. Includes amounts for the Transitional Assistance program of $0.4, $1.0, and $0.1 billion in 2004-2006, respectively.

[5]See text concerning nature of general revenue allocations process and implications for con ingency reserve assets.

[6]Section 708 of the Social Security Act modifies he provisions for the payment of Social Security benefits when the regularly designated day falls on a Saturday, Sunday, or legal public holiday. Payment of hose benefits normally due January 3, 2010 actually occurred on December 31, 2009; consequently, he Part D premiums withheld from these benefits were added to the Part D account on December 31, 2009. The premium income for 2010 excludes this amount. Similarly, the expected payment date for those benefits normally due January 3, 2016 is December 31, 2015, and the expected date for those benefits normally due January 3, 2021 is December 31, 2020.

Note: Totals do not necessarily equal the sums of rounded components.

Table III.D4 shows prescription drug payment amounts in the aggregate, on a per capita basis, and relative to the Gross Domestic Product (GDP). It also shows rates of growth for the next 10 years based on the intermediate set of assumptions.

Over the past 6 years, Part D expenditures have increased by an annual rate of 5.9 percent in aggregate and only 0.7 percent on a per enrollee basis. These results reflect the rapid growth in enrollment as the new program began, together with a substantial increase in the proportion of prescriptions filled with low-cost generic drugs and patent expiration for some major drugs in 2012.

Table III.D4.—Growth in Part D Benefits (Cash Basis) through December 31, 2022

Calendar year	Aggregate benefits [billions]	Percent change	Per capita benefits	Percent change	Part D benefits as a percentage of GDP
Historical data:					
2004	$0.4	—	$362	—	0.0%
2005	1.1	—	596	—	0.0
2006	47.1	—	1,708	—	0.4
2007	48.8	3.7%	1,556	−8.9%	0.3
2008	49.0	0.4	1,504	−3.3	0.3
2009[1]	60.5	23.4	1,798	19.6	0.4
2010[1]	61.7	2.0	1,775	−1.3	0.4
2011	66.7	8.1	1,868	5.3	0.4
2012	66.5	−0.4	1,779	−4.8	0.4
Intermediate estimates:					
2013	71.8	8.1	1,846	3.8	0.4
2014	83.2	15.9	2,077	12.5	0.5
2015	89.1	7.0	2,165	4.2	0.5
2016	95.8	7.6	2,267	4.7	0.5
2017[1]	104.9	9.4	2,412	6.4	0.5
2018[1]	114.6	9.2	2,562	6.2	0.5
2019	125.0	9.2	2,720	6.2	0.6
2020	137.7	10.1	2,904	6.7	0.6
2021	149.9	8.9	3,079	6.0	0.6
2022	164.5	9.7	3,287	6.8	0.6

[1] See footnote 6 of table III.D3.

The relatively rapid projected cost increases shown in table III.D4 result in part from further increases in Part D enrollment, changes in the distribution of enrollees by coverage category, and the expected resumption of per capita drug cost growth rates that exceed the rate of increase in other categories of medical spending, in part due to expected slowing of the trend toward greater generic use. Over the next 10 years, aggregate benefits are projected to increase at 9.5 percent annually, on average, while the per enrollee rate is 6.3 percent.

The payment structure of the Part D program causes the somewhat volatile pattern of annual growth rates; prospective payments to the plans are made based on the plan bids and then reconciled with actual prescription drug expenditures after the end of the year. For example, since actual prescription drug expenditures in 2006 were substantially less than the plan bids, the plans owed the Part D program over $4 billion in the form of risk-sharing returns and reimbursement of overpayments for reinsurance and low-income subsidy capitation amounts. These reconciliation payments reduced Part D spending in 2007 and 2008, resulting in per capita drug cost growth rates that are lower than normal for those years. In contrast, actual drug spending exceeded the plan bids in 2008, which resulted in more than $2 billion in additional Part D outlays for 2009. It is expected that for 2013, spending will exceed plan bids by about $4 billion, which will be paid by Part D in 2014.

Legislation also contributes to the volatility of the annual growth rates. For example, the Affordable Care Act imposed an insurance premium fee starting in 2014, which is expected to increase the bid amounts.

The Trustees prepared high- and low-cost estimates using two alternative sets of assumptions that reflect variation from the intermediate assumptions in both the projection and the level of incurred costs in the 2012 base year. Table III.D5 summarizes the estimated operations of the Part D account for all three alternatives. Section IV.B2 presents in detail the assumptions underlying the intermediate estimates, as well as the assumptions used in preparing estimates under the low-cost and high-cost alternatives. Estimated Part D expenditures grow significantly faster than GDP under the intermediate, low-cost, and high-cost assumptions.

Table III.D5.—Estimated Operations of the Part D Account in the SMI Trust Fund during Calendar Years 2012-2022, under Alternative Sets of Assumptions
[In billions]

Calendar year	Premiums from enrollees	Other income[1]	Total income	Total expenditures	Balance in account at end of year
Intermediate:					
2012	$8.3	$58.6	$66.9	$66.9	$1.0
2013	9.9	62.0	71.9	72.2	0.7
2014	11.6	72.1	83.6	83.6	0.7
2015	13.5[2]	76.0	89.5	89.5	0.8
2016	14.6[2]	81.7	96.3	96.3	0.8
2017	16.5	88.9	105.4	105.3	0.9
2018	18.3	96.8	115.1	115.0	0.9
2019	20.3	105.4	125.6	125.5	1.0
2020	22.5[2]	115.8	138.3	138.2	1.1
2021	23.8[2]	126.8	150.6	150.5	1.2
2022	26.6	138.7	165.2	165.1	1.3
Low-cost:					
2012	8.3	58.6	66.9	66.9	1.0
2013	9.9	60.5	70.4	70.7	0.7
2014	9.8	63.2	73.0	73.0	0.7
2015	11.0[2]	66.2	77.2	77.2	0.7
2016	11.5[2]	69.5	81.0	81.0	0.7
2017	12.8	73.6	86.4	86.4	0.7
2018	14.1	77.9	92.0	92.0	0.8
2019	15.3	82.4	97.8	97.7	0.8
2020	16.8[2]	88.3	105.1	105.0	0.8
2021	17.5[2]	94.0	111.6	111.5	0.9
2022	19.3	100.2	119.5	119.4	0.9
High-cost:					
2012	8.3	58.6	66.9	66.9	1.0
2013	9.9	63.5	73.5	73.7	0.7
2014	13.4	81.5	94.8	94.8	0.8
2015	16.1[2]	86.7	102.8	102.8	0.8
2016	17.7[2]	95.3	113.1	113.0	0.9
2017	20.3	106.6	126.9	126.8	1.0
2018	22.8	119.3	142.1	142.0	1.1
2019	25.6	133.6	159.2	159.1	1.3
2020	28.9[2]	150.8	179.7	179.5	1.5
2021	31.0[2]	169.8	200.8	200.6	1.6
2022	35.0	191.0	225.9	225.7	1.9

[1]Other income contains Federal and State government contributions and interest.
[2]See footnote 6 of table III.D3.
Note: Totals do not necessarily equal the sums of rounded components.

The Trustees selected the three sets of assumptions in order to indicate the general range in which one might reasonably expect the cost to fall. The low- and high-cost alternatives provide for a wide range of possible experience. Actual experience is likely to fall within the range, but there can be no assurance that this will be the case, especially since Part D is a relatively new, voluntary program for which there is little experience.

The alternative projections shown in table III.D5 illustrate two important aspects of the financial operations of the Part D account:

· Despite the widely differing assumptions underlying the three alternatives, the balance between Part D income and expenditures remains relatively stable. Under the low-cost assumptions, for example, by 2022 both income and expenditures would be around 28 percent lower than projected under the intermediate assumptions. The corresponding amounts under the high-cost assumptions would be around 37 percent higher than the intermediate estimates.

This result occurs because the premiums and general revenue contributions underlying the Part D financing will be reestablished annually. Thus, Part D income will automatically track Part D expenditures fairly closely, regardless of the specific economic and other conditions.

- As a result of the close matching of income and expenditures described above, together with anticipated continuing flexibility in the apportionment of general revenues, the need for a contingency reserve to handle unanticipated fluctuations is minimal. The next section describes this issue in more detail.

Adequacy of Part D Financing Established for Calendar Year 2013

As noted previously, the Part D account in the SMI trust fund will be in financial balance indefinitely because the premiums paid by enrollees and the amounts apportioned from the general fund of the Treasury are determined each year so as to adequately finance Part D expenditures. Moreover, the appropriation language transferring funds to the Part D account provides substantial flexibility in the amount of general revenues available to the account. Although an apportioned amount is provided, based on estimates from the President's Budget, the financing method also allows indefinite budget authority for Part D in the event that the apportioned amount is insufficient. As a result of this process, further Congressional action would not be necessary to cover a higher-than-expected level of Part D expenditures.[49] Similar flexibility is anticipated for Part D in the future.

This basis for appropriations was used for the 2004-2005 transitional drug card subsidies and has been used for the Part D payment transactions since 2006. It has also been used for many years in setting appropriations for Federal matching funds for the Medicaid program.

---

[49]The indefinite authority applies to all Part D outlays other than Federal administrative expenses. Those amounts are appropriated each year.

As a consequence of this approach to the general fund financing for Part D, the Department of Treasury transfers general revenues to the account in the amount necessary to cover expenditures. The indefinite authority provision allows such apportionments to change without additional Congressional action if the amount previously apportioned was insufficient. Consequently, no deficit will occur in the Part D account, and no contingency fund will be necessary to cover deficits.

As described in the section on the financial status of the Part B account, it is important to maintain an appropriate level of assets to cover the liability for claims that have been incurred but not yet reported or paid. In the case of Part D, however, most such claims are the responsibility of the prescription drug plans rather than the Part D program. Accordingly, the Part D account is generally not at risk for incurred-but-unreported claim amounts, and no asset reserve is necessary for this purpose.

Another potential Part D liability exists to the extent that Part D reinsurance payments and low-income cost-sharing subsidy payments are based on plan estimates.[50] Since actual Part D costs, as subsequently determined, will generally differ somewhat from the plan bids, payment adjustments are made after the close of the year as necessary to reconcile the accounts. Medicare has made such settlements in favor of the plans from the following year's appropriated general revenues; thus, creation of a reserve for payment of such settlement amounts is unnecessary.

For these reasons, the Trustees have concluded that maintenance of Part D account assets for contingency or liability purposes is unnecessary at this time. Accordingly, evaluation of the adequacy of Part D assets is also unnecessary, and the Part D account is considered to be in satisfactory financial condition for 2012 (and all future years under current law) as a consequence of its basis for financing.

To the extent that actual future account transactions and apportionment measures differ from the current expectations, it may be necessary to reconsider this conclusion.

---

[50]These estimates are subject to actuarial review by the Office of the Actuary at CMS.

3. Long-Range Estimates

Section III.D2 presented the expected operations of the Part D account over the next 10 years. This section describes the long-range expenditures of the account under the intermediate assumptions. Due to its automatic financing provisions, the Trustees expect adequate financing of the Part D account into the indefinite future and so have not conducted a long-range analysis using high-cost and low-cost assumptions.

Table III.D6 shows the estimated Part D incurred expenditures under the intermediate assumptions expressed as a percentage of GDP, for selected years over the calendar-year period 2012-2087.[51] The 75-year projection period fully allows for the presentation of likely future trends, such as the large increase in enrollees after 2010 as the baby boom generation begins to receive benefits.

Table III.D6.—Part D Expenditures (Incurred Basis) as a Percentage of the Gross Domestic Product[1]

Calendar year	Part D expenditures as a percentage of GDP
2012	0.45%
2013	0.45
2014	0.47
2015	0.49
2016	0.50
2017	0.51
2018	0.53
2019	0.55
2020	0.58
2021	0.61
2022	0.64
2025	0.71
2030	0.83
2035	0.92
2040	0.97
2045	1.02
2050	1.07
2055	1.12
2060	1.18
2065	1.24
2070	1.29
2075	1.35
2080	1.38
2085	1.42

[1]Expenditures are the sum of benefit payments and administrative expenses.

The Trustees assume that increases in Part D costs per enrollee during the initial 25-year period will decline gradually to the growth rates described in sections II.C and IV.D. Based on these assumptions and projected demographic changes, incurred Part D expenditures as

---

[51]These estimated incurred expenditures are for benefit payments and administrative expenses combined, unlike the values in table III.D4, which express only benefit payments on a cash basis as a percentage of GDP.

a percentage of GDP would increase rapidly from 0.45 percent in 2012 to 1.42 percent in 2085.

The long-range Part D projections are based on the "baseline" cost-growth assumptions described previously. More information on these assumptions is available in section IV.D of this report. Section IV.B2 describes the data sources and assumptions underlying the updated Part D estimates.

Figure III.D1 compares the year-by-year Part D costs as a percentage of GDP for the current annual report with the corresponding projections from the 2012 report. The estimates in this report are slightly lower than in last year's report. The percentage differential is −0.01 percent of GDP in 2012 and grows to −0.07 percent of GDP in 2087, primarily due to the lower-than-expected prescription drug expenditures for 2012 in the U.S. overall, and a lower projected trend for 2013.

Figure III.D1.—Comparison of Part D Projections as a Percentage of the Gross Domestic Product: Current versus Prior Year's Reports

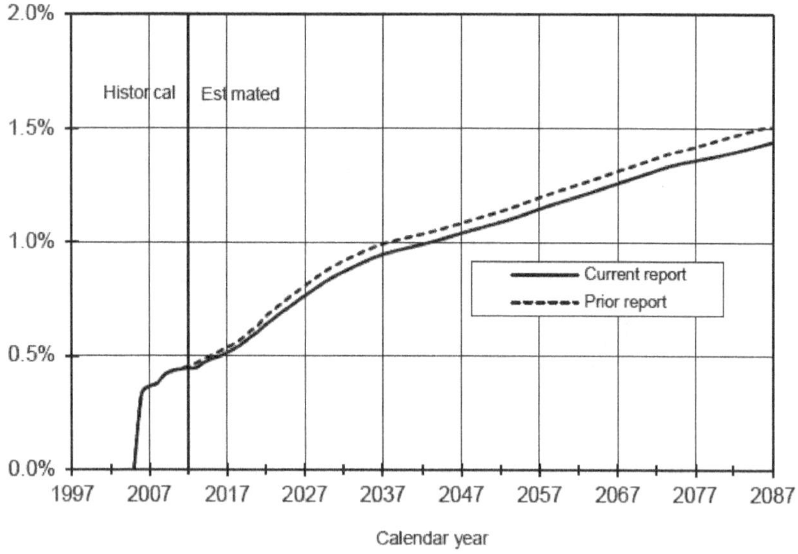

Calendar year

IV. ACTUARIAL METHODOLOGY AND PRINCIPAL ASSUMPTIONS FOR COST ESTIMATES FOR THE HOSPITAL INSURANCE AND SUPPLEMENTARY MEDICAL INSURANCE TRUST FUNDS

This section describes the basic methodology and assumptions used in the estimates for the HI and SMI trust funds under the intermediate assumptions and presents projections of HI and SMI costs under two alternative sets of assumptions.

The economic and demographic assumptions underlying the projections of HI and SMI costs shown in this report are consistent with those in the 2013 Annual Report of the Board of Trustees of the Federal Old-Age and Survivors Insurance and Federal Disability Insurance Trust Funds. That report describes these assumptions in more detail.

A. HOSPITAL INSURANCE

1. Cost Projection Methodology

The principal steps involved in projecting future HI costs are (i) establishing the present cost of services provided to beneficiaries, by type of service, to serve as a projection base; (ii) projecting increases in HI payments for inpatient hospital services; (iii) projecting increases in HI payments for skilled nursing, home health, and hospice services covered; (iv) projecting increases in payments to private health plans; and (v) projecting increases in administrative costs.

a. Projection Base

To establish a suitable base from which to project future HI costs, the incurred payments for services provided must be constructed for the most recent period for which a reliable determination can be made. Accordingly, payments to providers must be attributed to dates of service, rather than to payment dates; in addition, the nonrecurring effects of any changes in regulations, legislation, or administration, and of any items affecting only the timing and flow of payments to providers, must be eliminated. As a result, the rates of increase in the HI incurred costs differ from the increases in cash expenditures shown in the tables in section III.B.

For those expenses still reimbursed on a reasonable-cost basis, the costs for covered services are determined on the basis of provider cost reports. Due to the time required to obtain cost reports from providers, to verify these reports, and to perform audits (where appropriate), final settlements have lagged behind the original costs by as much as several years for some providers. Additional complications arise from legislative, regulatory, and administrative changes, the effects of which cannot always be determined precisely.

The process of allocating the various types of HI payments made to the proper incurred period—using incomplete data and estimates of the impact of administrative actions—presents difficult problems, and the solutions to these problems can be only approximate. Under the circumstances, the best that one can expect is that the actual HI incurred cost for a recent period can be estimated within a few percent. This process increases the projection error directly by incorporating any error in estimating the base year into all future years.

b. Fee-for-Service Payments for Inpatient Hospital Costs

Payment for almost all inpatient hospital services for fee-for-service beneficiaries occurs under a prospective payment system. The law stipulates that the annual increase in the payment rate for each admission relate to a hospital input price index (also known as the hospital market basket), which measures the increase in prices for goods and services purchased by hospitals for use in providing care to hospital inpatients. For fiscal year 2013, the prospective payment rates have already been determined. For fiscal years 2014 and later, the statute mandates that the annual increase in the payment rate per admission equal the annual increase in the hospital input price index (for those hospitals submitting required quality measure data), minus a specified percentage. For this report, the Trustees assume that all hospitals will submit these data.

Increases in aggregate payments for inpatient hospital care covered under HI can be analyzed in five broad categories, presented in table IV.A1:

(1) Labor factors—the increase in the hospital input price index attributable to increases in hospital workers' hourly compensation (including fringe benefits);

(2) Non-labor factors—the increase in the hospital input price index attributable to factors other than hospital workers' hourly compensation, such as the costs of energy, food, and supplies;

(3) Unit input intensity allowance—an amount added to or subtracted from the input price index (generally called for in legislation) to yield the prospective payment update factor;

(4) Volume of services—the increase in total output of units of service (as measured by covered HI hospital admissions);

(5) Case mix—the financial effect of changes in the average complexity of hospital admissions; and

(6) Other sources—a residual category reflecting all other factors affecting hospital cost increases (such as legislative increases).

Table IV.A1 shows the estimated historical values of these principal components, as well as the projected trends used in the estimates. Unless otherwise indicated, the following discussions apply to projections under the intermediate assumptions.

Table IV.A1.—Components of Historical and Projected Increases in HI Inpatient Hospital Payments[1]

Calendar year	Average hourly compensation	Labor Hospital hourly compensation differential	Hospital hourly compensation	CPI	Non-labor Hospital price differential	Non-labor hospital prices	Input price index	Unit input intensity allowance[2]	HI enrollment	Units of service Managed care shift effect	Admission incidence	Case mix	Other sources	HI inpatient hospital payments
Historical data:														
2003	5.0%	−0.8%	4.2%	2.2%	1.5%	3.7%	4.0%	−0.8%	1.7%	0.9%	−0.1%	1.1%	−1.9%	4.8%
2004	4.5	−0.6	3.9	2.6	1.4	4.0	3.9	−0.6	1.8	0.1	−0.7	0.5	0.8	5.9
2005	3.7	0.2	3.9	3.5	0.7	4.2	4.0	−0.6	1.8	−0.9	−0.3	0.4	1.3	5.8
2006	3.9	−0.1	3.8	3.2	0.7	3.9	3.8	−0.2	2.0	−3.7	−1.3	0.7	−0.7	0.4
2007	3.2	0.4	3.6	2.9	0.6	3.5	3.6	−0.3	2.2	−3.4	1.0	−0.2	−2.2	0.6
2008	3.6	−0.3	3.3	4.1	1.0	5.1	4.1	−0.3	2.6	−3.1	−3.8	1.9	2.2	3.4
2009	1.4	1.3	2.7	−0.7	2.1	1.4	2.1	0.7	2.5	−2.4	−2.5	2.7	−1.3	1.6
2010	3.3	−1.3	2.0	2.1	0.7	2.8	2.3	−0.3	2.4	−0.9	−0.8	0.6	−1.7	1.6
2011	2.6	−0.8	1.8	3.6	0.4	4.0	2.7	−0.3	2.5	−1.1	−0.8	0.0	−0.8	2.1
2012	1.7	−0.1	1.6	2.1	0.8	2.9	2.2	−0.5	3.6	−2.0	−3.1	0.7	0.8	1.7
Intermediate estimates:														
2013	2.1	0.1	2.2	1.8	0.6	2.4	2.3	−0.6	3.3	−2.1	0.0	0.5	−2.1	1.1
2014	4.2	0.0	4.2	2.2	0.6	2.8	3.6	−0.8	3.2	−0.6	−0.4	0.5	−3.2	2.1
2015	5.0	0.0	5.0	2.4	0.5	2.9	4.1	−0.7	3.1	1.5	−0.6	0.5	−3.5	4.4
2016	5.1	0.0	5.1	2.5	0.4	2.9	4.2	−0.9	3.0	2.2	−0.5	0.5	−1.2	7.4
2017	4.9	0.0	4.9	2.7	0.3	3.0	4.1	−1.4	3.0	2.8	−0.4	0.5	0.0	8.8
2018	4.8	0.0	4.8	2.8	0.2	3.0	4.1	−1.6	2.9	1.1	−0.3	0.5	1.3	8.3
2019	4.5	0.0	4.5	2.8	0.1	2.9	3.9	−1.5	2.9	0.0	−0.2	0.5	0.1	5.8
2020	4.5	0.0	4.5	2.8	0.0	2.8	3.8	−0.9	2.9	−0.3	−0.2	0.5	0.2	6.1
2021	4.4	0.0	4.4	2.8	0.0	2.8	3.8	−0.9	2.9	−0.6	−0.1	0.5	0.2	5.9
2022	4.2	0.0	4.2	2.8	0.0	2.8	3.7	−0.9	2.8	−0.6	0.0	0.5	1.7	7.4
2025	4.1	0.0	4.1	2.8	0.0	2.8	3.6	−1.0	2.6	−0.0	0.1	0.5	0.0	5.9
2030	4.1	0.0	4.1	2.8	0.0	2.8	3.6	−1.1	1.7	0.0	0.7	0.5	0.0	5.5
2035	4.1	0.0	4.1	2.8	0.0	2.8	3.7	−1.1	1.1	0.0	1.0	0.5	0.0	5.2

[1]Percent increase in year indicated over previous year, on an incurred basis.

[2]Reflects the allowances provided for in the prospective payment update factors. Also reflects the downward adjustments to price updates based on the 10-year moving average of private, non-farm business multifactor productivity growth in 2012 and later, and additional decreases in updates ranging from 0.1 percentage point to 0.75 percentage point from 2010 through 2019, as introduced by the Affordable Care Act. Historical values also include any difference between the official payment update, which is based on an estimate for the following year, and subsequent actual data.

Note: Historical and projected data reflect the hospital input price index, which was recalibrated to a 2002 base year in 2005.

Increases in hospital workers' hourly compensation can be analyzed and projected in terms of (i) the assumed increases in hourly compensation in employment in the general economy; and (ii) the difference between increases in hourly compensation in the general economy and the hospital hourly compensation used in the hospital input price index. Since HI began, the differential between hospital workers' hourly compensation and hourly compensation in the general economy has fluctuated widely and averaged about −0.2 percent since 2003. After 2013, this differential is assumed to be zero for the entire projection period.

Non-labor cost increases can similarly be analyzed in terms of a known, economy-wide price measure (the Consumer Price Index, or CPI) and a differential between the CPI and hospital-specific prices. This differential reflects price increases for hospital-purchased non-labor goods and services that do not parallel increases in the CPI. Although the price differential has fluctuated erratically in the past, it averaged about 1.0 percent during 2003-2012. Over the next few years, the hospital price differential is assumed to decrease from recent levels and by 2020 to level off at zero for the remainder of the projection period.

The final input price index is calculated as a weighted average of the labor and non-labor factors described above. The weights reflect the relative use of each factor by hospitals (currently about 60 percent labor and 40 percent non-labor).

The unit input intensity allowance is generally a downward adjustment provided for by law in the prospective payment update factor; that is, it is the amount subtracted from the input price index to yield the update factor.[52] Beginning in fiscal year 2004, the law provides that increases in payments to prospective payment system hospitals for covered admissions will equal the increase in the hospital input price index for those hospitals that submit the required quality measure data. For other hospitals, the increase will be slightly smaller. For this report, the Trustees assume that all hospitals will submit these data. Beginning in fiscal year 2010, the

---

[52]The update factors are generally prescribed on a fiscal-year basis, while table IV.A1 is on a calendar-year basis. Calculations have therefore been performed to estimate the unit input intensity allowance on a calendar-year basis. Also, because the displayed input price index amounts are the latest estimates available, as opposed to the estimates used when each prospective payment update factor was originally prescribed, the unit input intensity allowance includes, if necessary, an adjustment to offset this change. Accordingly, the sum of the input price index and the unit input intensity allowance generally reflects the prescribed prospective payment update factor, but on a calendar-year, rather than a fiscal-year, basis.

Affordable Care Act mandates amounts to be subtracted from the input price index, including the increase in economy-wide multifactor productivity in 2012 and later, and amounts ranging from 0.1 percentage point to 0.75 percentage point for 2010 through 2019. As a result of these adjustments, the unit input intensity allowance, as indicated in table IV.A1, is negative throughout the first 25-year projection period.

Increases in payments for inpatient hospital services also reflect growth in the number of inpatient hospital admissions covered under HI. As shown in table IV.A1, increases in admissions are attributable to growth in both HI fee-for-service enrollment and admission incidence (admissions per beneficiary).[53] The historical and projected growth in enrollment reflects a more rapid increase in the population aged 65 and over than in the total population of the United States, as well as increasing numbers of disabled beneficiaries and persons with end-stage renal disease. Growth in enrollment is expected to continue and to mirror the ongoing demographic shift into categories of the population eligible for HI benefits.

In the 1990s the choice of more beneficiaries to join private health plans was an offsetting factor to the HI enrollment growth, as shown in the "managed care shift effect" column of table IV.A1. In other words, greater enrollment in private health plans reduced the number of beneficiaries with fee-for-service Medicare coverage and thereby reduced hospital admissions paid through fee-for-service. This factor reversed during 2000-2003, when significant numbers of beneficiaries left private health plans. More recently, with the changes introduced in the Medicare Modernization Act, enrollment in Medicare Advantage plans accelerated rapidly. Private Medicare health plan membership is projected to continue to grow through 2014. Annual decreases in enrollment are projected to begin in 2015 and continue through 2018 as a result of the benchmark and rebate provisions of the Affordable Care Act.

Since the beginning of the prospective payment system (PPS), inpatient hospital payments have varied based on the complexity of admissions. These variations are primarily due to (i) the changes in diagnosis-related group (DRG) coding as hospitals continue to adjust to the PPS and (ii) the trend toward treating less complicated (and

---

[53]For 2010-2021, this factor is estimated to be negative, reflecting the influx of beneficiaries aged 65 (and the resulting reduction in the average age of beneficiaries) due to the retirement of the baby boom generation. By 2025, the aging of this group is expected to increase the incidence of admissions.

thus less expensive) cases in outpatient settings, which results in an increase in the average prospective payment per admission.

The average complexity of hospital admissions (case mix) is expected to increase by 0.5 percent annually in fiscal years 2013 through 2037 as a result of an assumed continuation of the current trend toward treating less complicated cases in outpatient settings, ongoing changes in DRG coding, and the overall impact of new technology. This assumption is based on the recommendation of the 2010-2011 Medicare Technical Review Panel.

Hospital payments are also affected by other factors, as reflected in the "other sources" column of table IV.A1. A complicating factor is the advent of the new MS-DRG system, which led to significant increases in case mix as a result of claims coding. Statutory budget neutrality adjustments have offset much of the MS-DRG impact. Although the law limited the size of these adjustments in 2008 and 2009, it allows subsequent recovery of any extra payments that resulted. The "other sources" column reflects all of these actual and anticipated effects and adjustments. In addition, one can attribute part of the increase from "other sources" to the increase in payments for certain costs, not included in the DRG payment, that are generally growing at a rate slower than the input price index. These other costs include capital, medical education (both direct and indirect), "disproportionate share (DSH)" payments, and payments to hospitals not included in the prospective payment system. A particularly important change affecting these costs is the reduction in Medicare DSH payments under the ACA. This change reflects the major coverage expansions beginning in 2014 that will result in significantly fewer uninsured hospital patients.

Additional possible sources of changes in payments include (i) a shift to higher cost or lower cost admissions due to changes in the demographic characteristics of the covered population; (ii) changes in medical practice patterns; and (iii) adjustments in the relative payment levels for various DRGs, or addition/deletion of DRGs, in response to changes in technology.

The "other sources" column reflects, as appropriate, the impact of certain enacted legislation, including the sequestration process required by the Budget Control Act of 2011 as amended by the American Taxpayer Relief Act of 2012, which requires a reduction in Medicare expenditures of 2 percent for April 2013 through March 2022. Also reflected in this column is the impact of the estimated bonus payments and penalties for hospitals due to the health information technology incentive provisions of the American Recovery and Reinvestment Act of 2009.

The increases in the input price index (less any intensity allowance specified in the law), units of service, and other sources are compounded to calculate the total increase in payments for inpatient hospital services. The last column of table IV.A1 shows these overall increases.

c. Fee-for-Service Payments for Skilled Nursing Facility, Home Health Agency, and Hospice Services

Historically, the number of days of care covered in skilled nursing facilities (SNFs) under HI has varied widely. This extremely volatile experience has resulted, in part, from legislative and regulatory changes and from judicial decisions affecting the scope of coverage. At the start of the prospective payment system (PPS) in 1998 and 1999, there were large decreases in utilization. Since that time, utilization rates have increased at fairly high rates. The intermediate projections assume that these increases will decline until the increases in covered SNF days reflect the growth and aging of the population plus 1 percent annually, as an underlying trend. This assumption is based on the recommendation of the 2010-2011 Medicare Technical Review Panel.

Rising payroll costs for nurses and other required skilled labor are the principal cause of increases in the average HI cost per day[54] in SNFs. For 1998 and later, such costs reflect the implementation of the new PPS for SNFs, as required by the Balanced Budget Act of 1997. Increases in reimbursement per day also reflect the implementation and expiration of special provisions from the Balanced Budget Refinement Act of 1999 and the Benefits Improvement and Protection Act of 2000. The implementation of the new RUG-53 system of payment in 2006 was accompanied by an increase of over 7 percent in case mix for 2006 and more than 3 percent for 2007 through 2009. In 2010, a reduction of about 3.3 percent was applied to all the rates to better match payments from the old payment system to the new payment system. The implementation of a new RUG system again caused a very large increase in case mix in 2011, and a reduction of about 12.6 percent was applied in 2012 to once again match payments. The Budget Control Act of 2011, as amended by the American Taxpayer Relief Act of 2012, requires a 2-percent reduction in expenditures during fiscal

---

[54]Cost is defined to be the total of HI reimbursement and beneficiary cost sharing.

years 2013 through 2021, as reflected in the projected expenditures. The case mix increases are assumed to gradually slow down to a level of 1.5 percent annually, based on the recommendation of the 2010-2011 Medicare Review Panel. These assumed trends result in projected rates of increase in cost per day that are assumed to decline to a level slightly higher than increases in general earnings throughout the projection period.

Table IV.A2 shows the resulting increases in fee-for-service expenditures for SNF services.

Table IV.A2.—Relationship between Increases in HI Expenditures and Increases in Taxable Payroll[1]

Calendar year	Inpatient hospital[2,3]	Skilled nursing facility[3]	Home health agency[3,7]	Private plans	Weighted average[3,4]	HI admin-istrative costs[3,5]	HI expendi-tures[3,6]	HI taxable payroll	Growth rate differential[6]
Historical data:									
2003	5.1%	2.5%	-12.7%	0.1%	4.0%	-0.5%	4.0%	2.7%	1.2%
2004	5.7	13.6	9.5	10.5	7.7	18.3	7.9	6.0	1.8
2005	5.6	10.7	6.9	21.0	8.6	-2.6	8.4	5.5	2.8
2006	0 5	7.8	2.4	28.0	6.0	0.0	5.9	6.2	-0.4
2007	0.6	8.3	3.9	22.6	5.9	-1.0	5.8	5.4	0.3
2008	2 9	9.0	7.6	21.6	7.7	10.6	7.7	1.8	5.8
2009	1.6	5.4	4.3	19.2	6.4	-2.5	6.3	-4.6	11.4
2010	1.6	5.6	3.3	2.9	2.7	8.0	2.7	2.2	0.6
2011	2 0	10.6	-5.4	6.6	4.3	7.0	4.3	3.8	0.5
2012	1.7	-6.6	-1.2	9.0	2.7	7.8	2.8	4.0	-1.2
Intermediate estimates									
2013	1.1	3.6	1.5	4.3	2.4	-2.1	2.3	3.8	-1.4
2014	2.1	6.5	3.1	-2.6	1.5	8.1	1.6	5.8	-3.9
2015	4 5	9.5	5.9	-2.6	3.4	10.5	3.5	7.0	-3.2
2016	7 5	10.7	6.0	0.2	6.2	11.2	6.3	7.1	-0.8
2017	8 9	11.5	7.3	-2.0	6.6	11.5	6.7	6.7	0.1
2018	8.4	9.7	9.6	4.1	7.6	9.4	7.6	6.1	1.4
2019	5 8	8.5	8.2	6.8	6.4	7.5	6.5	5.3	1.1
2020	6.1	8.2	8.1	8.4	7.0	6.9	7.0	4.8	2.0
2021	5 9	8.1	8.0	9.2	7.1	7.8	7.1	4.7	2.3
2022	7.4	9.9	9.7	11.0	8.8	10.1	8.8	4.4	4.2
2025	5 9	8.7	8.3	6.6	6.2	6.6	6.2	4.4	1.8
2030	5 5	8.7	8.1	6.3	6.5	5.7	6.5	4.4	2.0
2035	5 2	8.5	7.8	6.1	6.3	5.0	6.2	4.5	1.7

[1]Percent increase in year indicated over previous year.
[2]This column may differ slightly from the last column of table IV.A1, since table IV.A1 includes all persons eligible for HI protection while this table excludes noninsured persons.
[3]Costs attributable to insured beneficiaries only, on an incurred basis. Benefits and administrative costs for noninsured persons are expected to be financed through general revenue transfers and premium payments, rather than through payroll taxes.
[4]Includes costs for hospice care.
[5]Includes costs of Quality Improvement Organiza ions.
[6]The ratio of the increase in HI costs to the increase in taxable payroll. This ratio is equivalent to the percent increase in the ratio of HI expenditures to taxable payroll (the cost rate).
[7]Includes the declining share of costs drawn from HI for coverage of certain home health services transferred from HI to SMI Part B.

Historically, HI experience with home health agency (HHA) payments had shown a generally upward trend, frequently with sharp increases in the number of visits from year to year. The enactment of the Balanced Budget Act of 1997, which introduced interim per beneficiary cost limits at levels that resulted in substantially lower aggregate payments, also heavily affected the growth in the benefit. These cost limits were used until the implementation of the prospective payment system in October 2000. For 1998 through 2001, data show large decreases in utilization, with utilization leveling off in 2002 and 2003. For 2004 through 2009, the increases were slightly larger. Moreover, in certain areas of the country, outlier payments for treatment episodes increased at extraordinary rates during this period, prompting special rules to limit abusive practices. In 2010, limits were placed on the proportion of total payments that an agency could receive in the form of outlier payments, and prosecution of fraud cases resulted in the closing of a number of purported home health agencies. There was a slight decrease in utilization in 2010, followed by a large decrease in 2011. Preliminary data show another decrease in 2012. For 2013 and later, these utilization and intensity increases are expected to rebound, and increases are assumed for the rest of the projection period equal to the growth and aging of the population plus 1 percent annually. This assumption is based on the recommendation of the 2010-2011 Medicare Technical Review Panel. As is the case for all types of Medicare benefits, the projected home health expenditures reflect a 2-percent reduction during fiscal years 2013 through 2021 based on the provisions of the Budget Control Act of 2011, as amended by the American Taxpayer Relief Act of 2012.

Reimbursement per episode of care[55] is assumed to increase at a slightly higher rate than increases in general earnings, but adjustments to reflect statutory limits on HHA reimbursement per episode are included where appropriate. In particular, payments were set to be equivalent to a 15-percent reduction in the prior interim cost limits, effective October 2002. Under the Affordable Care Act, HHA payment rates will be "rebased" starting in 2014, with an estimated 14-percent reduction in payments phased in over a 4-year period. Reimbursement per episode also includes any change in the mix of services being provided. During 2001, the first year that the prospective payment system was in effect, this mix of services was much higher than anticipated. Since then the case mix increases have been more modest. CMS adjusted HHA payment levels from 2008 through 2013 to offset gradually the financial effect of the unduly high mix of services in the first and subsequent years. Projected HHA costs reflect these regulatory adjustments. Based on the recommendation of the 2010-2011 Medicare Technical Review Panel,

---

[55]Under the HHA prospective payment system, Medicare payments are made for each episode of care, rather than for each individual home health visit.

HHA case mix is projected to increase at 1.5 percent annually. Table IV.A2 shows the resulting increases in fee-for-service expenditures for HHA services.

HI covers certain hospice care for terminally ill beneficiaries. Hospice payments were originally very small relative to total HI benefit payments, but they have grown rapidly in most years and now substantially exceed the level of HI home health expenditures. This growth rate slowed dramatically in the mid-to-late 1990s but rebounded sharply during the 1999-2007 period. From 2008 to 2012 the growth slowed, and this growth rate is expected to continue at this level for the remainder of the projection period. Although detailed hospice data are scant at this time, estimates for hospice benefit payment increases are based on mandated daily payment rates and annual payment caps, and these estimates assume a deceleration in the growth in the number of covered days. Table IV.A2 does not show increases in hospice payments separately but includes them in the weighted average increase for all HI types of service.

d. Private Health Plan Costs

HI payments to private health plans have generally increased significantly from the time that such plans began to participate in the Medicare program in the 1970s. Most of the growth in expenditures has been attributable to the increasing numbers of beneficiaries who have enrolled in these plans. Section IV.C of this report contains a description of the private health plan assumptions and methodology.

e. Administrative Expenses

Historically, the cost of administering the HI trust fund has remained relatively small in comparison with benefit amounts. The ratio of administrative expenses to benefit payments has generally fallen within the range of 1 to 3 percent. The short-range projection of administrative cost is based on estimates of workloads and approved budgets for intermediaries and CMS. In the long range, administrative cost increases are based on assumed increases in workloads, primarily due to growth and aging of the population, and on assumed unit cost increases of slightly less than the increases in average hourly compensation that appear in table IV.A1.

2. Financing Analysis Methodology

Because payroll taxes are the primary basis for financing the HI trust fund, HI costs can be compared on a year-by-year basis with the taxable payroll in order to analyze costs and evaluate the financing. Since the vast majority of total HI costs relate to insured beneficiaries, and since general revenue appropriations and premium payments are expected to support the uninsured segments, the remainder of this section will focus on the financing for insured beneficiaries only.

a. Taxable Payroll

Taxable payroll increases occur as a result of increases in both average covered earnings and the number of covered workers. The taxable payroll projection used in this report is based on the same economic assumptions used in the 2013 Annual Report of the Board of Trustees of the Federal Old-Age and Survivors Insurance and Federal Disability Insurance Trust Funds (OASDI). Table IV.A2 shows the projected increases in taxable payroll for this report, under the intermediate assumptions.

b. Relationship between HI Costs and Taxable Payroll

The most meaningful measure of HI cost increases, with regard to the financing of the system, is the relationship between cost increases and taxable payroll increases. If costs increase more rapidly than taxable payroll, either income rates must be increased or costs reduced (or some combination thereof) to finance the system in the future. Table IV.A3 shows the projected increases in HI costs relative to taxable payroll over the first 25-year projection period. These relative increases fluctuate, starting at −1.4 percent per year in 2013, remaining negative as the assumed economic recovery leads to faster growth in employment and earnings, and then changing to a positive differential of about 1.7 percent per year by 2035 for the intermediate assumption.

The result of these relative growth rates is an initial decrease, followed by a steady increase, in the year-by-year ratios of HI expenditures to taxable payroll, as shown in table IV.A3. Under the low-cost alternative, increases in HI expenditures follow a similar pattern relative to increases in taxable payroll, but at a somewhat lower rate; the rate becomes about 4.0 percent less than the rate for taxable payroll by 2013 but then increases, reaching about 0.2 percent less per year than taxable payroll by 2035. The high-cost alternative follows a comparable pattern but at a somewhat higher rate than under the intermediate assumptions, sharply decreasing from about 2.2 percent more than taxable payroll in 2013 before returning to about 3.9 percent more than taxable payroll by 2035.

Table IV.A3.—Summary of HI Alternative Projections

Calendar year	Increases in aggregate HI inpatient hospital payments[1]				Changes in the rela ionship between expenditures and payroll[1]			Expenditures as a percent of taxable payroll[3,4,5]
	Average hourly compensation	CPI	Other factors[2]	Total[3]	HI expendi- tures[3,4,5]	Taxable payroll	Ratio of expenditures to payroll	
Intermediate:								
2013	2.1%	1.8%	−0.8%	1.1%	2.3%	3.8%	−1.4%	3.62%
2014	4.2	2.2	−1.2	2.1	1.6	5.8	−3.9	3.48
2015	5.0	2.4	0.5	4.4	3.5	7.0	−3.2	3.37
2016	5.1	2.5	3.2	7.4	6.3	7.1	−0.8	3.34
2017	4.9	2.7	4.6	8.8	6.7	6.7	0.1	3.34
2018	4.8	2.8	4.1	8.3	7.6	6.1	1.4	3.39
2019	4.5	2.8	1.9	5.8	6.5	5.3	1.1	3.43
2020	4.5	2.8	2.2	6.1	7.0	4.8	2.0	3.50
2021	4.4	2.8	2.0	5.9	7.1	4.7	2.3	3.58
2022	4.2	2.8	3.6	7.4	8.8	4.4	4.2	3.73
2025	4.1	2.8	2.2	5.9	6.2	4.4	1.8	3.99
2030	4.1	2.8	1.8	5.5	6.5	4.4	2.0	4.45
2035	4.1	2.8	1.4	5.2	6.2	4.5	1.7	4.86
Low-cost:								
2013	3.0	1.7	−3.8	−1.4	1.3	5.5	−4.0	3.51
2014	4.6	1.7	−2.0	1.3	0.4	7.3	−6.4	3.28
2015	4.5	1.7	−0.7	2.6	1.9	7.1	−4.8	3.12
2016	4.5	1.8	1.6	5.1	4.1	6.8	−2.6	3.04
2017	4.1	1.8	2.9	6.2	4.2	6.0	−1.7	2.99
2018	3.8	1.8	2.3	5.4	4.8	5.1	−0.3	2.98
2019	3.8	1.8	−0.1	3.0	3.7	4.5	−0.8	2.96
2020	3.8	1.8	0.4	3.5	4.4	4.3	0.1	2.96
2021	3.8	1.8	0.4	3.5	4.8	4.4	0.4	2.97
2022	3.6	1.8	2.1	5.0	6.5	4.1	2.4	3.04
2025	3.5	1.8	0.6	3.5	3.9	4.0	−0.2	3.08
2030	3.5	1.8	0.3	3.2	4.3	4.0	0.2	3.14
2035	3.5	1.8	−0.1	2.9	4.0	4.2	−0.2	3.13
High-cost:								
2013	1.1	1.9	2.0	3.5	4.1	1.9	2.2	3.77
2014	3.7	2.7	−0.8	2.4	2.8	3.7	−0.8	3.74
2015	5.0	3.2	1.1	5.4	4.5	5.7	−1.1	3.70
2016	5.4	3.3	4.4	9.2	8.0	6.6	1.4	3.75
2017	5.8	3.6	6.3	11.5	9.4	7.2	2.0	3.83
2018	5.9	3.8	6.1	11.4	10.8	7.2	3.4	3.95
2019	5.6	3.8	4.1	9.1	9.9	6.6	3.1	4.08
2020	5.6	3.8	4.4	9.5	10.5	6.4	3.8	4.24
2021	5.2	3.8	4.0	8.9	10.2	5.7	4.2	4.42
2022	4.9	3.8	5.3	10.0	11.5	5.1	6.2	4.69
2025	4.7	3.8	3.7	8.3	8.9	4.8	3.9	5.33
2030	4.7	3.8	3.4	8.0	9.1	4.7	4.2	6.57
2035	4.7	3.8	3.0	7.5	8.8	4.8	3.9	7.98

[1]Percent increase for the year indicated over the previous year.
[2]Other factors include hospital hourly earnings, hospital price input intensity, unit input intensity allowance, units of service as measured by admissions, and additional sources.
[3]On an incurred basis.
[4]Includes expenditures attributable to insured beneficiaries only.
[5]Includes hospital, SNF, HHA, private heal h plan, and hospice expenditures; administrative costs; and costs of Quality Improvement Organizations.

3. Projections under Alternative Assumptions

In almost every year since the trust fund was established, average HI expenditures per beneficiary have increased substantially faster than increases in average earnings and prices in the general economy. Table IV.A2 shows the estimated past experience of HI from 2003 to 2012. As mentioned earlier, HI now makes payments to the great majority of providers on a prospective basis. The prospective payment systems have made (and are expected to continue to make) HI outlays potentially less vulnerable to excessive rates of growth in the health care industry. However, there is still considerable uncertainty in projecting HI expenditures—for inpatient hospital services as well as for other types of covered services—due to the uncertainty of the underlying economic assumptions and utilization increases. Uncertainty in projecting HI expenditures also exists because of the possibility that future legislation will affect unit payment levels, particularly for inpatient hospital services. Legislation has been enacted affecting the inpatient PPS payment levels to hospitals in most of the past 25 years. For future market basket updates for hospitals and most other providers, the Affordable Care Act mandates reductions that are estimated to average 0.8 percent through 2029 and 1.1 percent per year thereafter.

In view of the uncertainty of future cost trends, projected HI costs based on current law have been prepared under three alternative sets of assumptions. Table IV.A3 shows a summary of the assumptions and results. Increases in the economic factors (average hourly compensation and Consumer Price Index) for the three alternatives are consistent with those underlying the OASDI report.

Under the intermediate assumptions, HI costs beyond the first 25-year projection period are based on the assumption that average per beneficiary expenditures (excluding demographic impacts) will increase at the baseline rates determined by the economic model described in sections II.C and IV.D less the economy-wide productivity adjustments. This rate is about 0.4 percent faster than the increase in Gross Domestic Product (GDP) per capita in 2037 but would decelerate to about 0.5 percent slower than GDP per capita by 2087. HI expenditures, which were 3.7 percent of taxable payroll in 2012, increase to 4.9 percent by 2035 and to 5.9 percent by 2087 under the intermediate assumptions. Accordingly, if all of the projection assumptions are realized over time, the HI income rates provided in current law (3.83 percent of taxable payroll) would be inadequate to support the HI cost.

During the first 25-year projection period, the low-cost and high-cost alternatives contain assumptions that result in HI costs increasing, relative to taxable payroll increases, approximately 2 percentage points less rapidly and 2 percentage points more rapidly, respectively, than the results under the intermediate assumptions. Costs beyond the first 25-year projection period assume that the 2-percentage-point differential gradually decreases until 2062, when HI cost increases relative to taxable payroll are approximately the same as under the intermediate assumptions. Under the low-cost alternative, HI expenditures would be 3.1 percent of taxable payroll in 2035, decreasing to 2.7 percent of taxable payroll by 2087 (only about four-fifths of the current level). Under the high-cost alternative, HI expenditures would increase to 8.0 percent of taxable payroll in 2035 and to 12.8 percent of taxable payroll in 2087.

B. SUPPLEMENTARY MEDICAL INSURANCE

SMI consists of Part B and, since 2004, Part D. The benefits provided by each part are quite different. The actuarial methodologies used to produce the estimates for each part reflect these differences and thus appear in separate sections.

1. Part B

a. Cost Projection Methodology

Estimates under the intermediate assumptions are calculated separately for each category of enrollee and for each type of service. The estimates are prepared by establishing the allowed charges or costs incurred per enrollee for a recent year (to serve as a projection base) and then projecting these charges through the estimation period. The per enrollee charges are then converted to reimbursement amounts by subtracting the per enrollee values of the deductible and coinsurance. Aggregate reimbursement amounts are calculated by multiplying the per enrollee reimbursement amounts by the projected enrollment. In order to estimate cash expenditures, an allowance is made for the delay between receipt of, and payment for, the service.

The current-law Part B projections include a very large negative update to physician payments, and yearly adjustments for economy-wide productivity growth applied to most other Part B types of service. The physician payment reduction is likely to be overridden by lawmakers, as similar updates have been for every year since 2003.

Accordingly, the projected Part B estimates under current law are likely understated to a considerable degree.

(1) Projection Base

To establish a suitable base from which to project the future Part B costs, the incurred payments for services provided must be constructed for the most recent period for which a reliable determination can be made. Accordingly, payments to providers must be attributed to dates of service, rather than to payment dates; in addition, the nonrecurring effects of any changes in regulations, legislation, or administration, and of any items affecting only the timing and flow of payments to providers, must be eliminated. As a result, the rates of increase in the Part B incurred cost differ from the increases in cash expenditures.

(a) Carrier Services

Organizations acting for the Centers for Medicare & Medicaid Services (CMS) pay reimbursement amounts for physician services, durable medical equipment (DME), laboratory tests performed in physician offices and independent laboratories, and other services (such as physician-administered drugs, free-standing ambulatory surgical center facility services, ambulance, and supplies). These organizations, referred to as "carriers," determine whether Part B covers billed services, establish the allowed charges for covered services, and transmit to CMS a record of the allowed charges, the applicable deductible and coinsurance, and the amount reimbursed after reduction for coinsurance and the deductible.

The data are tabulated on an incurred basis. As a check on the validity of the projection base, incurred reimbursement amounts are compared with carrier cash expenditures.

(b) Intermediary Services

The same "fiscal intermediaries" that pay for HI services pay reimbursement amounts for institutional services under Part B. Institutional care covered under Part B includes outpatient hospital services, home health agency services, laboratory services performed in hospital outpatient departments, and such services as renal dialysis performed in free-standing dialysis facilities, services in outpatient rehabilitation facilities, and services in rural health clinics.

Separate payment systems exist for almost all the Part B institutional services. For these systems, the intermediaries determine whether Part B covers billed services, establish the allowed payment for covered services, and send to CMS a record of the allowed payment, the applicable deductible and coinsurance, and the amount reimbursed after reduction for coinsurance and the deductible.

For those services still reimbursed on a reasonable-cost basis, the costs for covered services are determined on the basis of provider cost reports. Reimbursement for these services occurs in two stages. First, bills are submitted by providers to the intermediaries, and interim payments are made on the basis of these bills. The second stage takes place at the close of a provider's accounting period, when a cost report is submitted and lump-sum payments or recoveries are made to correct for the difference between interim payments and final settlement amounts for providing covered services (net of coinsurance and deductible amounts). Tabulations of the bills are prepared by date of service, and the lump-sum settlements, which are reported only on a cash basis, are adjusted (using approximations) to allocate them to the time of service.

(c) Private Health Plan Services

Private health plans with contracts to provide health services to Medicare beneficiaries are reimbursed directly by CMS on either a reasonable-cost or capitation basis. Section IV.C of this report contains a description of the assumptions and methodology used to estimate payments to private plans.

(2) Projected Fee-for-Service Payments for Aged Enrollees and Disabled Enrollees without End-Stage Renal Disease

Part B enrollees with end-stage renal disease (ESRD) have per enrollee costs that are substantially higher and quite different in nature from those of most other beneficiaries. Accordingly, the analysis in this section excludes their Part B costs. Those costs are discussed later in this section, as well as costs associated with beneficiaries enrolled in private health plans.

(a) Carrier Services

i. Physician Services

Medicare payments for physician services are based on a fee schedule, which reflects the relative level of resources required for each service.

The fee schedule amount is equal to the product of the procedure's relative value, a conversion factor, and a geographic adjustment factor. Payments are based on the lower of the actual charge and the fee schedule amount. Increases in physician fees are based on growth in the Medicare Economic Index (MEI),[56] plus an update adjustment factor (UAF) that reflects whether past growth in the volume and intensity of services met specified targets under the sustainable growth rate (SGR) mechanism. Table IV.B1 shows the actual and projected MEI increases and update adjustment factors for 2003 through 2022. The physician fee updates and MEI increases shown through 2013 are actual values. For 2014, the physician update reflects the 24.7-percent payment reduction required under current law. The modified update shown in column 4 reflects the growth in the MEI, the update adjustment factor, and all legislative impacts, such as the addition of certain preventive services under the Affordable Care Act. The expected 2-percent reduction in all Medicare payments in 2014 through 2022 does not affect allowed charges, so is not reflected in table IV.B1. Its impact is included in table IV.B2.

---

[56]The MEI is a measure of inflation in physician practice costs and general wage levels. It includes a reduction for economy-wide "private nonfarm business multifactor productivity."

Table IV.B1.—Components of Increases in Total Allowed Charges per Fee-for-Service Enrollee for Carrier Services
[In percent]

Calendar year	MEI	UAF[1]	Physician fee schedule				CPI	DME	Lab	Other carrier
			Increase due to price changes							
			Physician update[2]	Modified update[3]	Residual factors	Total increase[4]				
Aged:										
2003	3.0%[5]	−1.1%[5]	1.4%[5]	1.4	4.5%	6 0%	2.2%	13.8%	6.9%	16.2%
2004	2.9	−1.4	1.8	3.8	5.9	10.0	2.6	−0.5	7.6	7.6
2005	3.1	−1.6	1.5	2.1	3.2	5.4	3.5	1.4	6.3	3.1
2006	2.8	−2.6	0.2	0.2	4.6	4.7	3.2	5.0	7.7	5.5
2007	2.1	−2.1	0.0	−1.4	3.5	2.1	2.9	2.9	9.8	4.7
2008	1.8	−1.3	0.5	0.4	3.3	3.7	4.1	6.4	7.2	4.2
2009	1.6	−0.5	1.1	1.6	1.4	3 0	−0.7	−7.5	8.5	7.9
2010	1.2[5]	0.1[5]	1.3[5]	2.5	1.4	4 0	2.1	1.7	1.4	3.4
2011	0.4	0.5	0.9	0.9	2.4	3.4	3.6	−3.7	−2.8	4.8
2012	0.6	−0.6	0.0	−1.0	1.2	0 2	2.1	2.0	5.8	2.3
2013	0.8	−0.8	0.0	−0.1	0.4	0 3	1.8	−5.1	2.0	4.3
2014	0.7	−25.2	−24.7	−25.0	7.1	−19.7	2.2	−3.7	4.5	4.2
2015	1.7	1.9	3.6	3.6	0.8	4 5	2.4	3.6	4.6	2.8
2016	2.9	−0.3	2.6	2.6	1.0	3.6	2.5	−4.9	6.3	2.7
2017	3.7	−1.6	2.0	2.0	2.1	4 2	2.7	4.8	6.2	4.1
2018	3.7	−2.1	1.5	1.5	2.7	4 3	2.8	5.4	6.2	4.2
2019	3.5	−2.4	1.0	1.0	3.0	4 0	2.8	5.3	6.1	4.2
2020	2.9	−1.9	0.9	0.9	3.0	4 0	2.8	5.1	5.9	4.6
2021	2.5	−1.5	1.0	1.0	3.0	4 0	2.8	5.4	6.3	4.8
2022	2.7	−1.4	1.3	1.3	3.1	4.4	2.8	5.5	6.4	4.9
Disabled (excluding ESRD):										
2003	3.0[5]	−1.1[5]	1.4[5]	1.4	4.6	6.1	2.2	14.9	6.8	23.3
2004	2.9	−1.4	1.8	3.8	5.5	9.6	2.6	−0.3	8.6	12.8
2005	3.1	−1.6	1.5	2.1	−1.7	0.4	3.5	−0.8	−2.8	1.1
2006	2.8	−2.6	0.2	0.2	3.5	3.7	3.2	7.2	10.0	−3.4
2007	2.1	−2.1	0.0	−1.4	4.1	2.6	2.9	2.6	15.8	7.8
2008	1.8	−1.3	0.5	0.4	3.0	3.4	4.1	6.6	11.3	8.6
2009	1.6	−0.5	1.1	1.6	4.7	6.4	−0.7	−1.5	21.0	9.5
2010	1.2[5]	0.1[5]	1.3[5]	2.5	2.8	5.4	2.1	2.0	−4.0	3.1
2011	0.4	0.5	0.9	0.9	1.9	2 9	3.6	−2.9	3.1	3.2
2012	0.6	−0.6	0.0	−1.0	5.4	4.4	2.1	3.9	25.2	4.5
2013	0.8	−0.8	0.0	−0.1	0.6	0.6	1.8	−5.0	2.3	3.4
2014	0.7	−25.2	−24.7	−25.0	7.3	−19.6	2.2	−3.6	4.7	4.5
2015	1.7	1.9	3.6	3.6	1.0	4.7	2.4	3.7	4.8	2.7
2016	2.9	−0.3	2.6	2.6	1.1	3 8	2.5	−4.9	6.4	2.5
2017	3.7	−1.6	2.0	2.0	2.1	4 2	2.7	4.7	6.2	4.1
2018	3.7	−2.1	1.5	1.5	2.7	4 2	2.8	5.2	6.1	4.0
2019	3.5	−2.4	1.0	1.0	3.0	4 0	2.8	5.2	6.1	4.0
2020	2.9	−1.9	0.9	0.9	3.0	4 0	2.8	5.1	5.9	4.5
2021	2.5	−1.5	1.0	1.0	3.0	4 0	2.8	5.4	6.3	4.7
2022	2.7	−1.4	1.3	1.3	3.0	4 3	2.8	5.4	6.3	4.7

[1]Update adjustment factor.
[2]Reflects the growth in the MEI, the update adjustment, and legislation that impacts the physician fee schedule update. The legislative impact is −0.2 percent in 2001-2003. For 2004 and 2005, the Medicare Modernization Act of 2003 established a minimum update of 1.5 percent. For 2006, the Deficit Reduction Act of 2005 froze the physician fee schedule conversion factor. The conversion factor freeze, along with refinements to the relative value units, results in an update of 0.2 percent for 2006. The conversion factor was frozen again for 2007 by the Tax Relief and Health Care Act of 2006. The Medicare, Medicaid, and SCHIP Extension Act of 2007, together with the Medicare Improvements for Patients and Providers Act (MIPPA) of 2008, specified an update of 0.5 percent for 2008. MIPPA also specified an update of 1.1 percent for 2009. The Department of Defense Appropria ions Act of 2009, the Temporary Extension Act of 2010, and the Continuing Extension Act of 2010 established a 0.0-percent update for January to May 2010. The Preservation of Access to Care for Medicare Beneficiaries and Pension Relief Act of 2010, and the Physician Payment and Therapy Relief Act of 2010, established a 2.2-percent update for June to December 2010. The Medicare and Medicaid Extenders Act of 2010 specified an update of 0 percent for 2011. The Temporary Payroll Tax Cut Continuation Act of 2011 and the Middle

Class Tax Relief and Job Creation Act of 2012, established a 0-percent update for 2012. The American Tax Payer Relief Act of 2012 established a 0% update for 2013.
[3]Reflects the growth in the MEI, the update adjustment, and all legislation affec ing physician services—for example, the addition of new preventative services enacted in 1997, 2000, and 2010. The legislative impacts would include those listed in footnote 2.
[4]Equals combined increases in allowed fees and residual factors.
[5]A physician payment price change occurred on March 1, 2003.
[6]A physician payment price change occurred on June 1, 2010.

Under current law, the SGR requires an adjustment to future physician payment increases for past actual physician spending relative to a target spending level. For 2003 through 2013, the system would have led to significant reductions in physician fee schedule rates in multiple years. The Consolidated Appropriation Resolution established a 1.7-percent update beginning in March 2003 that applied to the rest of calendar year 2003. To avoid the reductions from 2004 through 2006, the Medicare Modernization Act established minimum updates of 1.5 percent for 2004 and 2005, and the Deficit Reduction Act established a 0.2-percent update for 2006.[57] However, there was no adjustment to the target spending level for the amendments that avoided the reductions in 2004, 2005, and 2006, and thus the cumulative actual physician expenditures were substantially above the cumulative SGR targets at the end of 2006.

The Tax Relief and Health Care Act (TRA) established a zero-percent update for 2007, increased the target spending level for 1 year, and specified computation of the 2008 physician fee schedule conversion factor as if the TRA had not changed the 2007 physician update. The Medicare, Medicaid, and SCHIP Extension Act (MMSEA) established a 0.5-percent update for the first 6 months of 2008. The Medicare Improvements for Patients and Providers Act (MIPPA) extended the 0.5-percent update for the rest of calendar year 2008 and provided for a 1.1-percent update for 2009. The MMSEA and the MIPPA also increased the target spending level for 2008 and 2009 and specified calculation of the conversion factor for 2010 as if the MMSEA and the MIPPA had not changed the physician updates for 2008 and 2009. The Department of Defense Appropriations Act (DODDA), the Temporary Extension Act (TEA), and the Continuing Extension Act (CEA) established a zero-percent update for January through May 2010 and specified determination of the conversion factor for June 1, 2010 as if the DODAA, the TEA, and the CEA had not changed the scheduled updates for January through May 2010. The Preservation of Access to Care for Medicare Beneficiaries and Pension Relief Act of 2010 (PACMBPRA) and the Medicare and Medicaid

---

[57]The Deficit Reduction Act froze the conversion factor for 2006. Changes in relative value units (RVUs), which increased the average RVU by about 0.2 percent, resulted in a physician fee schedule update of 0.2 percent for 2006.

Extenders Act of 2010 (MMEA) established a 2.2-percent update for June through December 2010. The MMEA also established a 0-percent update for 2011. The DODAA, the TEA, the CEA, the PACMBPRA, and the MMEA together specified determination of the conversion factor for 2012 as if there had been no change to the scheduled updates for 2010 and 2011. The Temporary Payroll Tax Cut Continuation Act of 2011 and the Middle Class Tax Relief and Job Creation Act of 2012 established a 0-percent update for 2012 and specified determination of the conversion factor for 2013 as if there had been no change to the scheduled update for 2012. The American Taxpayer Relief Act of 2012 established a 0-percent update for 2013 and specified that the conversion factor for 2014 be determined as if there had been no change to the scheduled update for 2013.

Under current law, these recent amendments would cause the physician update to be an estimated −24.7 percent in 2014.[58] In contrast, the MEI is expected to increase by about 0.7 percent in 2014. Lawmakers are nearly certain to override such substantial reductions in physician payments per service. (Lawmakers have overridden the scheduled negative update for each of the past 11 years.) Since the physician estimates are based on current law, they are of limited use after 2013 for assessing the likely future state of Part B.[59]

The current-law projections in this report reflect only the direct impacts of the SGR provisions and not potential secondary SGR effects on Parts A, B, and D; accordingly, these projections do not illustrate the full consequences of the current-law physician payment mechanism on Medicare beneficiaries, providers, and financial operations.[60] The secondary impacts have been excluded because of the minimal likelihood that the physician payment reductions will occur in practice and because of the speculative nature of these possible effects.

---

[58]Additional information about the SGR system and the physician spending targets is available at http://www.cms.gov/Medicare/Medicare-Fee-for-Service-Payment/SustainableGRatesConFact/index.html.

[59]Part B projections under an illustrative alternative to the current-law estimates are available on the CMS website at http://www.cms.gov/Research-Statistics-Data-and-Systems/Statistics-Trends-and-Reports/ReportsTrustFunds/Downloads/2013TRAlternativeScenario.pdf. One should not infer any endorsement of this alternative by the Board of Trustees, CMS, or the Office of the Actuary.

[60]Such secondary effects could include (i) substantially reduced beneficiary access to physicians; (ii) a significant shift in enrollment to Medicare private health plans; (iii) an increase in emergency room services; (iv) an increase in mortality rates; and/or (v) an increase in hospital services.

Per capita physician charges also have changed each year as a result of a number of other factors besides fee increases, including more physician visits and related services per enrollee, the aging of the Medicare population, greater use of specialists and more expensive techniques, and certain administrative actions. The fifth column of table IV.B1 shows the increases in charges per enrollee resulting from these residual factors. Because the measurement of increased allowed charges per service is subject to error, residual causes implicitly include any such errors. Residual cost growth for physician services has generally increased rapidly over the last 10 years, averaging almost 4 percent annually during this period. Residual growth slowed abruptly in 2009 and continued to be slow in 2010 and 2011.

Based on the increases in table IV.B1, and incorporating a 2-percent reduction in all Medicare expenditures for April 2013 through March 2022 required by the American Taxpayer Relief Act of 2012, table IV.B2 shows the estimates of the average incurred reimbursement for carrier services per fee-for-service enrollee.

Table IV.B2.—Incurred Reimbursement Amounts per Fee-for-Service Enrollee
for Carrier Services

Calendar year	Fee-for-service enrollment [millions]	Physician fee schedule	DME	Lab	Other carrier
Aged:					
2003	28.232	$1,484.88	$214.19	$89.84	$396.38
2004	28.440	1,638.83	212.88	96.88	426.24
2005	28.433	1,724.29	215.43	103.01	440.39
2006	27.613	1,801.14	225.20	110.95	464.47
2007	26.936	1,836.65	231.39	121.85	486.45
2008	26.457	1,905.33	246.10	130.68	506.47
2009	26.230	1,963.27	227.71	141.76	546.24
2010	26.427	2,037.79	230.59	143.76	564.57
2011	26.589	2,120.41	222.21	139.77	592.79
2012	26.900	2,146.88	230.09	147.87	603.86
2013	27.235	2,109.11	213.45	148.54	615.18
2014	27.893	1,674.69	204.41	154.42	638.22
2015	29.299	1,744.00	211.71	161.46	655.72
2016	31.007	1,800.69	200.71	171.67	673.32
2017	33.049	1,873.09	210.24	182.29	701.13
2018	34.595	1,951.48	221.50	193.68	730.75
2019	35.777	2,028.19	233.11	205.50	761.10
2020	36.924	2,107.27	245.08	217.71	796.31
2021	37.931	2,190.71	258.34	231.38	834.27
2022	38.939	2,320.12	276.64	249.91	888.05
Disabled (excluding ESRD):					
2003	4.847	1,274.29	323.72	85.31	374.44
2004	5.100	1,403.27	322.26	92.61	422.60
2005	5.309	1,403.82	319.37	90.00	428.83
2006	5.236	1,453.03	341.66	99.00	413.59
2007	5.264	1,495.41	350.03	114.65	445.74
2008	5.277	1,548.48	372.81	127.59	482.93
2009	5.337	1,648.84	367.18	154.45	528.83
2010	5.518	1,748.15	374.03	148.30	545.81
2011	5.684	1,806.63	363.40	152.93	564.85
2012	5.663	1,917.13	379.86	191.46	591.75
2013	5.648	1,878.60	359.76	192.91	608.87
2014	5.738	1,495.27	344.83	200.96	633.46
2015	5.915	1,560.36	357.53	210.54	650.48
2016	6.096	1,612.75	339.29	224.07	666.73
2017	6.293	1,678.03	355.09	237.93	693.68
2018	6.370	1,746.52	373.71	252.54	721.25
2019	6.348	1,815.05	393.29	267.94	750.07
2020	6.286	1,885.76	413.47	283.85	784.08
2021	6.190	1,960.30	435.79	301.65	820.59
2022	6.082	2,073.97	466.23	325.49	871.77

ii. Durable Medical Equipment (DME), Laboratory, and Other Carrier Services

As with physician services, unique fee schedules or reimbursement mechanisms have been established for virtually all other non-physician carrier services. Table IV.B1 shows the increases in the allowed charges per fee-for-service enrollee for DME, laboratory services, and other carrier services before application of the 2-percent sequestration required by the Budget Control Act of 2011, as amended by the American Taxpayer Relief Act of 2012. Based on the increases in table IV.B1, table IV.B2 shows the corresponding estimates of the average incurred reimbursement for these services per fee-for-service enrollee, including the sequestration impact in 2013-2022. The fee schedules for each of these expenditure categories are updated by increases in the CPI, together with any applicable legislated limits on payment updates. In particular, under the Affordable Care Act, starting in 2011 these fees are updated by the increase in the CPI minus the increase in the 10-year moving average of private, non-farm business multifactor productivity. Per capita charges for these expenditure categories have also grown as a result of a number of other factors, including increased number of services provided, the aging of the Medicare population, more expensive services, and certain administrative actions. This growth is projected based on recent past trends in growth per enrollee.

(b) Intermediary Services

Over the years, legislation has established new payment systems for virtually all Part B intermediary services, including a fee schedule for tests performed in laboratories in hospital outpatient departments. The Balanced Budget Act (BBA) of 1997 implemented a prospective payment system (PPS), which began August 1, 2000, for services performed in the outpatient department of a hospital. It also implemented a PPS for home health agency services, which began October 1, 2000.

In 2007, accounting errors were discovered among the payments for intermediary services. A transition to a new national accounting system for intermediaries began in early 2005. This new accounting system mistakenly paid Part A hospice claims from the Part B account of the SMI trust fund, rather than from the HI trust fund. Intermediaries that had been transitioned to the new accounting system continued to make these accounting errors until the process was corrected on October 1, 2007.[61]

Table IV.B3 shows the historical and projected increases in charges and costs per fee-for-service enrollee for intermediary services, excluding the impact of the 2-percent sequestration.

---

[61]The Part B account and the HI trust fund were restored to their correct asset position on July 1, 2008, when $9.3 billion was paid into the Part B account and a similar amount was paid from the HI trust fund.

Table IV.B3.—Components of Increases in Recognized Charges and Costs
per Fee-for-Service Enrollee for Intermediary Services

[In percent]

Calendar year	Outpatient hospital	Home health agency	Outpatient lab	Other intermediary
Aged:				
2003	4.4%	4.5%[1]	6.7%	3.9%
2004	11.1	14.6[1]	7.1	15.6
2005	10.8	15.9	5.4	13.5
2006	5.1	17.6	4.4	7.5
2007	8.3	18.9	3.0	7.5
2008	6.3	12.4	5.1	6.0
2009	8.7	14.9	8.1	8.2
2010	5.0	2.5	2.2	3.1
2011	8.1	−4.9	5.2	3.0
2012	8.0	−2.1	4.2	5.8
2013	6.2	−0.2	0.7	6.0
2014	7.1	1.1	4.3	−9.0
2015	7.7	0.9	4.4	5.5
2016	7.9	0.3	6.2	9.6
2017	7.2	0.9	6.2	4.6
2018	6.9	5.0	6.3	5.1
2019	6.5	4.9	6.1	4.8
2020	7.3	5.1	6.0	5.3
2021	7.5	5.6	6.4	5.3
2022	7.3	7.3	6.4	5.4
Disabled (excluding ESRD):				
2003	6.0	5.0[1]	7.4	−3.7
2004	12.7	14.2[1]	8.8	14.9
2005	10.7	16.8	6.6	13.2
2006	5.4	20.3	6.1	11.5
2007	8.0	20.2	6.4	14.3
2008	7.4	14.4	6.1	6.0
2009	9.7	16.8	9.7	8.7
2010	5.2	0.8	0.3	−0.1
2011	8.2	−3.0	6.7	1.5
2012	10.7	−1.5	6.6	6.1
2013	6.3	1.7	0.8	6.8
2014	7.2	2.0	4.3	−1.6
2015	7.8	1.7	4.5	6.4
2016	7.9	1.0	6.2	6.2
2017	7.1	1.4	6.1	5.8
2018	6.8	5.4	6.2	5.9
2019	6.5	5.4	6.1	5.7
2020	7.3	5.8	6.0	6.0
2021	7.4	5.9	6.3	5.9
2022	7.2	7.3	6.3	6.0

[1]Does not reflect the impact of monies transferred from the Part A trust fund for HHA costs, as provided for by the Balanced Budget Act of 1997

Based on the increases in table IV.B3, table IV.B4 shows the estimates of the incurred reimbursement for the various intermediary services per fee-for-service enrollee. Each of these expenditure categories is projected on the basis of recent trends in growth per enrollee, along with applicable legislated limits on payment updates and the 2-percent reduction in payments to providers required by the American Taxpayer Relief Act of 2012.

Table IV.B4.—Incurred Reimbursement Amounts per Fee-for-Service Enrollee
for Intermediary Services

Calendar year	Fee-for-service enrollment [millions]	Outpatient hospital	Home health agency	Outpa ient lab	Other intermediary
Aged:					
2003	28.232	$419.43	$163.78[1]	$86.93	$207.86
2004	28.440	482.14	187.68	93.14	238.85
2005	28.433	555.13	217.43	98.14	267.20
2006	27.613	604.29	255.72	102.43	284.40
2007	26.936	664.56	303.92	105.51	304.20
2008	26.457	723.78	341.56	110.89	323.05
2009	26.230	801.76	392.49	119.89	348.04
2010	26.427	845.58	402.40	122.51	356.46
2011	26.589	922.79	382.79	128.83	364.37
2012	26.900	1,002.06	374.59	134.23	385.76
2013	27.235	1,056.71	375.34	133.12	406.26
2014	27.893	1,135.11	378.02	138.10	368.29
2015	29.299	1,230.61	381.32	144.20	388.58
2016	31.007	1,331.29	382.65	153.18	426.81
2017	33.049	1,427.43	386.09	162.67	446.09
2018	34.595	1,525.94	405.34	172.86	468.86
2019	35.777	1,624.74	425.25	183.45	491.31
2020	36.924	1,744.16	447.08	194.40	517.31
2021	37.931	1,875.15	471.92	206.85	544.65
2022	38.939	2,042.93	506.16	223.46	582.76
Disabled (excluding ESRD):					
2003	4.847	485.26	125.31[1]	93.63	144.71
2004	5.100	561.94	143.06	101.91	163.96
2005	5.309	642.26	167.11	108.59	181.52
2006	5.236	698.06	200.97	115.25	198.83
2007	5.264	762.03	241.55	122.66	226.48
2008	5.277	834.02	276.44	130.09	239.37
2009	5.337	932.03	322.87	142.77	257.95
2010	5.518	983.48	325.53	143.22	254.36
2011	5.684	1,071.95	315.87	152.85	253.11
2012	5.663	1,194.22	310.99	162.99	268.22
2013	5.648	1,260.65	317.57	161.77	289.53
2014	5.738	1,355.68	322.68	167.95	283.30
2015	5.915	1,472.89	328.12	175.53	301.45
2016	6.096	1,598.27	331.48	186.48	320.32
2017	6.293	1,714.30	336.06	197.85	338.77
2018	6.370	1,830.84	354.21	210.04	358.64
2019	6.348	1,949.17	373.22	222.89	379.08
2020	6.286	2,092.43	394.71	236.19	401.84
2021	6.190	2,247.18	417.86	251.05	425.52
2022	6.082	2,445.59	448.45	270.94	457.93

[1]See footnote 1 of table IV.B3.

As indicated in table IV.B4, expenditures for outpatient hospital services increased significantly due to provisions in the BBA, the Balanced Budget Refinement Act of 1999, and the Benefits Improvement and Protection Act of 2000 that reduced beneficiaries' coinsurance payments to normal levels but maintained the same total payment to the hospital. The result is that Medicare pays a larger portion of the total outpatient hospital costs.

Part B expenditures for home health services had been increasing very rapidly through 2010, in part due to suspected fraud and abuse in South Florida and certain other parts of the country. In late 2008, CMS suspended payments to a number of home health agencies and increased program integrity efforts for this category of services. From 2010 onward, outlier payments to agencies have been capped as a percentage of total payments. Assumed growth rates for home health expenditures reflect this initiative, along with the ongoing effects of growth in the number of beneficiaries, payment rates, utilization of services, and legislated changes affecting future payments.

(3) Projected Fee-for-Service Payments for Persons with End-Stage Renal Disease

Most persons with ESRD are eligible to enroll for Part B coverage. For analytical purposes, this section includes both enrollees who qualify for Medicare due to ESRD and those who are also eligible as Disability Insurance beneficiaries because their per enrollee costs are both higher and different in nature from those of most other disabled persons. Specifically, most of the Part B reimbursements for both groups are related to kidney transplants and renal dialysis.

The estimates under the intermediate assumptions reflect the payment mechanism for reimbursing ESRD services. Payment for dialysis services occurs through a bundled payment system, which began in 2011. The bundled payment rate is updated annually by an annual ESRD market basket less the increase in economy-wide productivity. Also, the estimates assume a continued increase in enrollment. Table IV.B5 shows the historical and projected enrollment and costs for Part B benefits, including the effects of the 2-percent sequestration.

Table IV.B5.—Enrollment and Incurred Reimbursement for End-Stage Renal Disease

Calendar year	Average enrollment [thousands]		Reimbursement [millions]	
	Disabled	Non-disabled	Disabled	Non-disabled
2003	118	84	$2,365	$1,714
2004	124	84	2,800	1,812
2005	130	87	3,200	2,408
2006	132	89	3,507	2,533
2007	137	89	3,543	2,503
2008	140	90	3,748	2,585
2009	144	92	4,056	2,694
2010	150	95	4,176	2,653
2011	153	98	4,353	2,746
2012	155	101	4,627	2,903
2013	158	104	4,736	2,987
2014	161	106	4,551	2,873
2015	165	107	4,882	3,063
2016	168	109	5,564	3,474
2017	171	110	5,930	3,674
2018	173	111	6,249	3,876
2019	173	112	6,508	4,073
2020	172	113	6,772	4,286
2021	171	114	7,032	4,509
2022	169	114	7,398	4,807

(4) Private Health Plan Costs

Part B payments to private health plans have generally increased significantly from the time that such plans began to participate in the Medicare program in the 1970s. Most of the growth in expenditures has been due to the increasing numbers of beneficiaries who have enrolled in these plans. Section IV.C of this report contains a description of the assumptions and methodology for the private health plans that provide coverage of Part B services for certain enrollees.

(5) Administrative Expenses

The ratio of Part B administrative expenses to total expenditures has declined to roughly 1.5 percent in recent years. Projections of administrative costs are based on estimates of changes in average annual wages and fee-for-service enrollment.

b. Summary of Aggregate Reimbursement Amounts on a Cash Basis under the Intermediate Assumptions

Table IV.B6 shows aggregate historical and projected reimbursement amounts by type of service on a cash basis under the intermediate assumptions. The difference between reimbursement amounts on a cash versus incurred basis results from the lag between the time of service and the time of payment. This lag has gradually decreased.

Table IV.B6.—Aggregate Part B Reimbursement Amounts on a Cash Basis

[In millions]

Calendar year	Physician fee schedule	Carrier				Hospital	Lab	Intermediary			Total FFS	Private health plans	Total Part B
		DME	Lab	Other	Total			Home health agency	Other	Total			
Historical data:													
2003	$48,325	$7,534	$2,983	$12,933	$71,775	$14,774	$2,998	$5,096[1]	$9,687	$32,556[1]	$104,331[1]	$17,250[1]	$121,582[1]
2004	54,080	7,739	3,318	14,177	79,314	16,861	3,297	5,852	10,856	36,865	116,179	18,672	134,851
2005	57,678	8,007	3,548	15,283	84,516	18,692	3,354	7,080	11,403	40,529[2]	125,045	22,012	147,057
2006	58,145	8,314	3,694	15,509	85,662	20,836	3,541	7,814	12,392	44,583[2]	130,245	31,460	161,704
2007	58,785	8,163	4,144	15,801	86,894	22,022	3,471	9,191	13,033	47,716[2]	134,610	38,858	173,468
2008	60,556	8,627	4,260	16,583	90,026	23,571	3,615	10,303	13,005	50,494	140,520	48,106	188,626
2009	61,801	8,211	4,671	17,760	92,443	26,232	3,982	11,757	14,608	56,578	149,021	53,378	202,400
2010	63,894	8,272	4,808	18,261	95,236	27,933	4,110	12,067	14,930	59,039	154,275	55,186	209,460
2011	67,474	8,171	4,579	19,260	99,485	30,890	4,351	12,356	15,265	62,862	162,347	59,124	221,471
2012	69,645	8,378	5,080	19,961	103,063	34,420	4,661	11,787	16,333	67,201	170,265	65,968	236,233
Intermediate estimates:													
2013	69,640	8,070	5,174	20,598	103,482	36,450	4,633	11,977	17,274	70,334	173,815	73,110	246,926
2014	57,431	7,858	5,477	21,794	92,560	39,877	4,886	12,303	16,458	73,524	166,084	83,053	249,137
2015	61,151	8,425	5,979	23,411	98,967	45,085	5,321	12,967	17,768	81,141	180,107	83,209	263,317
2016	66,597	8,461	6,681	25,302	107,041	51,349	5,934	13,724	20,492	91,499	198,541	83,722	282,262
2017	73,262	9,267	7,508	27,867	117,905	58,294	6,666	14,673	22,639	102,271	220,177	83,163	303,340
2018	79,565	10,142	8,304	30,261	128,272	64,942	7,377	15,999	24,573	112,891	241,164	87,161	328,325
2019	85,160	10,955	9,057	32,431	137,603	71,143	8,051	17,311	26,325	122,830	260,434	94,425	354,859
2020	90,782	11,774	9,828	34,779	147,162	78,162	8,741	18,697	28,200	133,801	280,963	103,522	384,485
2021	96,209	12,603	10,626	37,122	156,560	85,522	9,462	20,132	30,053	145,170	301,730	114,062	415,792
2022	104,155	13,746	11,714	40,377	169,991	95,146	10,436	22,098	32,632	160,312	330,303	128,333	458,636

[1]See footnote 2 of table IV.B3.
[2]Amounts shown exclude payments inadvertently made from the Part B account in 2005-2007 to cover the costs of certain Part A hospice benefits.

c. Projections under Alternative Assumptions

Projections of Part B cash expenditures under current law for the low-cost and high-cost alternatives were developed by modifying the growth rates estimated under the intermediate assumptions. Beginning in calendar year 2013, the low-cost and high-cost incurred benefits for the following 4 quarters reflect some variation relative to the intermediate assumptions. Thereafter, the low-cost and high-cost alternatives contain assumptions that result in incurred benefits increasing, relative to the Gross Domestic Product (GDP), 2 percent less rapidly and 2 percent more rapidly, respectively, than the results under the intermediate assumptions. Administrative expenses under the low-cost and high-cost alternatives are projected on the basis of their respective wage series growth. Based on the above methodology, cash expenditures as a percentage of GDP were calculated for all three sets of assumptions, as displayed in table IV.B7.

**Table IV.B7.—Part B Cash Expenditures as a Percentage
of the Gross Domestic Product for Calendar Years 2012-2022[1]**

		Alternatives	
Calendar year	Intermediate assumptions	Low-cost	High-cost
2012	1.53%	1.53%	1.53%
2013	1.55	1.52	1.58
2014	1.50	1.44	1.56
2015	1.49	1.41	1.58
2016	1.51	1.40	1.63
2017	1.54	1.39	1.69
2018	1.58	1.40	1.77
2019	1.62	1.41	1.86
2020	1.68	1.43	1.96
2021	1.74	1.45	2.07
2022	1.80	1.48	2.19

[1]Expenditures are the sum of benefit payments and administrative expenses.

2. Part D

Part D is a voluntary Medicare prescription drug benefit that offers beneficiaries enrolled in either Part A or Part B a choice of private drug insurance plans in which to enroll. Medicare substantially subsidizes the cost of the drug coverage. Low-income beneficiaries can receive additional assistance on the cost sharing and premiums, depending on their resource levels. Each year drug plan sponsors submit bids that include estimated total plan costs, prospective reinsurance payments (which are roughly 80 percent of the cost above the Part D catastrophic threshold), and low-income cost-sharing subsidies according to their experience and their expectations for the coming year. Upon approval of these bids, a national average bid amount and premium are calculated, and, based on the plan's bid relative to the national average bid, the individual plan premiums are determined dollar-for-dollar above or below the national average premium.

Each drug plan receives direct subsidies (calculated as the risk-adjusted plan bid amount minus the plan premium), prospective reinsurance payments, and prospective low-income cost-sharing subsidies from Medicare, as well as premiums from the beneficiaries and premium subsidies from Medicare on behalf of low-income enrollees. At the end of the year, the prospective reinsurance and low-income cost-sharing subsidy payments are reconciled to match the plan's actual experience. In addition, if actual experience differs from the plan's bid beyond specified risk corridors, Medicare shares in the plan's experience gain or loss.

Expenditures for this voluntary prescription drug benefit, which started on January 1, 2006, were determined by combining estimated Part D enrollment with projections of per capita spending. Actual Part D spending information for 2012 was used as the projection base.

a. Participation Rates

All individuals enrolled in Medicare Part A or Part B are eligible to enroll in the voluntary prescription drug benefit.

(1) Employer-Sponsored Plans

There are several ways that employer-sponsored retiree health plans can benefit from the Part D program. One way is the retiree drug subsidy (RDS), in which, for qualifying employer-sponsored plans, Medicare subsidizes a portion of their qualifying retiree drug expenses. In 2012 this subsidy covered about 15 percent of beneficiaries participating in Part D. Effective with 2013 under the Affordable Care Act, employers are no longer able to deduct retiree health plan costs reimbursed by the RDS. In addition, RDS claims are not eligible for the 50-percent brand-name drug discount, and the 28-percent RDS subsidy rate remains constant even though the coverage gap will be closing over time for other Part D drug plan participants. As a result of these changes, RDS program participation is assumed to decline quickly to about 2 percent of total Part D enrollment in 2016 and beyond. It is expected that the majority of the retirees losing drug coverage through qualifying employer plans will participate in other Part D plans.

Other ways that an employer-sponsored plan can benefit from Part D are to enroll in an employer/union-only Part D group welfare plan, wrap around an existing Part D plan, or become a prescription drug plan itself. The subsidies for these types of arrangements will generally be calculated in the same way as for other Part D plans. It is expected that such plans will offer additional benefits beyond the standard Part D benefit package, resulting in somewhat lower Part D reinsurance payments than those for the non-employer plans. In 2012 these employer-sponsored plans covered 9 percent of all beneficiaries participating in Part D. This proportion is estimated to increase to about 20 percent in 2016 and beyond, primarily due to a large percentage of RDS beneficiaries switching to employer-sponsored plans.

(2) Low-Income Subsidy

Qualifying low-income beneficiaries can receive additional Part D subsidies to help finance premium and cost-sharing payments. Subsidies are estimated for beneficiaries who apply for this assistance and meet the income and asset requirements. Most beneficiaries who qualify for both Medicare and Medicaid are automatically enrolled in plans with premiums below the low-income premium benchmarks within their regions, thereby receiving full subsidization of their Part D premiums. After several years of the continuing outreach effort and the enactment of MIPPA, which expanded the number of individuals eligible for low-income status, the estimated number of low-income enrollees is projected to stay at around 29 percent of total beneficiaries participating in Part D from 2012 to 2022.

(3) Other Part D Beneficiaries

Medicare beneficiaries not covered by employer plans and not qualified for the low-income subsidy can choose to enroll in any Part D plan. Once enrolled, they will pay for premiums and any applicable deductible, coinsurance, and/or copayment. After one accounts for the enrollees discussed above, about 56 percent of the remaining beneficiaries eligible[62] for Part D were enrolled in 2012. This participation rate is projected to grow to 58 percent by 2022. Table IV.B8 provides a summary of the estimated average enrollment in Part D, by category.

---

[62]A significant portion of the remaining eligible beneficiaries who do not participate in Part D plans receive creditable coverage through another source (such as the Federal Employees Health Benefits Program, TRICARE for Life, the Veterans Administration, and the Indian Health Service).

Table IV.B8.—Part D Enrollment
[In millions]

Calendar year	Employer subsidy[1]	Low-income subsidy			Total	All others	Total
		Medicaid full dual eligible	Other, with full subsidy	Other, with partial subsidy			
Historical data:							
2006	7.2	5.7	2.3	0.2	8.3	12.1	27.6
2007	7.1	5.9	3.0	0.3	9.2	15.1	31.4
2008	6.8	6.3	3.2	0.3	9.7	16.0	32.6
2009	6.7	6.4	3.3	0.3	10.0	16.9	33.6
2010	6.8	6.6	3.5	0.3	10.4	17.5	34.8
2011	6.2	6.6	3.7	0.3	10.6	18.9	35.7
2012	5.6	6.9	3.7	0.3	11.0	20.7	37.4
Intermediate estimates:							
2013	3.2	6.9	4.1	0.4	11.3	24.4	38.9
2014	2.1	7.1	4.2	0.4	11.7	26.2	40.1
2015	1.5	7.3	4.3	0.4	12.1	27.6	41.1
2016	0.8	7.5	4.5	0.4	12.4	29.0	42.3
2017	0.8	7.8	4.6	0.4	12.8	29.9	43.5
2018	0.9	8.0	4.7	0.4	13.2	30.7	44.7
2019	0.9	8.2	4.9	0.4	13.5	31.5	46.0
2020	0.9	8.4	5.0	0.5	13.9	32.6	47.4
2021	0.9	8.7	5.2	0.5	14.3	33.4	48.7
2022	1.0	8.9	5.3	0.5	14.7	34.4	50.1

[1]Excludes Federal Government and military retirees covered by either the Federal Employees Health Benefit Program or the TRICARE for Life program. Such programs qualify for the Medicare employer subsidy, but the subsidy will not be paid since it would amount to the Federal Government subsidizing itself.

b. Cost Projection Methodology on an Incurred Basis

(1) Drug Benefit Categories

Projected drug expenses are allocated to the beneficiary premium, direct subsidy, and reinsurance subsidy by the Part D premium formula based on the benefit formula specifications (deductible, coinsurance, initial benefit limit, and catastrophic threshold) for beneficiaries in prescription drug plans and Medicare Advantage drug plans. Low-income beneficiaries receive additional subsidies to help finance premium and cost-sharing payments. Subsidies are estimated for beneficiaries who meet the income and asset requirements.

The statute specifies that the base beneficiary premium is equal to 25.5 percent of the sum of the national average monthly bid amount and the estimated catastrophic reinsurance. The actual premium is greater, dollar for dollar, for plans with bids above the national average and lower for plans with lower bids. The average premium amount per enrollee is estimated based on the base beneficiary premium with an adjustment to reflect enrollees' tendency to select plans with below-average premiums. Beginning in 2011, Part D collects "income-related" premiums (in addition to the premiums charged by the plans) for individuals whose modified adjusted gross income exceeds a specified threshold. The amount of the "income-related" premium depends upon the individual's income level. The extra premium amount is the difference between 35, 50, 65, or 80 percent and 25.5 percent applied to the national average monthly bid amount adjusted for reinsurance.

(2) Projection Base

The projections in this year's report are based in part on actual Part D spending data through 2012. These data included amounts for total prescription drug costs, costs above the catastrophic threshold, plan payments, and low-income cost-sharing payments.

Estimates under the intermediate assumptions were calculated by establishing the total prescription drug costs for 2012 and then projecting these costs through the estimation period. The drug trends for 2012 through 2015 are relatively low since a number of commonly used drugs will be losing patent protection in those years. The projected Part D growth rates for those years are slightly different from the national health expenditure (NHE) trends to account for the different proportion of spending for those drugs in Part D versus the NHE. The per capita drug expenses for the total U.S. population from the NHE accounts are transitioned to by 2016.[63] In addition, the financial effects of the Affordable Care Act on Part D were then estimated and translated to an additional growth rate factor. The combined growth rates were used as the Part D per capita cost trends to project the future drug expenses. Table IV.B9 shows the Part D per capita growth rates along with the NHE trends.

To determine the estimated benefits for Part D, the total per capita drug costs are adjusted for two key factors. First, Part D benefit costs are reduced for the total amount of rebates that the prescription drug plans receive from drug manufacturers. Second, these plans incur administrative costs for plan operation and earn profits. Since drug expenses grow faster than administrative costs, the administrative expenses as a percentage of benefits slowly decrease over time. However, beginning in 2014 health insurance plans will be assessed an annual insurer fee that will be calculated based on their applicable premiums written in the prior year. As a result, administrative costs are projected to increase from 2014 through 2017. Table IV.B9 displays these key factors affecting Part D expenditure estimates.

---

[63]The CMS Office of the Actuary expects to publish full information on the NHE projections later in 2013.

Table IV.B9.—Key Factors for Part D Expenditure Estimates[1]

Calendar year	National health expenditure (NHE) drug projections[2]	Part D per capita cost trend[3]	Manufacturer rebates	Plan administrative expenses and profits[4]
Historical data:				
2006	—	—	8.6%	12.4%
2007	4.3%	1.4%	9.6	13.6
2008	1.9	3.7	10.4	13.2
2009	4.1	3.1	11.1	12.7
2010	−0.4	1.3	11.3	13.6
2011	2.1	3.7	11.5	13.0
Intermediate es imates:				
2012	1.8	−1.6	11.1	12.0
2013	2.0	0.4	10.9	12.2
2014	3.3	4.1	10.9	13.6
2015	4.5	4.6	10.4	14.1
2016	5.3	4.6	10.2	14.1
2017	5.4	5.6	10.3	14.4
2018	5.7	5.8	10.3	14.3
2019	6.0	6.2	10.3	14.1
2020	6.0	6.0	10.3	13.9
2021	6.2	6.3	10.3	13.7
2022	6.3	6.4	10.3	13.5

[1]These factors do not reflect the impact of the 2-percent sequestration for 2013-2022, as required by the Budget Control Act of 2012 and amended by the American Taxpayer Relief Act of 2012.
[2]The CMS Office of he Actuary expects to publish full information on the updated national health expenditure projections later in 2013. Values do not reflect the additional Part D expenditure growth that will result from the gradual elimination of the coverage gap from 2011 to 2020. This impact is accounted for separately in the projection.
[3]Values reflect ACA add-on and other law changes.
[4]Expressed as a percentage of plan benefit payments.

(3) Manufacturer Rebates

Prescription drug plans can negotiate rebates with drug manufacturers. Actual rebates for 2011 were approximately 11.5 percent of total prescription drug costs, which was somewhat higher than the plans estimated in their bid submissions. However, some of the drugs with the highest Part D rebate amounts will lose patent protection in the next several years. As a result, rebates are projected to decrease from 11.1 percent in 2012 to 10.3 percent in 2022, as shown in table IV.B9.[64]

(4) Administrative Expenses

The plans' expected administrative costs and projected profit margins from their bids are used to determine base-year amounts for these factors. Administrative expenses are projected forward with wage increases. The plan profit margins are projected using the per capita benefit trend. Beginning in 2014, the ACA requires insurers,

---

[64]These are average rebate percentages across all prescription drugs. Generic drugs, which represent about 81 percent of all Part D drug use in 2012, typically do not carry manufacturer rebates. Many brand-name prescription drugs carry substantial rebates, often as much as 20-30 percent.

including Part D plans, to pay a fee based on their applicable premiums from the prior year. This requirement results in an increase in administrative expenses included in plan bids beginning in 2014 as shown in table IV.B9.

(5) Incurred Per Capita Reimbursements

Table IV.B10 shows estimated enrollments and average per capita reimbursements for beneficiaries in private prescription drug plans, low-income beneficiaries, and beneficiaries in employer-sponsored retiree health plans. Due to a requirement of the Budget Control Act of 2011, as amended by the American Taxpayer Relief Act of 2012, the direct subsidy and employer subsidy are reduced by 2 percent from April 2013 through March 2022.

Table IV.B10.—Incurred Reimbursement Amounts per Enrollee for Part D Expenditures

| | Private plans (PDPs and MA-PDs) | | | | | Retiree drug subsidy | |
| | All beneficiaries | | | Low-income | | | |
Calendar year	Enrollment (millions)	Direct subsidy	Reinsur- ance	Enrollment (millions)	Low-income subsidy	Enrollment (millions)	Employer subsidy
Historical data:							
2006	20.3	$867	$297	8.3	$1,817	7.2	$527
2007	24.3	744	330	9.2	1,820	7.1	548
2008	25.8	687	366	9.7	1,856	6.8	552
2009	26.9	702	376	10.0	1,955	6.7	578
2010	28.0	705	400	10.4	2,020	6.8	572
2011	29.5	681	468	10.6	2,104	6.2	584
2012	31.8	658	492	11.0	2,053	5.6	592
Intermediate estimates:							
2013	35.7	575	473	11.3	2,045	3.2	585
2014	37.9	656	486	11.7	2,124	2.1	605
2015	39.6	706	509	12.1	2,213	1.5	632
2016	41.4	746	531	12.4	2,306	0.8	660
2017	42.6	804	559	12.8	2,428	0.8	696
2018	43.8	863	589	13.2	2,562	0.9	736
2019	45.1	924	620	13.5	2,702	0.9	777
2020	46.5	1,001	649	13.9	2,869	0.9	825
2021	47.8	1,060	693	14.3	3,040	0.9	876
2022	49.1	1,139	739	14.7	3,226	1.0	946

c. Cost Projection Methodology on a Cash Basis

(1) Prospective Payments

Prospective payments are made to the drug plans each month based on their actuarial bid submissions for that year. These data represent the plans' expectations of costs for pharmacy expenses (including discounts, rebates, and utilization management savings) and administrative costs (including profit margins). Separate amounts are determined for the direct subsidy, reinsurance, and low-income cost-sharing payments. All Part D plans initially receive the same direct subsidy for beneficiaries with an average risk profile. In contrast, the prospective payments for reinsurance and low-income cost sharing are unique to each plan.

For 2011, the average plan bid was somewhat higher than actual prescription drug spending. In 2012, bids declined slightly, but were still higher than the expected costs. Plan bids declined for the third consecutive year in 2013 and are expected to fall below the actual costs. For 2014 and beyond, the bids are assumed to be about 1 percent higher than actual spending.

A new prospective payment began in 2011 under the brand-name drug discount program introduced by the Affordable Care Act. This program requires drug manufacturers to provide a 50-percent ingredient cost discount on brand-name drugs used by non-low-income subsidy enrollees whose spending reaches the coverage gap. The annual expected discount amounts are determined for each non-employer Part D plan based on their bids. Medicare initially pays these amounts to the plans prospectively, on a monthly basis, and the plans use these amounts to pay half of the ingredient costs for brand-name drugs purchased by beneficiaries with spending in the coverage gap. The Part D drug plans then pay back the prospective payments once they receive the actual discount amounts from the drug manufacturers.

(2) Reconciliation

After each plan year, the prospective payments are reconciled with actual plan costs. Either additional payments to plans or refunds to Part D will result from this reconciliation. Since the Federal Government fully funds the reinsurance and low-income benefits, the prospective reinsurance and low-income cost-sharing payments to drug plans will be reconciled with actual expenses on a dollar-for-dollar basis. Costs for the basic Part D benefit are subject to an arrangement in which the Federal Government shares the risk that these costs will differ from the plan's expectation.

For 2011, the total prospective reinsurance payments were below the actual reinsurance costs. As a result, Medicare net reconciliation payments amounted to $1.5 billion to the Part D plans. The Part D plans' estimate of reinsurance for 2012 is expected to again be lower than the actual reinsurance costs. In addition, enrollment in the employer-sponsored Part D plans is projected to increase significantly in the next several years. Because prospective reinsurance payments are not paid to the employer-sponsored Part D plans, all reinsurance payments to employer-sponsored plans will be paid through the reconciliation process. As a result, the Trustees project that Medicare will pay reconciliation payments to the Part D plans in future years.

The prospective low-income cost-sharing payments in 2011 were slightly lower than the actual low-income cost-sharing amounts. As a result, there were modest net reconciliation payments totaling $0.3 billion from Medicare to the Part D plans. For 2012 through 2014, the Trustees expect that the actual low-income cost-sharing subsidies will continue to somewhat exceed the bid expectations. Thereafter, the two amounts are estimated to be nearly equal, resulting in smaller net reconciliation payments to the drug plans.

Risk-sharing payments are calculated based on the actual level of expenditures compared to the expected level of expenditures included in the plan bids for the basic Part D benefit. Each plan's differential is allocated to the appropriate risk corridor using the statutory formula and the risk corridor thresholds for each year, together with the risk-sharing percentages within each threshold layer. To estimate aggregate net risk-sharing amounts, payments or receipts are calculated for each plan and then aggregated.

The drug plans made net risk-sharing payments of $0.9 billion to Medicare in 2012 because the 2011 bids were slightly higher than the actual experience. For 2012, plan bids are again expected to be higher than the actual costs, but to a lesser extent. As a result, about $0.7 billion of net payments by Part D plans are anticipated. The bids for 2013 are projected to be lower than the actual cost, and accordingly Medicare will make net payments of about $1.0 billion to the Part D plans. Beyond 2013, actual costs are estimated to be slightly lower than the plan bids. Therefore, small net risk corridor receipts from plans are estimated.

As mentioned in section III.D, a new program of brand-name drug discounts began in 2011, requiring prospective payments from Part D to the drug plans. Part D does not ultimately bear the cost of the discounts, and the prospective payments and plans' repayments will be reconciled after the year end. The reconciliation amounts are expected to be minimal.

For each category of prospective payments, reconciliation payments for a particular year have typically been made in the latter part of the following year. Future reconciliation payments are also assumed to be made in the same time frame.

(3) Aggregate Reimbursements

Table IV.B11 shows aggregate projected reimbursements to plans and employers by type of payment. The 2014 Part D cash reimbursements are expected to have a higher growth rate from the 2013 level for the following reasons: (i) the return to a drug trend without major brand-name drug patent expirations; (ii) the projected increase in 2014 in the administrative expenses in the bid amounts due to the aforementioned ACA-imposed insurance premium fees; and (iii) higher reconciliation payments based on the assumption that 2013 bids will be lower than actual experience. After 2014, plan bids are expected to more closely match actual spending, resulting in cash and incurred amounts increasing at generally the same rate for 2015 and beyond. The direct subsidy and employer subsidy are reduced by 2 percent from April 2013 through March 2022, as required by the sequestration process enacted in the Budget Control Act of 2011 as amended by the American Taxpayer Relief Act of 2012.

Table IV.B11.—Aggregate Part D Reimbursement Amounts on a Cash Basis
[In billions]

Calendar year	Premiums[1]	Direct subsidy	Rein-surance	Low-income subsidy	Employer subsidy	Risk sharing[2]	Advanced discount payment[3]	Other[4]	Total
Historical data:									
2006	$3.5	$17 3	$8.6	$15.1	$2.1	—	—	$0.3	$47 0
2007	4.1	18.4	7.1	16.5	3.5	−$0.7	—	0.0	48.8
2008	5.0	17.5	6.7	17.4	3.8	−1.3	—	—	49.0
2009	6.1	18.8	11.4	20.3	4.0	−0.1	—	—	60.5
2010	6.7	19.9	10.4	20.9	3.8	−0.7	—	0.7	61.7
2011	7.3	20.1	12.8	22.3	3.2	−1.0	$1.8	0.3	66.7
2012	7.8	20.9	14.0	22.5	3.4	−1.0	−1.1	—	66.5
Intermediate estimates:									
2013	9.3	20.6	17.5	22.4	2.5	−0.6	0.1	—	71.8
2014	11.0	25.0	18.9	25.7	1.7	0.8	0.1	—	83.2
2015	12.6	28.0	20.4	27.1	1.1	−0.2	0.1	—	89.1
2016	14.0	30.9	21.7	28.6	0.7	−0.2	0.1	—	95.8
2017	15.4	34.3	23.7	31.0	0.6	−0.2	0.1	—	104 9
2018	16.9	37.8	25.7	33.7	0.6	−0.3	0.2	—	114 5
2019	18.5	41.7	27.8	36.6	0.7	−0.3	0.2	—	125 0
2020	20.4	46.6	30.1	40.0	0.7	−0.3	0.2	—	137.7
2021	22.3	50.6	32.8	43.5	0.8	−0.3	0.2	—	149 9
2022	24.4	55.9	36.0	47.5	0.9	−0.4	0.2	—	164 5

[1]Total premiums paid to Part D plans by enrollees (directly, or indirectly through premium withholding from Social Security benefits).
[2]Positive amounts represent net loss-sharing payments to plans, and negative amounts are net gain-sharing receipts from plans. These amounts may include the delayed set lement of risk sharing from prior years.
[3]The advanced discount payment serves as loans to plans for the 50-percent ingredient cost discount on brand-name drugs in the coverage gap. The plan sponsors will reimburse Part D once they receive the payments from the drug manufacturers.
[4]Other payments are one-time in nature. Amount shown in 2006 is the reimbursement of State costs under the Medicare Part D transition demonstration. Amounts in 2010 and 2011 represent the $250 rebate to beneficiaries spending more than the initial coverage limit.

d. Projections under Alternative Assumptions

Part D expenditures for the low-cost and high-cost alternatives were developed by modifying the estimates under the intermediate assumptions. The 2012 per capita estimates increased by about 3 percent under the high-cost scenario and decreased by about 3 percent under the low-cost scenario.

The 2012 base modifications include the following adjustments, since final data for 2012 will not be available until later in 2013:

- ±2 percent to account for the uncertainty of the completeness of the actual spending in 2012. The high-cost scenario increases the spending by 2 percent, and the low-cost scenario decreases the spending by 2 percent.

- ±1 percent for the average manufacturer rebate that drug plans negotiate. The high-cost scenario decreases the average rebate by 1 percent, and the low-cost scenario increases the average rebate by 1 percent.

For the projections beyond 2012, the increases in per capita drug costs from the intermediate projections are increased by 2 percent for the high-cost scenario and decreased by 2 percent for the low-cost scenario. In addition, assumptions regarding employer-sponsored plan participation, participation in the low-income subsidies, and the participation rate for individuals who do not qualify for the low-income subsidy or receive coverage through an employer-sponsored retiree plan vary in the alternative scenarios. Table IV.B12 compares these varying assumptions.

Table IV.B12.—Part D Assumptions under Alternative Scenarios for Calendar Years 2012-2022

Calendar year	Intermediate assumptions	Low-cost	High-cost
Par icipation of retiree drug subsidy as a percentage of Part D enrollees			
2012	15.0%	15.0%	15.0%
2013	8.1	8.1	8.1
2014	5.4	8.4	4.4
2015	3.7	8.5	1.8
2016	1.9	8.5	—
2017	1.9	8.6	—
2018	1.9	8.6	—
2019	1.9	8.6	—
2020	1.9	8.6	—
2021	1.9	8.7	—
2022	1.9	8.7	—
Par icipation of low-income as a percentage of Part D enrollees			
2012	29.5	29.5	29.5
2013	29.1	29.1	29.1
2014	29.2	29.4	28.9
2015	29.3	28.8	29.6
2016	29.4	28.1	30.3
2017	29.4	27.5	31.1
2018	29.4	26.9	31.8
2019	29.5	26.3	32.6
2020	29.4	25.6	33.3
2021	29.4	25.0	34.1
2022	29.4	24.5	34.9
Par icipation of all non-employer, non-low-income beneficiaries in Part D			
2012	56.4	56.4	56.4
2013	58.1	58.1	58.1
2014	58.1	54.3	62.2
2015	57.7	54.1	62.0
2016	57.5	54.0	61.9
2017	57.5	53.9	61.9
2018	57.4	53.8	61.8
2019	57.3	53.7	61.7
2020	57.6	54.0	62.0
2021	57.4	53.8	61.8
2022	57.4	53.8	61.8

Table IV.B13 compares Part D expenditures as a percentage of the Gross Domestic Product under the intermediate, low-cost, and high-cost alternatives.

Table IV.B13.—Part D Cash Expenditures as a Percentage of the Gross Domestic Product for Calendar Years 2012-2022[1]

Calendar year	Intermediate assumptions	Low-cost	High-cost
2012	0.43%	0.43%	0.43%
2013	0.44	0.43	0.46
2014	0.49	0.41	0.57
2015	0.49	0.41	0.59
2016	0.50	0.41	0.61
2017	0.51	0.41	0.65
2018	0.53	0.42	0.68
2019	0.55	0.43	0.72
2020	0.58	0.44	0.77
2021	0.61	0.45	0.81
2022	0.64	0.46	0.87

[1] Expenditures are the sum of benefit payments and administrative expenses.

C. PRIVATE HEALTH PLANS

1. Legislative History

Dating back to the 1970s, some Medicare beneficiaries have chosen to receive their coverage for Part A and Part B services through private health plans. Initially, this coverage was available only through demonstrations and plans reimbursed on a reasonable cost basis.

The Tax Equity and Fiscal Responsibility Act (TEFRA) of 1982 mandated that CMS negotiate with private health maintenance organizations (HMOs) to offer Medicare A/B coverage on a risk basis.[65] TEFRA set the capitated reimbursement amount to plans at 95 percent of the estimated county-level fee-for-service cost adjusted for enrollee demographics.

The Balanced Budget Act (BBA) of 1997 expanded the coverage options and payment rules of the Medicare risk system and named the program Medicare+Choice. The BBA also permitted CMS to enter into risk contracts with preferred provider organizations (PPOs), provider-sponsored organizations (PSOs), and private fee-for-service (PFFS) plans. Although the BBA required other Medicare health plans to establish provider networks, it did not require PFFS products to do so; it did, however, require them to set provider payment rates that were at least equal to Medicare fee-for-service payment rates.

Another effect of the BBA was that it eliminated the direct link between Medicare plan payments and county-level fee-for-service costs. Beginning in 1998, annual payment rates were based on the largest of three amounts: a minimum payment amount, or "floor"; a blended national and local rate; or a 2-percent minimum increase over the prior year's rate. The BBA also began the process of risk adjusting the plan payment rates to account for beneficiary health status.

The Medicare Modernization Act (MMA) of 2003 revamped Medicare+Choice and renamed the system Medicare Advantage (MA).

---

[65]Under these arrangements, the private health plan is paid a prospectively determined capitation amount per enrollee and accepts the insurance risk that actual costs could prove to be greater than expected.

The MMA also formally designated all private health insurance coverage options available through Medicare as "Part C."[66]

One of the goals of the Medicare Modernization Act was to increase the number of beneficiaries enrolled in private plans. The MMA accomplished this aim by significantly increasing the level of the payment rates for private health plans for 2004 and 2005. These increases carried forward to 2006 and beyond since the new cost "benchmarks" were based on the prior year's payment rates increased with growth in per capita spending for Medicare Parts A and B. The higher payment rates enabled Medicare Advantage plans to offer attractive benefit packages with lower cost-sharing requirements and/or additional benefits, compared to the standard Medicare fee-for-service benefit package. Although the additional benefits were very valuable to beneficiaries choosing to enroll in Medicare Advantage plans, they increased Medicare costs substantially compared to fee-for-service beneficiary costs. Other Medicare Modernization Act changes included adding a fourth factor—the local fee-for-service cost—to the ratebook "greater of" formula; increasing the existing minimum update to the greater of the growth in Medicare per capita costs overall or 2 percent; and implementing several other steps to increase payment rates.

Prior to 2006, payments to private health plans were directly based on a published capitation ratebook. Beginning in 2006, payments are based on competitive bids and their relationship to corresponding benchmarks, which are based on the ratebook. Also, rebates were introduced and are used to provide additional benefits not covered under Medicare, reduce cost sharing, and/or reduce Part B or Part D premiums. Prior to the passage of the Affordable Care Act, rebates were calculated as 75 percent of the difference, if any, between the benchmark and the bid.

In addition to the plan types that already existed, the MMA provided for the establishment of Regional Preferred Provider Organizations (RPPOs) and special needs plans (SNPs). Unlike other MA plans, which define their own service areas, RPPOs operate in pre-defined service areas referred to as "regions." RPPOs are available to all beneficiaries residing in their region, and the plans must ensure that enrollees have appropriate access to care. RPPOs also have special rules for capitation payment benchmarks, and they received special

---

[66]Of Medicare beneficiaries enrolled in private plans, about 97 percent are in Medicare Advantage plans, with the remainder in certain holdover plans reimbursed on a cost basis, rather than through capitation payments.

incentives under the MMA, including Medicare risk-sharing arrangements for 2006 and 2007.

SNPs are products designed for, and marketed to, these special population groups: Medicaid dual-eligible beneficiaries, individuals with specialized chronic conditions, and institutionalized beneficiaries. The statutory authority for SNPs will expire January 1, 2014.

The Deficit Reduction Act of 2005 eliminated the minimum update of 2 percent in the ratebook.

The Medicare Improvement for Patients and Providers Act (MIPPA) of 2008 mandated that, beginning in 2011, all non-group PFFS plans must establish provider networks in counties in which they operate that have two or more competing coordinated care plans. Also, MIPPA required that PFFS plans available only to employer or union groups must have networks in each county of their service area beginning in 2011.

The Affordable Care Act made fundamental changes to MA funding by linking the benchmark rates to Medicare fee-for-service costs and by requiring the use of quality measures to determine eligibility for bonuses and the share of bid savings versus benchmarks to be provided as a rebate.

The ACA held MA benchmarks for 2011 at the 2010 levels. Beginning in 2012, it requires the MA county-level benchmarks to be based on a multiple of estimated fee-for-service costs in the county. The multiple applied for a given county is based on the ranking of its fee-for-service cost relative to that for other counties, and the multiplier factors are phased in. The 25 percent, or quartile, of counties with the highest fee-for-service costs will have a multiple of 95 percent of county fee-for-service costs; the second quartile, 100 percent; the third quartile, 107.5 percent; and the lowest quartile, 115 percent. Prior to the ACA, most county benchmarks were in the range of 100-140 percent of local fee-for-service costs.

Starting in 2012, plans are eligible to receive specified increases to their benchmark based on their quality rating scores. For calendar years 2012 through 2014, the bonuses will be paid under demonstration authority initially approved in November 2010 and enhanced in April 2011. During this period, bonuses will range from 3 percent of the local Medicare fee-for-service cost for plans with a quality score of 3 stars (out of 5) to 5 percent for plans with a quality score of 5 stars. Also, for plans with at least 3 stars during 2012 through 2014 the demonstration waives the statutory cap on the phased-in benchmark, including bonuses, at the pre-ACA level. Beginning in 2015, the statutory provisions will apply, which call for a bonus of 5 percent for plans with at least a 4-star rating.

The bonuses are doubled for health plans in a "qualifying county," defined as a county in which (i) per capita spending in original Medicare is lower than average; (ii) 25 percent or more of eligible beneficiaries enrolled in Medicare Advantage as of December 2009; and (iii) the benchmark rate in 2004 was based on the minimum amount applicable to an urban area. There are special bonus provisions for newly established and low-enrollment plans.

The ACA benchmarks will phase in over 2, 4, or 6 years, depending upon the size of the benchmark reduction, with a longer phase-in schedule for areas in which the benchmark decreases by larger amounts. After the demonstration period is over in 2015, the phased-in benchmarks, including bonuses, will be capped at the pre-ACA level.

The ACA also makes changes regarding the share of the excess of benchmarks over bids to be paid to the plan sponsors as rebates. Prior to the ACA, the rebate share was 75 percent. The ACA varies plan rebates based on quality. The highest quality plans (4.5 stars or higher) will receive a 70-percent rebate, plans with a quality rating of at least 3.5 stars and less than 4.5 stars will receive a 65-percent rebate, and plans with a rating of less than 3.5 stars will receive a 50-percent rebate. The change in rebate from the fixed 75-percent level to the variable ACA percentages phases in over 3 years beginning in 2012.

Finally, the ACA requires that private insurers pay an assessment, or fee, based on their revenues from the prior year. The fees, which will be first collected in 2014, apply to most health insurance sectors, including the majority of Medicare private health plans.

The basis for the 2014 MA benchmarks has been calculated reflecting an assumption that Congress will act to prevent the scheduled 25-percent reduction in Medicare physician payment rates from occurring. The precedent establishes a higher baseline for Medicare Advantage payments that is reflected throughout these projections.

It is important to note that Medicare coverage provided through private health plans, or Part C, does not have separate financing or an associated trust fund. Rather, the Part A and Part B trust funds are the source for payments to such private health plans.

2. Participation Rates

a. Background

To account for the distinct benefit, enrollment, and payment characteristics of private health plans, enrollment and spending trends for such plans are analyzed at the product level:

- Local coordinated care plans (LCCPs), which include HMOs, HMOs with a point-of-service option, local PPOs, PSOs, and Medical Savings Accounts.

- Private Fee-for-Service (PFFS) plans.

- Regional PPO (RPPO) plans.

- Special needs plans (SNPs).

- Other products, which include cost plans and Program of All-Inclusive Care for the Elderly (PACE) plans.

All types of coverage except for those represented in the "other" category are Medicare Advantage plans. Also, the values represented in each category include enrollment not only in plans available to all beneficiaries residing in the plan's service area, but also in plans available only to members of employer or union groups.

b. Historical

One can trace the past trend in private health plan enrollment largely to the corresponding legislated payment policies. During the period 1985 through 1999, private plan enrollment grew steadily and reached a peak in 1999 shortly after the passage of the BBA in 1997.

One intent of the BBA was to expand the availability of plans by providing for new coverage options and by increasing payment rates in rural areas through the addition of the payment floors. However, instead of increasing plan availability, many of the contracts existing in 1997 were eventually withdrawn, primarily because their costs were growing faster than the annual payment, which generally rose at 2 percent.[67] As a direct consequence of the plan terminations, the percentage of Medicare beneficiaries who enrolled in private health plans declined each year from 2000 through 2004.

These declines reversed after the MMA established higher payment rates in 2005, which was the first post-MMA opportunity for plan expansion. Between 2004 and 2012, private plan enrollment grew by 8.2 million or 153 percent, which compares to growth in the overall Medicare population of 21 percent for the same period.

The Trustees previously estimated that plan enrollment would decrease, starting in 2011, as a result of the benchmark and rebate changes in the Affordable Care Act. In practice, enrollment continued to increase from 2011 through 2013 in part because of the quality bonus demonstration and the lack of further payment adjustments in these years to offset excess risk score coding intensity.[68]

PFFS enrollment dropped 78 percent between 2009 and 2012 primarily due to plan reaction to new statutory provider network requirements beginning in 2011. Most of the terminating enrollees transferred to a LCCP or RPPO plan.

The 2012 enrollment includes 2.3 million beneficiaries with coverage through employer-only or union-only plans, the vast majority of whom are in LCCPs, with few remaining in either RPPO or PFFS plans.

c. Projected

Consistent with the recommendations of the 2010-2011 Medicare Technical Panel, two key processes are involved in the projection of private Medicare health plan membership. The first step is a forecast of the ultimate share of the eligible beneficiaries—those with coverage for Medicare Parts A and B—who would enroll in private plans absent the benchmark reductions, and other payment reduction provisions, of the Affordable Care Act (ACA). Among other factors, this projection takes into account recent trends in enrollment growth.

---

[67]The BBA included numerous provisions affecting Medicare fee-for-service payment rates. As a result, the "floor" payment levels and "blended" private plan payment rates increased very slowly for several years, and the statutory rates for most plans increased by the 2-percent minimum.

[68]The risk-adjustment formula is calibrated using detailed data on beneficiaries in fee-for-service Medicare. If the nature of diagnosis coding changes over time in a different way for Medicare Advantage plans than in fee-for-service, then the risk-adjustment process becomes distorted. Periodic adjustments to overall MA risk scores are now authorized to minimize such distortions.

The Trustees assume that, absent the effects of the ACA, the private plan membership will plateau at 36 percent in calendar year 2019.

The second phase of the membership projection is based on forecasted changes in the net rebates relative to bids. This projection is performed at the county level, and the national results are an aggregation of county forecasts.

Private Medicare health plan membership is projected to continue to grow through 2014. Annual decreases in enrollment are projected to begin in 2015 and continue through 2018 as a result of the benchmark and rebate provisions of the ACA. Beginning in 2019, private plan enrollment is projected to increase annually primarily due to growth in the MA eligible population—those with coverage for Medicare Part A and Part B.

The share of Medicare enrollees in private health plans is projected to peak in 2014 at 28.8 percent and to reach a low of 23.3 percent in 2018. Modest increases are expected in private plan penetration rates between 2019 and 2025 due to higher relative bonus payments stemming from assumed improvements in quality rating scores. Overall, total health plan membership is expected to increase by 22 percent between 2022 and 2030 due to the large increase in total Medicare beneficiaries during those years. (The total Medicare population is expected to increase by 20 percent between 2022 and 2030.)

SNP enrollment is expected to increase (17 percent) between 2012 and 2014. The statutory authority for SNPs will expire as of January 1, 2015 under current law.[69] Beginning in 2015, it is expected that the majority of existing SNP enrollees will join local coordinated care plans and that the remaining enrollees will transfer to the Medicare fee-for-service program.

The growth in LCCPs is expected to be 10 percent in 2013 after increasing 15 percent in 2012. The expected increase in LCCPs in 2013 follows closely the overall 2013 increase in private Medicare health plan membership of 9 percent. A further spike in enrollment of 13 percent is expected in 2015 due to the influx of enrollees from terminating SNPs under current law.

RPPO enrollment, which experienced rapid growth from 2006 to 2011 and small declines from 2011 to 2013, is projected to increase by

---

[69]In practice, the SNP authority has been set to expire as far back as 2008 but has been extended by lawmakers.

13 percent in 2013. The recent fluctuations in the RPPO enrollment are due primarily to the migration of beneficiaries of employer-sponsored plans to either RPPO (in 2013) or LCCP (in 2012) offerings stemming from changes in sponsors' marketing strategies. Table IV.C1 shows past and projected enrollment for private health plans.

The current projection of private plan enrollment is considerably higher than that reflected in last year's report. Projected enrollment for calendar year 2013 has increased from 13.7 million estimated in the 2012 report to 14.8 million as shown below in table IV.C1. This increase is primarily due to higher MA rebates for 2013, which, in part, contributed to more successful plan marketing. The larger rebates are a result of relatively low bid trends for 2013 as compared to per capita growth in Medicare fee-for-service (FFS).

Stemming from this recent experience, the Trustees have updated the assumptions supporting the MA enrollment growth in this report. First, the pre-ACA ultimate penetration rate projection has been updated from 34 percent in 2019 to 36 percent in 2020. Next, the 2014 penetration rate reflects that the 2014 MA benchmarks have been calculated based on an assumption that Congress will act to prevent the scheduled 25-percent reduction in Medicare physician payment rates. Also, to account for the competitive plan bids, relative to the Medicare FFS trend, the bid growth assumption for the remainder of the ACA benchmark phase-in period (through 2017) has been updated to be the average of the benchmark and FFS growth rates for each plan. Beginning in 2018, the bid growth rate is assumed to match the per capita growth in Medicare FFS.

Table IV.C1.—Private Health Plan Enrollment[1]
[In thousands]

Calendar year	Local CCP	PFFS	Regional PPO	SNP	Other	Total private health plan	Total Medicare	Ratio of private health plan to total Medicare
1985	498	—	—	—	773	1,271	31,081	0.0%
1990	1,263	—	—	—	754	2,017	34,251	5.9
1995	2,735	—	—	—	732	3,467	37,594	9.2
2000	6,435	1	—	—	420	6,856	39,688	17.3
2005	5,248	125	—	—	421	5,794	42,606	13.6
2006	5,428	712	74	660	417	7,291	43,436	16.8
2007	5,529	1,623	183	930	403	8,667	44,368	19.5
2008	5,966	2,244	290	1,148	362	10,010	45,500	22.0
2009	6,605	2,433	422	1,270	373	11,104	46,604	23.8
2010	7,546	1,674	833	1,227	412	11,692	47,720	24.5
2011	8,925	602	1,153	1,256	446	12,382	48,884	25.3
2012	10,246	526	955	1,376	483	13,586	50,655	26.8
2013	11,275	424	1,079	1,536	522	14,837	52,294	28.4
2014	11,831	446	1,133	1,607	545	15,562	53,962	28.8
2015	13,324	443	1,125	—	547	15,439	55,629	27.8
2016	12,925	431	1,093	—	560	15,010	57,289	26.2
2017	12,236	411	1,037	—	576	14,260	58,987	24.2
2018	12,125	409	1,029	—	592	14,156	60,713	23.3
2019	12,460	421	1,058	—	609	14,549	62,470	23.3
2020	12,951	439	1,100	—	627	15,117	64,272	23.5
2021	13,583	460	1,154	—	644	15,842	66,105	24.0
2022	14,259	483	1,212	—	662	16,617	67,976	24.4
2025	15,807	536	1,344	—	715	18,402	73,527	25.0
2030	17,475	593	1,485	—	791	20,343	81,482	25.0
2035	18,515	628	1,574	—	838	21,554	86,480	24.9

[1]Most private plan enrollees are eligible for Medicare Part A and enrolled in Medicare Part B. Some enrollees have coverage for only Medicare Part B. For example, in 2009 the Part B-only private plan enrollment consisted of 3,000 in local CCPs, 2,000 in PFFS plans, and 68,000 in the "other" coverage category.

3. Cost Projection Methodology

a. Background

Benchmarks form the foundation for payments to Medicare Advantage plans. Along with geographic, demographic, and risk characteristics of plan enrollees, these values determine the monthly prospective payments made to private health plans. Medicare Advantage benchmarks vary substantially by county. Historically, benchmarks have been in the range of 100 percent of local fee-for-service costs (for Parts A and B) to more than 200 percent of such costs in a few areas. Under the Affordable Care Act, benchmarks will transition to the range of 95-115 percent of fee-for-service costs, plus applicable quality bonuses.

For non-RPPO plans, a plan's benchmark is an average of the statutory capitation ratebook values, weighted by projected plan enrollment in each county in the plan's service area. For RPPOs, the benchmark is a blend of the weighted ratebook values for all Medicare-eligible beneficiaries in the region and an enrollment-weighted average of RPPO bids for the region. The weight applied to the bid component to calculate the blended benchmark is the national Medicare Advantage participation rate.

Plans submit bids equal to their projected per enrollee cost of providing the standard Medicare Part A and Part B benefits. Plans with bids below the benchmark apply the rebate share of the "savings" to aid plan enrollees through coverage of Part A and Part B cost sharing, coverage of additional non-drug benefits, and/or reduction in the Part B or Part D premium. From 2006 to 2011, the rebate share of the difference between a plan's benchmark and bid was 75 percent. For 2012 and later, the rebate percentage is based on the quality rating of the health plan and will range from 50 to 70 percent once fully phased in for 2014. Beneficiaries choosing plans with bids above the benchmark must pay for both the full amount of the difference between the bid and the benchmark and the projected cost of the plans' supplemental benefits.

Medicare capitation payments to a Medicare Advantage plan are a product of the standardized plan bid, which is equal to the bid divided by the plan's projected risk score, and the actual enrollee risk score, which is based on demographic characteristics and medical diagnosis data. The risk score for a given enrollee may be adjusted retrospectively since CMS receives diagnosis data after the payment date.

Rebate payments are based on the projected risk profile of the plan and are not adjusted based on subsequent actual risk scores.

b. Incurred Basis

Private health plan expenditures are forecast on an incurred basis by coverage type. The bid-based expenditures for each quarter are a product of the average enrollment and the projected average per capita bid. Similarly, the rebate expenditures are a product of enrollment and projected average rebates.

Annual per capita benchmarks, bids, and rebates were determined on an incurred basis for calendar years 2006-2012 for each coverage category. These amounts include adjustments processed after the payment due date for retroactive enrollment and risk score updates. The annual per capita benchmark values are calculated as the prior year's value increased with the projected increase in the benchmark rates for each plan category. The rebates are equal to the applicable percent of the positive difference, if any, between the benchmarks and bids.

Factors accounted for in the benchmark growth trend include the projected increase in the fee-for-service per capita costs (USPCCs), the scheduled phase-out of the ratebook indirect medical expenses, and assumed changes in the risk-coding practices of private health plans relative to Medicare fee-for-service providers.

For the period 2006 through 2009, aggregate payments for bids and rebates experienced double-digit annual growth resulting from rapid increases in private plan enrollment, growth in per capita Medicare fee-for-service costs affecting the benchmarks, inflation in plan costs, and growth in private plan risk scores.

Growth in bids for 2010 and 2011 slowed to 6 percent per annum primarily due to flattening of the enrollment trend and relatively flat growth in the per capita bids. During the period, the aggregate rebates decreased by 4 percent per annum. The reduction in rebates was primarily attributable to a decrease in 2010 risk scores due to the application of an across-the-board reduction to account for differences in coding between private plans and Medicare fee-for-service providers.

Benchmark growth for 2012 and later will be significantly lower than historical trends because of the phase-in of the fee-for-service based ratebook beginning in 2012, which will result in lower benchmark rates in most areas. Also, the productivity offsets to Medicare fee updates and other savings provisions of the Affordable Care Act will dampen the projected increase in the per capita fee-for-service base of the benchmark.

The trend in the per capita bids for 2014 through 2017 is estimated to be equal to the average of the fee-for-service trend and the benchmark trend plus the incremental cost of the ACA insurer fees. The expectation is that bids will grow faster than benchmarks but more slowly than fee-for-service rates, which results in lower per capita rebates in 2014 and 2015. For years 2018 and later, the trend in the per capita bids is estimated to be equal to that of beneficiaries enrolled in Medicare fee-for-service.

c. *Cash Basis*

Cash Medicare Advantage expenditures are largely identical to incurred amounts, since both arise primarily from the monthly capitation payments to plans. Small cash payment adjustments are developed from incurred spending by accounting for the payment lag that results from CMS' receipt of post-payment diagnosis data, retroactive enrollment notifications, and corrections in enrollees' demographic characteristics.

Table IV.C2 shows Medicare private plan expenditures on an incurred and cash basis, separately for the Part A and Part B trust funds. The incurred payments are reported separately for the bid-related and rebate expenditures. As noted, most payments to plans are made as they are incurred, and cash and incurred amounts are generally the same.

Table IV.C2.—Medicare Payments to Private Health Plans, by Trust Fund
[In billions]

| Calendar year | Incurred basis [1] | | | Cash basis |
	Bid	Rebate	Total	
Expenditures from the HI (Part A) trust fund:				
2006	$29.7	$3.5	$33.2	$32.9
2007	36.4	4.3	40.7	39.0
2008	44.1	5.4	49.5	50.6
2009	52.7	6.3	59.0	59.4
2010	55.5	5.2	60.7	60.7
2011	59.1	5.7	64.8	64.6
2012	64.4	6.2	70.6	70.2
2013	68.4	6.4	74.8	74.7
2014	68.3	4.9	73.2	73.2
2015	67.4	3.9	71.3	71.3
2016	67.5	3.9	71.4	71.4
2017	66.4	3.7	70.1	70.1
2018	68.8	4.1	72.9	72.8
2019	73.3	4.6	77.9	77.7
2020	79.2	5.2	84.4	84.2
2021	86.5	5.7	92.2	92.0
2022	94.5	6.3	100.8	100.6
Expenditures from the Part B account of the SMI trust fund:				
2006	28.8	3.2	32.0	31.5
2007	35.6	3.9	39.5	38.9
2008	43.0	5.0	48.0	48.1
2009	47.9	5.5	53.4	53.4
2010	50.7	4.6	55.3	55.2
2011	54.1	5.1	59.2	59.1
2012	60.8	5.6	66.4	66.0
2013	68.1	6.2	74.3	74.1
2014	79.3	5.6	84.9	84.7
2015	80.4	4.5	84.9	84.9
2016	80.9	4.6	85.5	85.4
2017	80.5	4.4	84.9	84.9
2018	84.3	4.8	89.1	88.9
2019	91.0	5.5	96.5	96.3
2020	99.5	6.3	105.8	105.6
2021	109.8	7.1	116.9	116.6
2022	121.4	7.9	129.3	129.0

[1] The bid category includes all expenditures for non-Medicare Advantage coverage.

d. Incurred Expenditures per Enrollee

Table IV.C3 shows estimated incurred per enrollee expenditures for beneficiaries enrolled in private health plans. It combines the values for expenditures from the Part A and Part B trust funds.

Table IV.C3.—Incurred Expenditures per Private Health Plan Enrollee[1]

Calendar year	Local CCP	PFFS	Regional PPO	SNP	Other	Total
Bid-based expenditures[2]						
2006	$8,203	$6,925	$7,624	$10,027	$4,852	$8,084
2007	8,547	7,367	8,315	9,989	5,044	8,342
2008	8,781	8,088	9,223	10,429	5,350	8,727
2009	9,019	8,753	9,196	11,012	5,314	9,092
2010	8,975	8,488	8,934	12,070	5,215	9,114
2011	8,965	8,281	8,966	12,511	4,872	9,162
2012	9,005	8,435	9,042	12,675	5,353	9,244
2013	8,911	8,870	9,354	12,743	5,176	9,222
2014	9,191	9,173	9,664	13,161	5,187	9,508
2015	9,756	9,232	9,775	n/a	5,267	9,598
2016	10,092	9,543	10,093	n/a	5,391	9,917
2017	10,527	9,927	10,518	n/a	5,570	10,328
2018	11,060	10,469	11,044	n/a	5,829	10,843
2019	11,549	10,980	11,524	n/a	6,086	11,321
2020	12,095	11,514	12,054	n/a	6,379	11,857
2021	12,666	12,059	12,621	n/a	6,695	12,421
2022	13,274	12,642	13,226	n/a	7,028	13,022
Rebate expenditures[2]						
2006	958	616	565	1,489	—	920
2007	947	703	952	1,777	—	951
2008	1,123	613	784	1,874	—	1,049
2009	1,211	478	663	1,833	—	1,064
2010	990	320	436	1,176	—	842
2011	955	450	510	1,158	—	878
2012	935	355	562	1,099	—	872
2013	906	256	549	1,132	—	854
2014	738	103	368	810	—	676
2015	615	—	221	n/a	—	546
2016	637	—	223	n/a	—	564
2017	646	—	207	n/a	—	567
2018	716	—	249	n/a	—	631
2019	790	—	298	n/a	—	699
2020	858	—	337	n/a	—	762
2021	911	7	364	n/a	—	810
2022	965	9	386	n/a	—	858
Total expenditures						
2006	9,162	7,541	8,189	11,515	4,852	9,004
2007	9,494	8,070	9,268	11,766	5,044	9,293
2008	9,904	8,701	10,007	12,303	5,350	9,775
2009	10,231	9,231	9,859	12,845	5,314	10,156
2010	9,965	8,808	9,371	13,246	5,215	9,955
2011	9,920	8,731	9,475	13,669	4,872	10,040
2012	9,940	8,790	9,603	13,775	5,353	10,115
2013	9,817	9,125	9,903	13,876	5,176	10,076
2014	9,930	9,276	10,032	13,971	5,187	10,184
2015	10,371	9,232	9,996	n/a	5,267	10,144
2016	10,729	9,543	10,316	n/a	5,391	10,481
2017	11,173	9,927	10,724	n/a	5,570	10,895
2018	11,777	10,469	11,293	n/a	5,829	11,474
2019	12,340	10,980	11,822	n/a	6,086	12,020
2020	12,954	11,514	12,391	n/a	6,379	12,619
2021	13,577	12,066	12,984	n/a	6,695	13,231
2022	14,239	12,650	13,612	n/a	7,028	13,880

[1]Values represent the sum of per capita expenditures for Part A and Part B.
[2]The bid category includes all expenditures for non-Medicare Advantage coverage.

Average Medicare payments per private plan enrollee vary by geographic location of the plan, plan efficiency, and average reported health status of plan enrollees. Local coordinated care plans and special needs plans tend to be located in urban areas where prevailing health care costs tend to be above average. Conversely, private fee-for-service plans and regional PPOs generally reflect a more rural enrollment. These factors complicate meaningful comparisons of average per capita costs by plan category.

In general, the per capita increases in bids for 2006 through 2009 were in the single-digit range and were correlated with the Medicare fee-for-service trend and the change in risk profile of the plan populations. Per capita bid payments in 2010 decreased for all types of coverage (except for SNP) since the application of the risk score coding intensity adjustment more than offset the relatively low Medicare fee-for-service growth. The primary factor driving the growth in SNP per capita bids for 2010 was the change in definition of "Medicare required" benefits, which takes into account the waiver of plan cost sharing for many beneficiaries who are dually eligible for Medicare and Medicaid. Per capita bid payments in 2011 and 2012 were relatively flat, increasing by 0.3 percent and 0.9 percent, respectively, in aggregate. Per capita bid payments are expected to remain relatively flat in 2013, decreasing by 0.2 percent.

Beginning in 2014 through 2017, the overall per capita bid trend is expected to be the average of the growth in Medicare fee-for-service expenditures and the benchmark growth plus the per capita growth in the ACA insurer fees. For years 2018 and later, the per capita bid trend is expected to be equal to the growth in Medicare fee-for-service expenditures. If MA plans are not able to hold their cost increases to a level consistent with the expected growth in trends as defined above—including the impact of the productivity adjustments to provider payment updates—then actual MA rebate levels and enrollment would be lower than the projections shown here.

After 2021, average Medicare payments to private plans per enrollee are assumed to follow the aggregate growth trends of the HI and SMI Part B per capita benefits, as described in section IV.D of this report.

There was significant variation in the per capita trend in rebates for 2006 through 2009; this variation reflected the difference in the annual trend between bids and benchmarks. All types of coverage experienced significant decreases in rebates for 2010 as a result of the reduction in risk-adjusted benchmarks—both in absolute terms and relative to the change in bids. Per capita rebates increased in aggregate by 4 percent in 2011 due to the flat bid payments in 2011 and an increase in the plans' average risk scores. Per capita rebates were relatively flat in 2012, declining by less than 1 percent due to the introduction of the phase-in period of the fee-for-service based ratebook. Rebates are projected to decline in 2013 and 2014 as a result of the mandated benchmark reductions and the lower statutory share of benchmark-versus-bid savings to be provided as a rebate. Beginning in 2016, modest annual increases in per capita rebates are forecast.

D. LONG-RANGE MEDICARE COST GROWTH ASSUMPTIONS

The prior three sections have described the detailed assumptions and methodology underlying the projected expenditures for HI (Part A) and SMI (Parts B and D) during 2013 through 2022. These projections are made for individual categories of Medicare-covered services, such as inpatient hospital care and physician services.

As the projection horizon lengthens, it becomes increasingly difficult to anticipate changes in the delivery of health care, the development of new medical technologies, and other factors that will affect future health care cost increases. With enactment of the Affordable Care Act, such increases are subject to greater uncertainty in the long term, especially for the Medicare program. Accordingly, rather than extending the detailed projections by individual type of service for all future years, the Trustees use a more aggregated basis for setting cost growth assumptions in the long range.

For this year's report, the assumed long-range rate of growth in annual Medicare expenditures per beneficiary under current law are based on statutory price updates and assumptions for volume and intensity growth derived from a "factors contributing to growth" model developed by the Office of the Actuary that decomposes the major drivers of historical and projected health spending growth into distinct factors. Additionally, the Trustees assume that the Medicare payment rates under current law will reduce volume and intensity growth slightly below the assumption from the factors model for impacted Medicare services. The Trustees' methodology is consistent with the recommendations by the 2010-2011 Technical Review Panel on the Medicare Trustees Report,[70] which incorporated a more refined analysis of the factors behind those assumptions. For this report, the Trustees have concluded that the factors approach is appropriate to use in developing the long-range Medicare projections and that the ultimate assumptions derived using the model should be checked for reasonableness by comparing them to results produced by an average "GDP plus" approach. The Trustees plan to continue to direct

---

[70]The Panel's final report is available at http://aspe.hhs.gov/health/reports/2013/ MedicareTech/TechnicalPanelReport2010-2011.pdf.

research into the factors approach and will consider additional refinements and improvements in forthcoming reports.

For the 2001-2005 Trustees Reports, the Trustees assumed that the increase in average expenditures per beneficiary for the 25th through 75th years of the projection would equal the growth in per capita GDP plus 1 percentage point,[71] as recommended by the 2000 Medicare Technical Review Panel. With the inclusion of infinite-horizon projections starting in the 2004 Trustees Report, per beneficiary expenditures after the 75th year were assumed to increase at the same rate as per capita GDP. The 2004 Technical Review Panel recommended that the Trustees continue to use these assumptions, given the limits of current knowledge, but also conduct further research.

Beginning with the 2006 report, the Trustees adopted a refinement of the long-range growth assumption that provided a more gradual transition from historical health cost growth rates, which had been roughly 2 to 3 percentage points above the level of GDP growth, to the ultimate assumed level of GDP plus zero percent just after the 75th year and for the indefinite future. The year-by-year growth assumptions were based on a simplified economic model and were determined in a way such that the 75-year actuarial balance for the HI trust fund was consistent with that generated by the constant "GDP plus 1 percent" assumption. An independent group of experts in health economics and long-range forecasting reviewed the model and advised that its use for this purpose was appropriate.

The stylized economic model made assumptions about (i) continuing improvements in medical technology; (ii) the extent to which new medical technology either increases health care costs or reduces them; and (iii) society's relative preference for improved health versus consumption of other goods and services. The theory behind the model was that, should innovations in medical technology continue to increase rapidly in the future and add substantially to costs as in the past, then eventually society would be unwilling and unable to devote a steadily increasing share of its income to obtaining better health. Such unwillingness could be expressed in a number of ways consistent with current law, such as private and public health plans' reluctance to cover expensive new technologies unless they offer significant health improvement over existing techniques, or the

---

[71]This assumed increase in the average expenditures per beneficiary excludes the impacts of the aging of the population and changes in the gender composition of the Medicare population, which the Trustees estimated separately.

inability on the part of individuals to afford health insurance premiums or cost-sharing payments.

For the 2010 and 2011 Medicare Trustees Reports, the Trustees assumed a "baseline" long-range Medicare cost growth assumption, using the process described above, and then incorporated the Affordable Care Act, which permanently modifies the annual increases in Medicare payment rates for most categories of health service providers by reducing them for 2011 and later by the 10-year moving average increase in private, non-farm business multifactor productivity.[72] This adjustment affects all HI (Part A) providers. On average, the resulting long-range growth assumption for HI was the increase in per capita GDP plus 1 percent, minus the productivity factor.

For SMI Part B, the productivity adjustment affects certain provider categories—for example, outpatient hospitals, ambulatory surgical centers, diagnostic laboratories, and most other non-physician services. These services had the same assumed long-range growth rate as did HI services. The sustainable growth rate formula in current law governs increases in average physician expenditures per beneficiary, which must increase at approximately the rate of per capita GDP growth. The remaining Part B services, and all Part D outlays, had an assumed average growth rate of per capita GDP plus 1 percent.

In December 2011, the 2010-2011 Medicare Technical Review Panel unanimously recommended a new approach that builds off of the longstanding "GDP plus 1 percent" assumption while incorporating several key refinements.[73] Specifically, the panel recommended two separate means of establishing long-range growth rates:

- The first approach is a refinement to the traditional "GDP plus 1 percent" growth assumption that better accounts for the level of payment rate updates for Medicare (prior to the effects of the ACA) compared to private health insurance and other payers of health care in the U.S. The details are discussed later in this section of the report, but most importantly this refinement results in an increase in the long-range pre-ACA "baseline" cost growth

---

[72]"Multifactor productivity" is a measure of real output per combined unit of labor and capital, reflecting the contributions of all factors of production.

[73]For convenience, the increase in Medicare expenditures per beneficiary, before consideration of demographic impacts, is referred to as the "Medicare cost growth rate." Similarly, these growth rate assumptions are described relative to the per capita increase in GDP and characterized simply as "GDP plus X percent."

assumption for Medicare to "GDP plus 1.4 percent." (The corresponding assumed average growth rate for all national health expenditures continues to be "GDP plus 1 percent.")

- The second approach recommended by the Technical Panel is the "factors contributing to growth" model developed by the Office of the Actuary at CMS as a possible replacement for the existing process. This model builds upon the key considerations used in establishing the earlier "GDP plus 1 percent" assumption, together with subsequent refinements in the analysis of growth factors, additional years of data on national health expenditures available since the 2000 Technical Panel's deliberations, and use of projected trends in the model's key factors. The model is based on economic research that decomposes health spending growth into its major drivers—income growth, relative medical price inflation, insurance coverage, and a residual factor that primarily reflects the impact of technological development.[74]

For the 2012 report, the Trustees based the average ultimate Medicare growth rate on the updated "GDP plus 1.4 percent" baseline assumption and used the "factors contributing to growth" model to create the specific, year-by-year declining growth rates during the last 50 years of the projection. For this report, the Trustees have decided (i) to use the statutory price updates and the volume and intensity assumptions from the factors model to derive the year-by-year Medicare cost growth assumptions for the last 50 years of the projection period and (ii) to check the ultimate Medicare cost growth assumptions derived from this approach for reasonableness by comparing them to results produced by an average "GDP plus" approach. The remainder of this section discusses the derivation of the assumption for overall health spending using the factors model, which produces results that are consistent with the "GDP plus 1 percent" approach. This section also explains the detailed long-range assumptions underlying the Medicare current-law projection. Appendix V.C provides the methods used to derive the long-range cost growth assumptions for the projections based on illustrative alternatives to current law.

---

[74]Smith, S., Newhouse, J., and Freeland, M., "Income, Insurance, and Technology: Why Does Health Spending Outpace Economic Growth?" *Health Affairs*, September/October 2009.

1. Long-Range Growth Assumptions for the Overall Health Sector

The first step to estimate the long-range Medicare trends is to determine the long-range assumptions affecting the overall health sector. For this report, as noted previously, the Trustees use the "factors contributing to growth" model to determine the year-by-year growth rates for the overall health sector over the last 50 years of the projection. This approach produces a result that is consistent with an ultimate average rate of per capita GDP plus 1 percent, as had been assumed since the 2001 report. Based on the factors model, the Trustees assume that the long-range per capita overall health spending growth is "GDP plus 1.15 percent" (or 5.21 percent) for 2037, gradually declining to "GDP plus 0.32 percent" by 2087 (or 4.35 percent). The per capita increase in overall health care costs is due to the combined effects of general inflation, medical-specific "excess" price inflation (above general price growth), and changes in the utilization of services per person and the "intensity" or average complexity per service. The Trustees assume that beginning in 2037 (i) general price inflation will remain constant at 2.4 percent per year, as measured by the GDP deflator; (ii) excess medical price inflation will remain constant at 0.8 percent per year, as discussed in more detail below; and (iii) the annual increase in the volume and intensity of services per person will decline gradually from approximately 2.0 percent in 2037 to 1.15 percent in 2087 based on the key economic assumptions and elasticity estimates from the factors model, as described below.

Excess medical price inflation for the overall health sector is assumed to grow at 0.8 percent annually. The method used by the Trustees for developing the medical price changes that the market will bear is to decompose this price into its two main factors[75]: (i) medical input price growth and (ii) resource-based health sector productivity growth.[76] The Trustees assume that medical input price growth for the overall health sector will equal the increase in the hospital input price index over the long run, which is estimated at about 3.6 percent per year, as seen previously in table IV.A1. For resource-based health

---

[75]A third factor, provider profit margins, is assumed to remain constant over the long run.

[76]Resource-based productivity is defined as the real value of provider goods and services divided by the real value of the resources (inputs) used to produce the goods and services, where price changes are measured across constant products—that is, defined health services with a constant mix of inputs. Resource-based productivity is used for this decomposition, rather than outcomes-based productivity (which incorporates the estimated value of improvements in health resulting from the services) because Medicare and most other payers reimburse providers based on their resource use.

sector productivity, the Trustees assume that the rate of growth will be equivalent to recently published research[77] on historical measures for hospitals and physicians and that productivity growth for all other provider categories, such as skilled nursing facilities, home health agencies, hospices, diagnostic laboratories, dialysis centers, and ambulance companies, will average to roughly zero. Taken together, the estimate of overall resource-based health sector productivity is determined to be 0.4 percent per year. Combining the 3.6-percent medical input price growth with the 0.4-percent health sector productivity growth results in medical sector price growth of 3.2 percent per year, which is 0.8 percentage point faster than growth in the GDP deflator.

As stated earlier, the factors model is based on economic research that separates health spending growth into its major drivers—income growth, relative medical price inflation, insurance coverage, and a residual that primarily reflects the impact of technological development. The factors model provides the ability to model the likely behavioral effects associated with a continuing increase in the share of national income devoted to consumption of health care services. In addition, this approach is easier to understand than the economic model used in the 2006 through 2011 reports and does not suffer from the same data limitations. (As noted above, for the 2012 report, the factors model was used to create the year-by-year growth rates.) In particular, it is based on historically estimated income and price elasticities and uses measurable key variables, thereby improving the underlying basis for developing the long-range growth assumptions.[78]

In the factors model, the sensitivity of health cost growth to each of the three factors must be estimated. Each such sensitivity is measured as an "elasticity," which is the percentage change in cost growth that is caused by a 1-percent change in a factor. The first elasticity, the income-technology elasticity, reflects the increase in demand for health care and new medical technologies in response to growth in income. This elasticity is estimated at 1.4 based on cross-country comparisons of the historical relationship between

---

[77]Cylus, Jonathan D., and Dickensheets, Bridget A.: "Hospital Multifactor Productivity: A Presentation and Analysis of Two Methodologies." *Health Care Financing Review* 29(2): 49-64, Winter 2007-2008; Fisher, Charles: "Multifactor Productivity in Physicians' Offices: An Exploratory Analysis." *Health Care Financing Review* 29(2): 15-32, Winter 2007-2008.

[78]Additional information on the "factors contributing to growth" model is available in a memorandum by the Office of the Actuary titled "The Long-Term Projection Assumptions for Medicare and Aggregate National Health Expenditures," available at http://www.cms.gov/Research-Statistics-Data-and-Systems/Statistics-Trends-and-Reports/ReportsTrustFunds/Downloads/ProjectionMethodology.pdf.

health spending and GDP growth for member countries in the Organisation for Economic Co-operation and Development. (A similar elasticity was determined using only U.S.-specific data.) The second elasticity, the relative medical price elasticity, reflects the sensitivity of consumers and purchasers in consuming health care to changes in excess medical price inflation. Based on the Office of the Actuary's national health expenditure (NHE) projection model for 1970-2009, which uses observed price changes, this price elasticity was estimated at −0.4. The final key elasticity is the insurance elasticity, which reflects the change in demand for medical care as the level of insurance coverage changes. Based on the RAND Health Insurance Experiment, the insurance elasticity is estimated at −0.2.[79]

The insurance elasticity is assumed to be unchanged over the long-range projection period at −0.2. The income-technology elasticity and price elasticity, in contrast, are assumed to vary over time. Both of these elasticities are assumed to equal their long-term historical average in the 25th year of the projection period (2037). After 2037, the income-technology elasticity is assumed to decline linearly and to reach 1.0 by the end of the 75-year projection period (2087) under the assumption that the preference for additional health care will lessen as health care continues to consume a greater proportion of income. The price elasticity, on the other hand, is assumed to become larger in absolute value as the share of income devoted to health care increases.[80] As the overall health sector share of GDP is projected to double during the projection period, and as the income-technology elasticity approaches 1.0, the price elasticity is assumed to reach −0.6 by the end of the 75-year projection period (2087). The decline in the price elasticity from −0.4 to −0.6 is assumed to occur linearly.

Two additional assumptions are required to complete the factors model determination. First, relative medical price inflation must be estimated over the long-range projection period. As discussed previously, the Trustees assume that relative medical price growth is 0.8 percent per year. Second, insurance coverage is assumed to be unchanged over the long run in order to maintain consistency with the concept of a Medicare current-law projection in which the Medicare benefit package cannot be altered.

---

[79]Newhouse, J., Health Insurance Experiment Group. *Lessons from the RAND Health Insurance Experiment.* Cambridge (MA): Harvard University Press; 1993. The coefficient of this elasticity is negative because the level of insurance coverage is measured using individuals' cost-sharing requirements (such as deductibles and coinsurance).

[80]Silberberg, Eugene, *The Structure of Economics: A Mathematical Analysis*, McGraw-Hill, 2000.

2. Long-Range Growth Assumptions for Medicare under Current Law

The Trustees have assumed since 2001 that it is reasonable to expect over the long range that the drivers of health spending will be similar for the overall health sector and for the Medicare program. This view was affirmed by the 2010-2011 Medicare Technical Review Panel, which recommended use of the same long-range assumptions for the increase in the volume and intensity of health care services for the total health sector and for Medicare. Therefore, the overall health sector long-range cost growth assumptions for volume and intensity are used as the starting point for developing the Medicare-specific assumptions under current law.

Prior to the Affordable Care Act, Medicare payment rates for most non-physician provider categories were updated annually by the increase in providers' input prices for the market basket of employee wages and benefits, facility costs, medical supplies, energy and utility costs, professional liability insurance, and other inputs needed to produce the health care goods and services. To the extent that health care providers can improve their productivity each year, their net costs of production (other things being equal) will increase more slowly than their input prices—but the Medicare payment rate updates prior to the ACA were not adjusted for potential productivity gains. Accordingly, Medicare costs per beneficiary would have increased somewhat faster than for the health sector overall.[81] In particular, the Trustees assume that the full market basket increase would be approximately 3.6 percent annually, or about 0.4 percent greater than the net price increase of 3.2 percent per year described above for the total health sector. The Affordable Care Act requires that many of these Medicare payment updates be reduced by the 10-year moving average increase in private, non-farm business multifactor productivity, which the Trustees assume will be 1.1 percent per year over the long range. The different statutory provisions for updating payment rates require the development of separate long-range Medicare cost growth assumptions for four categories of health care providers:

---

[81]Historically, lawmakers frequently reduced the payment updates below the increase in providers' input prices in an effort to slow Medicare cost growth or to offset unwarranted changes in claims coding practices. Prior to the ACA, the law did not specify any such adjustments after 2009.

(i) *All HI, and some SMI Part B, services that are updated annually by provider input price increases less the increase in economy-wide productivity.*

Under the Affordable Care Act, the annual increase in Medicare payment rates for these services will be reduced by the 10-year moving average increase in private, non-farm business multifactor productivity. These gains are estimated to average 0.8 percent from 2012 through 2029 and to be 1.1 percent per year thereafter. Combined with an assumed market basket increase of 3.6 percent, the statutory price update for these services is 2.5 percent per year over the long-range projection period. The initial projected increase in the volume and intensity of these Medicare services is assumed to be equivalent to the average projected growth in the volume and intensity of services for the overall health sector. The Trustees believe that the use of a common baseline rate of volume and intensity growth is reasonable, as there would be only a small likelihood that one part of the health sector could continue to grow indefinitely at significantly faster rates of growth than do other parts.

Additionally, the Trustees assume that the growth in Medicare payment rates under current law will reduce the volume and intensity growth of these services by 0.1 percent per year relative to the assumption from the factors model. The Trustees' assumption is also based on recommendations by the 2010-2011 Medicare Technical Review Panel, which concluded that there would likely be a small net negative impact on volume and intensity growth due to reduced incentives to develop new technologies, provider exits, and the impact of greater bundling of services for payment purposes.[82] For new technology that leads to new services, the ACA will result in lower fees than would otherwise be the case, and providers will be less likely to adopt new services and innovations, thereby lowering the demand for, and intensity of, the medical care provided. Regarding provider exits, as fee-for-service fees decline relative to the pre-ACA levels, facilities of marginal profitability are likely to exit the Medicare market, reducing capacity and volume. This change could also cause a more bifurcated health system in which only providers who can operate profitably under Medicare offer services to Medicare beneficiaries, with a tendency to provide only the more

---

[82]Other factors, such as reduced beneficiary cost-sharing requirements, would tend to increase the volume and intensity of services. The assumption of −0.1 percent reflects the Technical Panel's assessment that the overall impact would be a small net decrease in volume and intensity growth.

basic services not associated with new medical technologies. Finally, the innovations being tested under the ACA, such as bundled payments or accountable care organizations, could reduce incentives to adopt new technologies for those participating in these programs and/or could contribute to greater efforts to avoid services of limited or no value within the service bundle.

Reflecting all of these considerations, the year-by-year long-range current-law cost growth assumption for these HI and SMI Part B services starts at 4.5 percent in 2037, or "GDP plus 0.4 percent," and gradually declines to 3.6 percent by 2087, or "GDP minus 0.5 percent." On average over the long-range projection period, these services are assumed to increase at 4.3 percent per year under the intermediate assumptions, which is roughly equivalent to "GDP plus 0.2 percent." This average growth rate is consistent with Recommendation III-4 of the 2010-2011 Medicare Technical Review Panel's report.

(ii) *Certain SMI Part B services that are updated annually by the CPI increase less the increase in productivity.*

Such services include durable medical equipment, laboratory services, ambulatory surgical centers, ambulance services, and medical supplies, which are updated by the CPI and affected by the ACA productivity adjustment. For these services, the Trustees initially assume that the rate of per beneficiary volume and intensity growth is equivalent to that derived for the overall health sector using the factors model. This volume and intensity growth is assumed to be reduced by 0.1 percent per year to reflect the ACA impact, as described above. The post-ACA volume and intensity assumption is combined with the long-range CPI assumption (2.8 percent) minus the productivity factor (1.1 percent) to produce a long-range growth assumption for these SMI Part B services. The corresponding year-by-year growth rates are 3.6 percent in 2037, or "GDP minus 0.5 percent," gradually declining to 2.8 percent in 2087, or "GDP minus 1.3 percent." On average over the long range, the growth is about 3.5 percent per year, which equates to "GDP minus 0.6 percent."

(iii) *Services payable under the physician fee schedule, as governed by the sustainable growth rate formula in current law.*

The Trustees assume that per beneficiary expenditures for these services will increase at approximately the rate of per capita GDP growth in every year (or 4.1 percent), consistent with the requirements of the statutory SGR formula.

(iv) *All other Medicare services, for which payments are established based on market processes, such as prescription drugs provided through Part D and the remaining Part B services.*

The Trustees assume that per beneficiary outlays for these other Part B services, which constitute about 11 percent of total Part B expenditures in 2022, and for all Part D services grow at the same rate as the overall health sector as determined from the factors model. The services are assumed to grow similarly because their payment updates are determined by market forces, such as the competitive-bidding process for Medicare Part D. The year-by-year growth rates are 5.3 percent in 2037, or "GDP plus 1.2 percent," gradually declining to 4.4 percent by 2087, or "GDP plus 0.3 percent." On average over the long range, the growth rate is 5.1 percent, or "GDP plus 1 percent."

In addition, these long-range cost growth rates must be modified to reflect demographic impacts. For example, beneficiaries at ages 80 and above use Part A skilled nursing and home health services much more frequently than do younger beneficiaries. As the beneficiary population ages, Part A costs will grow at a faster rate due to increased use of these services. In contrast, the incidence of prescription drug use is more evenly distributed by age, and an increase in the average age of Part D enrollees has significantly less of an effect on Part D costs.

After combining the rates of growth from the four long-range assumptions, the weighted average growth rate for Part B is 4.1 percent per year for the last 50 years of the projection period, or "GDP plus 0 percent," on average. When Parts A, B, and D are combined, the weighted average growth rate is 4.3 percent over this same time period or "GDP plus 0.2 percent," while the growth rate in 2087 is 3.9 percent or "GDP minus 0.2 percent."

As in the past, the Trustees have established detailed growth rate assumptions for the initial 10 years of the projection period by individual type of service (for example, inpatient hospital care and physician services), reflecting recent trends and the impact of all provisions of the Affordable Care Act and other applicable statutory provisions. For each of Parts A, B, and D, the assumed growth rates for years 11 through 25 of the projection period are set by interpolating between the rate at the end of the short-range period and the rate at the start of the final 50 years of the long-range period described above.

V. APPENDICES

A. MEDICARE AMENDMENTS SINCE THE 2012 REPORT

Since the 2012 annual report was transmitted to Congress on April 23, 2012, one law has been enacted that has a significant effect on the Medicare trust funds.

The American Taxpayer Relief Act of 2012 (Public Law 112-240, enacted on January 2, 2013) included several provisions that affect the HI and SMI programs. The more important provisions, from an actuarial standpoint, are described in the following paragraphs. Certain provisions with a relatively minor financial impact, but which are important from a policy perspective, are described as well.

Provisions Affecting HI

- Medicare inpatient hospital add-on payments for "low-volume" hospitals (having less than 1,600 Medicare discharges annually and located 15 miles or greater from the nearest like hospital) are extended through December 31, 2013.

- The Medicare-Dependent Hospital Program, which enhances reimbursement for Medicare inpatient hospital services provided in small rural hospitals for which Medicare patients make up a significant percentage of inpatient days or discharges, is extended through September 30, 2013.

- The Secretary of HHS is authorized to continue reducing the standardized payment rates for hospitals under the Medicare inpatient prospective payment system to account for documentation and coding adjustments associated with the implementation of Medicare severity diagnosis-related groups (which replaced diagnosis-related groups beginning in fiscal year 2008) that do not reflect real changes in patient case-mix. Specifically, the Secretary is authorized to make adjustments to the payment rates for discharges occurring during fiscal years 2014-2017, in order to recoup $11 billion in overpayments associated with documentation and coding adjustments in fiscal years 2008-2010 that have not been recovered through previously implemented adjustments to payment rates (for discharges occurring during fiscal years 2008-2013). In addition, the legislation prohibits the Secretary from recouping any additional amounts associated with documentation and coding adjustments for discharges that occurred during fiscal years 2008 and 2009; however, it does not change the Secretary's authority to make future adjustments to payment rates to account for documentation and coding adjustments for discharges that occurred during fiscal year 2010.

Provisions Affecting Part B of SMI Only

- In the formula for determining physician payment rates, the update to the single conversion factor is set at 0 percent for all of 2013.

- For 2014 and subsequent calendar years, the physician fee schedule conversion factor will be computed as if the conversion factor for 2013 had not been changed by the American Taxpayer Relief Act.

- The 1.00 floor on the geographic index for physician work is extended through December 31, 2013.

- The exceptions process for limits on therapy services is extended through December 31, 2013.

- Certain ambulance add-on payments are extended through December 31, 2013. These add-on payments include a 3-percent bonus for services originating in rural areas, a 2-percent bonus for services originating in other locations, and a "super rural" bonus for rural areas with the lowest population densities. In addition, air ambulance services in areas considered rural on December 31, 2006 will continue to be classified and paid as rural through June 30, 2013.

- For physician fee schedule therapy services furnished on or after January 1, 2011, payments for multiple therapy procedures (that is, therapy services provided to the same patient on the same day) have been reduced by 20 percent, rather than by 25 percent as specified in the final rule in the November 29, 2010 *Federal Register*. For services furnished on or after April 1, 2013, the reduction will be 50 percent. For multiple therapy procedures furnished by other types of providers, the 25-percent reduction that has been in place will likewise increase to 50 percent for services furnished on or after April 1, 2013. (Budget neutrality is waived for all reductions.)

- Payments under the hospital outpatient prospective payment system are reduced for certain outpatient hospital stereotactic radiosurgery services furnished on or after April 1, 2013.

- The utilization rates used in determining fee schedules for the use of diagnostic imaging equipment are revised for 2014 and subsequent years.

- Medicare reimbursements for diabetic supplies that are non-mail order are made equal to the single payment amounts established under the national mail order competition for diabetic supplies.

- For renal dialysis services furnished on or after January 1, 2014, reductions are to be made to the ESRD bundled payment rate to reflect changes in the utilization of certain drugs and biologicals.

- For renal dialysis services for individuals with ESRD, Medicare payments are reduced by 10-percent for non-emergency, basic life support ambulance transport furnished on or after October 1, 2013.

- The Qualifying Individual program is extended through December 31, 2013. This program is part of Medicaid and pays the Medicare Part B premium on behalf of certain beneficiaries with relatively low income and assets, with the cost financed from the Part B account of the SMI trust fund.

Provisions Affecting Part C

- The authorization for specialized Medicare Advantage plans for special needs individuals is extended through December 31, 2014.

- The coding intensity adjustment factor used in determining payments to Medicare Advantage plans is revised.

Provisions Affecting All Parts of Medicare

- The start of the sequestration process, should Congress fail to address the budget deficit by certain deadlines, as discussed in last year's report as a provision of the Budget Control Act of 2011 (Public Law 112-25, enacted on August 2, 2011), is delayed 2 months. Specifically, the sequester, originally scheduled for January 2, 2013, is postponed until March 1, 2013, and the enforcement of the statutory limits on discretionary spending for fiscal year 2013 (through the sequester), originally scheduled for 15 days after Congress adjourns to end a session, is postponed until March 27, 2013. (In light of the sequestration process, CMS announced that, in general, Medicare benefit payments for services incurred on or after April 1, 2013 will incur a 2-percent payment reduction.)

- The length of time that the Secretary of HHS has to collect Medicare overpayments is extended from 3 years to 5 years, effective upon date of enactment.

- All funding for the Medicare Improvement Fund is eliminated, starting in fiscal year 2014.

B. TOTAL MEDICARE FINANCIAL PROJECTIONS

Medicare is the nation's second largest social insurance program, exceeded only by Social Security (OASDI). Although Medicare's two components—Hospital Insurance (HI) and Supplementary Medical Insurance (SMI)—are very different from each other in many key respects, it is important to consider the overall cost of Medicare and its financing. By reviewing Medicare's total expenditures, readers can assess the financial obligation created by the program. Similarly, the sources and relative magnitudes of HI and SMI revenues are an important policy matter.

The issues of Medicare's total cost to society and the means of financing that cost are different from the question of the financial status of the Medicare trust funds. The latter focuses on whether a specific trust fund's income and expenditures are in balance. The separate HI and SMI financial projections prepared for this purpose, however, can be usefully combined for the broader purposes outlined above. To that end, this section presents information on combined HI and SMI costs and revenues. Sections III.B, III.C, and III.D of this report present detailed assessments of the financial status of the HI trust fund, and the Part B and Part D accounts of the SMI trust fund, respectively.

1. 10-year Actuarial Estimates (2013-2022)

Table V.B1 shows past and projected Medicare income, expenditures, and trust fund assets in dollar amounts for calendar years,[83] with projections shown under the intermediate set of assumptions for the short-range projection period 2013 through 2022 based on current law.

---

[83]The table shows amounts on a "cash" basis, reflecting actual expenditures made during the year, even if the payments were for services performed in an earlier year. Similarly, income figures represent amounts actually received during the year, even if incurred in an earlier year.

Table V.B1.—Total Medicare Income, Expenditures, and Trust Fund Assets
during Calendar Years 1970-2022
[In billions]

Calendar year	Total income	Total expenditures	Net change in assets	Assets at end of year
Historical data:				
1970	$8.2	$7.5	$0.7	$3.4
1975	17.7	16.3	1.3	12.0
1980	37.0	36.8	0.1	18.3
1985	76.5	72.3	4.2	31.4
1990	126.3	111.0	15.3	114.4
1995	175.3	184.2	−8.9	143.4
2000	257.1	221.8	35.3	221.5
2005	357.5	336.4	21.0	309.8
2006	437.0	408.3	28.7	338.5
2007	462.1	431.7	30.4	368.9
2008	480.8	468.2	12.7	381.6
2009	508.3[1]	509.0	−0.7	380.8
2010	486.1[1]	522.9	−36.8	344.0
2011	530.0	549.1	−19.2	324.9
2012	536.9	574.2	−37.3	287.6
Intermediate es imates:				
2013	574.9	594.0	−19.0	268.6
2014	614.0	612.2	1.7	270.3
2015	674.9[1]	641.0	34.0	304.3
2016	705.3[1]	684.8	20.5	324.7
2017	771.6	734.5	37.1	361.8
2018	831.9	794.4	37.4	399.2
2019	894.0	853.4	40.6	439.8
2020	975.4[1]	921.9	53.5	493.3
2021	1,017.3[1]	994.5	22.8	516.1
2022	1,113.4	1,087.7	25.7	541.8

[1]Section 708 of the Social Security Act modifies he provisions for the payment of Social Security benefits when the regularly designated day falls on a Saturday, Sunday, or legal public holiday. Payment of those benefits normally due January 3, 2010 actually occurred on December 31, 2009. Consequently, he Part B and Part D premiums withheld from these benefits and the associated Part B general revenue contributions were added to the respective Part B or Part D account on December 31, 2009. The total income for 2010 excludes these amounts. Similarly, the payment date for those benefits normally due January 3, 2016 will be December 31, 2015, and the payment date for those benefits normally due January 3, 2021 will be on December 31, 2020.

Note: Totals do not necessarily equal the sums of rounded components.

As indicated in table V.B1, Medicare expenditures have increased rapidly during most of the program's history. From 1985 to 2012, expenditures grew at an average annual rate of 8.0 percent. The following factors affect health care cost increases, including those for Medicare, Medicaid, and private health insurance:

- Growth in the number of beneficiaries;

- Increases in the prices paid per service;

- Increases in the average number of services per beneficiary ("utilization"); and

- Increases in the average complexity of services ("intensity").

Projected Medicare expenditures increase at an average annual rate of 6.6 percent during 2013-2022. The average growth rate reflects the continuing impact of each of the factors listed above, together with the effects of the scheduled (but unrealistic) physician payment reductions, the changes in the Affordable Care Act that affect the level of Medicare costs (such as the phased-in reduction in Medicare Advantage payment benchmarks), and other ACA changes that affect cost growth rates (such as the productivity adjustments to annual payment updates for most providers).

Through most of Medicare's history, trust fund income has kept pace with increases in expenditures.[84] Under current law, the Trustees estimate that total Medicare income will increase at a significantly faster rate (7.6 percent annually) than expenditures during 2013-2022. This difference arises in part because of the lower expenditures under the Affordable Care Act, the Budget Control Act, and the physician payment reductions. It is also attributable to faster growth in HI payroll tax revenues because the income threshold for application of the additional 0.9-percent tax rate is not indexed for inflation (with the result that an increasing proportion of workers becomes subject to the additional tax rate over time).

The Department of Treasury has invested past excesses of income over expenditures in U.S. Treasury securities, with total trust fund assets accumulating to $288 billion at the end of calendar year 2012. Combined assets decreased during 2009 through 2012, and the Trustees estimate that they will do so again, in 2013, mainly due to the continuing deficits in the HI trust fund and an intentional drawdown of excess Part B assets to help ameliorate premium increases otherwise required in 2013. Although it remains positive, the change in assets fluctuates slightly over the remainder of the short-range projection period due to the timing of premium collections as described in the footnote to table V.B1. The shift from the actual and expected declines in total Medicare trust fund assets in 2009-2013 to significant growth in assets during 2014-2020 reflects two primary factors. First, the magnitude of the projected HI deficits decreases and becomes HI surpluses as key provisions of the Affordable Care Act phase in and as the lower provider payment updates compound over time. Such projected lower HI deficits and small HI surpluses would be added to large projected surpluses in the

---

[84]This balance resulted from periodic increases in HI payroll tax rates and other HI financing, from annual increases in SMI premium and general revenue financing rates (to cover the following year's estimated expenditures), and from frequent legislation designed to slow the rate of growth in expenditures.

Part B trust fund account. These latter surpluses would not materialize in the likely event that Congress continues to override the physician payment reductions required under current law. Under the illustrative alternative projections, combined trust fund deficits would generally continue throughout the short-range projection period.[85]

The Affordable Care Act of 2010 established a 15-member Independent Payment Advisory Board (IPAB) to develop and submit proposals to Congress aimed at extending the solvency of Medicare, slowing Medicare cost growth, and improving the quality of care delivered to Medicare beneficiaries. The Board is required to submit proposals to the President the year following a determination that the projected rate of growth in Medicare spending per beneficiary exceeds a target growth rate.[86] Determinations of the projected and target growth rates are to be made by the Chief Actuary at CMS beginning in 2013. If the Chief Actuary makes a determination that the projected Medicare per capita growth rate exceeds the per capita target growth rate in the implementation year, the Chief Actuary will establish a savings target for that year.

For a given determination year, the rates of growth for Medicare spending and the target are calculated as the 5-year average consisting of the 2 prior years, the current year, and the 2 following years. For example, for the 2013 determination year, 2014 is the proposal year, 2015 is the implementation year, and the 5-year period is 2011-2015. Table V.B2 presents the projected rates of growth that are used in the IPAB determination.

---

[85]See sections III.B, III.C, and III.D regarding the asset projections for HI and Part B and Part D of SMI, separately, including the reasons for the projected large increase in Part B assets under current law.

[86]Beginning in 2019, the ACA provides an exception to the requirement that the Board submit proposals if the projected rate of growth for Medicare is less than that for national health expenditures. This exception can occur only if the IPAB was required to submit a proposal in the prior year, and it may not be used in 2 consecutive years. In addition, when there is a determination that the projected increase in the medical CPI is less than the CPI for the implementation year, the Board is not required to submit a proposal.

Table V.B2.—Key Rates of Growth for IPAB Determination
[In percent]

Calendar year	Medicare per capita[1]	CPI	CPI medical care	GDP per capita	NHE per capita[2]	IPAB determination[3] Medicare	Target[4]
2011	2.2	3.6	3.0	3.2	3.1	—	—
2012	1.1	2.1	3.8	3.4	3.4	—	—
2013	−0.4	1.8	3.6	3.3	2.9	1.46	3.04
2014	2.7	2.2	3.9	4.3	6.4	1.74	3.06
2015	1.8	2.4	4.1	5.2	4.7	2.33	3.17
2016	3.6	2.5	4.2	5.2	5.3	3.38	3.36
2017	4.1	2.7	4.4	4.8	5.0	3.72	3.48
2018	4.8	2.8	4.5	4.5	5.2	4.31	5.48
2019	4.1	2.8	4.5	4.1	5.5	4.50	5.20
2020	4.7	2.8	4.5	3.8	5.8	4.92	4.97
2021	4.8	2.8	4.5	3.7	5.7	5.04	4.81
2022	6.2	2.8	4.5	3.7	5.7	5.20	4.75

[1]These amounts differ from those presented in section V.D because they are determined based on the methodology required for the IPAB determination. They are calculated as the sum of the average per capita spending under each of Parts A, B, and D. For Parts B and D, the spending is net of premiums. Since the projected update to the single conversion factor applicable to payments for physician fee schedule services is negative for 2014, the determination requires that the Medicare grow h rate be calculated as if the update for these services was 0 percent ra her than the nega ive percentage that would otherwise apply. In addition, the amounts represent spending based on the date the service is incurred rather han when it is paid, and they do not reflect the effects of the IPAB proposals.
[2]Source: National health expenditure (NHE) projec ions article published in June, 2012 (*Health Affairs*; Vol. 31, No. 7). The findings presented in this article, along with the paper outlining its methodology, are available at http://www.cms.gov/Research-Statistics-Data-and-Systems/Statistics-Trends-and-Reports/NationalHealthExpendData/NationalHealthAccountsProjected.html.
[3]5-year average starting 2 years prior to the determination year and ending 2 years after the determination year. An implementation year is 2 years after a determination year where Medicare per capita costs are projected to grow at a faster rate than the target, requiring a reduction in spending.
[4]For determinations made in 2013-2017, the target is equal to the average of the growth in the Consumer Price Index for all urban consumers (all items; United States city average) and the medical care expenditure category of he Consumer Price Index for all urban consumers (United States city average). For 2018 and later determinations, the target rate of growth is per capita GDP plus 1 percent.

2. 75-year Actuarial Estimates (2013-2087)

Table V.B3 shows past and projected Medicare expenditures expressed as a percentage of GDP.[87] This percentage provides a relative measure of the size of the Medicare program compared to the general economy and represents the portion of the nation's total resources dedicated each year to providing health care services to beneficiaries through Medicare. Expenditures represented 0.7 percent of GDP in 1970 and had grown to 2.7 percent of GDP by 2005, reflecting rapid increases in the factors affecting health care cost growth. Starting in 2006, Medicare provided subsidized access to prescription drug coverage through Part D, which caused most of the increase in Medicare expenditures to 3.1 percent of GDP in the first year. The Trustees project much more moderate continuing growth in the long range under current law, partially as a result of the lower

---

[87]In contrast to the expenditure amounts shown in table V.B1, table V.B3 shows historical and projected expenditures on an incurred basis. Incurred amounts relate to the expenditures for services performed in a given year, even if payment for those expenditures occurs in a later year.

price updates under the Affordable Care Act, with total Medicare expenditures projected to reach about 6.5 percent of GDP by 2085. Projected Medicare costs would slightly exceed those for Social Security in 2056 and later under current law.

Part of the projected increase is attributable to the prescription drug benefit in Medicare. In its first (partial) year of operation, this benefit increased aggregate Medicare costs by about one-eighth.[88] With continuing faster growth in drug costs, relative to the traditional HI and SMI Part B expenditures, the Trustees project that the prescription drug benefit will increase current-law Medicare costs by roughly 18 percent beginning in 2022 and by about 28 percent at the end of the projection period. The Affordable Care Act provisions reduce growth rates for all HI and most SMI Part B non-physician services by the productivity adjustments to price updates; these adjustments do not apply to Part D, since a bidding process establishes payments to drug plans.

The cost projections shown in table V.B3 for total Medicare are lower than those in the 2012 annual report mostly due to lower growth rates assumed for Part A providers and Part D plans. The differences arise for a number of reasons, which sections III.B, III.C, and III.D describe.

---

[88]Although the Part D drug benefit became available on January 1, 2006, beneficiaries had until May 15 to enroll. About 62 percent of the ultimate number of enrollees had enrolled as of January 1.

Table V.B3.—HI and SMI Incurred Expenditures as a Percentage
of the Gross Domestic Product

Calendar year	HI Part A	SMI Part B	SMI Part D	Total
Historical data:				
1970	0.52%	0.22%	—	0.74%
1975	0.73	0.30	—	1.03
1980	0.91	0.41	—	1.32
1985	1.12	0.56	—	1.68
1990	1.14	0.76	—	1.90
1995	1.58	0.90	—	2.47
2000	1.31	0.94	—	2.25
2005	1.46	1.22	0.01%	2.69
2006	1.46	1.27	0.33	3.07
2007	1.47	1.31	0.36	3.15
2008	1.56	1.28	0.38	3.22
2009	1.69	1.47	0.42	3.58
2010	1.68	1.48	0.43	3.59
2011	1.68	1.50	0.44	3.62
2012	1.66	1.54	0.45	3.65
Intermediate es imates:				
2013	1.63	1.54	0.45	3.62
2014	1.57	1.47	0.47	3.52
2015	1.54	1.48	0.49	3.50
2016	1.54	1.50	0.50	3.53
2017	1.55	1.52	0.51	3.59
2018	1.59	1.56	0.53	3.68
2019	1.61	1.60	0.55	3.76
2020	1.64	1.65	0.58	3.88
2021	1.68	1.71	0.61	4.00
2022	1.75	1.80	0.64	4.18
2025	1.86	1.98	0.71	4.56
2030	2.06	2.25	0.83	5.14
2035	2.24	2.39	0.92	5.55
2040	2.37	2.45	0.97	5.79
2045	2.44	2.45	1.02	5.91
2050	2.46	2.45	1.07	5.98
2055	2.46	2.46	1.12	6.04
2060	2.47	2.50	1.18	6.15
2065	2.50	2.53	1.24	6.27
2070	2.54	2.56	1.29	6.40
2075	2.57	2.58	1.35	6.50
2080	2.56	2.56	1.38	6.50
2085	2.54	2.56	1.42	6.53

The 75-year projection period fully allows for the presentation of anticipated future developments, such as the impact of a large increase in enrollees during 2010-2030. This increase in the number of beneficiaries will occur because the relatively large number of persons born during the period between the end of World War II and the mid-1960s (known as the baby boom generation) will reach eligibility age and begin to receive benefits. Moreover, as this generation ages, these individuals will experience greater health care utilization and costs, thereby adding further to growth in program expenditures. Table V.B4 shows past and projected enrollment in the Medicare program.

As indicated in table V.B4, the total number of Medicare beneficiaries approximately doubled over the last 35 years, and the Trustees expect the total to double again over approximately the next 35 years. During this same historical period, the number of covered workers also increased rapidly (by about 56 percent) but is projected to increase much more slowly (about 26 percent) over the next 35 years. This demographic shift and its implications for Medicare costs, relative to workers' earnings or to the GDP, are fairly well known.

The enrollment data also show that the number of Medicare beneficiaries enrolled in private health plans under Part C has increased substantially in recent years. This increase reflects the higher Medicare payments to Medicare Advantage plans specified by the Medicare Prescription Drug, Improvement, and Modernization Act of 2003, which enabled these plans to offer additional benefit coverage. From 2005 to 2009, the number of Part C enrollees increased by more than 90 percent (an average of about 18 percent per year). Enrollment growth continued in 2010 and 2011 but at a slower pace of about 5 to 6 percent annually. In 2012, enrollment growth was nearly 10 percent. (Section IV.C of this report describes the factors contributing to the acceleration and deceleration in enrollment growth during these periods.) In 2012, enrollment in private health plans represented over 26 percent of total Medicare beneficiaries, with nearly all such enrollees participating in Medicare Advantage health insurance plans. The Trustees expect enrollment in Medicare Advantage plans to peak in 2014, as a percent of total beneficiaries, because the Affordable Care Act reduces Medicare payments to private plans, which will result in less-generous plan benefit packages and/or higher enrollee premiums. By 2018, after these changes have fully phased in, just over 23 percent of Medicare beneficiaries are estimated to remain in private Part C health plans, with the balance reverting back to traditional "fee-for-service" Medicare. Modest increases are expected in private plan penetration rates between 2019 and 2025. Ultimately, the estimated proportion of beneficiaries in such plans stabilizes at about 25 percent.

Table V.B4.—Medicare Enrollment
[In thousands]

Calendar year	HI Part A	SMI Part B	SMI Part D	Part C	Total[1]
Historical data:					
1970	20,104	19,496	—	—	20,398
1975	24,481	23,744	—	—	24,864
1980	28,002	27,278	—	—	28,433
1985	30,621	29,869	—	1,271	31,081
1990	33,747	32,567	—	2,017	34,251
1995	37,175	35,641	—	3,467	37,594
2000	39,257	37,335	—	6,856	39,688
2005	42,233	39,752	1,841	5,794	42,606
2006	43,065	40,361	30,560	7,291	43,436
2007	44,010	41,093	31,392	8,667	44,368
2008	45,150	41,975	32,589	10,010	45,500
2009	46,256	42,908	33,644	11,104	46,604
2010	47,365	43,882	34,772	11,692	47,720
2011	48,528	44,906	35,720	12,382	48,884
2012	50,298	46,405	37,367	13,586	50,655
Intermediate es imates:					
2013	51,939	47,982	38,906	14,837	52,294
2014	53,608	49,459	40,063	15,562	53,961
2015	55,276	50,924	41,140	15,439	55,629
2016	56,938	52,390	42,256	15,010	57,289
2017	58,636	53,883	43,475	14,260	58,987
2018	60,362	55,404	44,709	14,156	60,713
2019	62,118	56,958	45,969	14,549	62,469
2020	63,919	58,611	47,420	15,117	64,272
2021	65,751	60,247	48,694	15,842	66,105
2022	67,619	61,921	50,057	16,617	67,975
2025	73,164	66,903	54,144	18,402	73,526
2030	81,111	74,090	60,003	20,343	81,482
2035	86,106	78,539	63,683	21,554	86,479
2040	88,519	80,770	65,459	[2]	88,891
2045	89,978	82,070	66,536	[2]	90,353
2050	92,003	83,918	68,032	[2]	92,385
2055	94,679	86,323	70,011	[2]	95,073
2060	98,152	89,512	72,582	[2]	98,563
2065	101,701	92,734	75,208	[2]	102,130
2070	105,597	96,286	78,092	[2]	106,046
2075	109,486	99,867	80,972	[2]	109,957
2080	112,114	102,257	82,919	[2]	112,601
2085	115,914	105,702	85,733	[2]	116,422

[1]Number of beneficiaries with HI and/or SMI coverage.
[2]The Trustees do not explicitly project enrollment in Part C beyond 2035.

Table V.B5 shows the past and projected amounts of Medicare revenues as a percentage of total non-interest Medicare income, based on the intermediate assumptions. The table excludes interest income, which would not be a significant part of program financing in the long range under current law.

Table V.B5.—Medicare Sources of Income as a Percentage of Total Income[1]

Calendar year	Payroll taxes	Tax on benefits	Premiums[1]	Brand-name drug fees	State transfers	General revenue
Historical data:						
1970	61.8%	—	13.7%	—	—	24.6%
1980	68.0	—	8.6	—	—	23.4
1990	62.2	—	9.8	—	—	27.9
2000	59.8	3.6%	9.1	—	—	27.6
2010	38.9	2.9	13.3	—	0.9%	44.0
2012	39.4	3.6	13.4	0.4%	1.6	41.6
Intermediate es imates:						
2013	38.5	2.6	13.8	0.5	1.5	43.1
2020	35.3	3.7	14.7	0.3	1.4	44.6
2030	30.9	4.4	15.5	0.2	1.7	47.4
2040	28.2	4.3	16.3	0.1	1.8	49.3
2050	28.1	4.2	16.4	0.1	1.9	49.4
2060	27.6	4.1	16.6	0.0	2.0	49.6
2070	27.0	4.1	16.9	0.0	2.1	49.9
2080	26.8	4.0	17.2	0.0	2.2	49.8

[1]Includes premium revenue from HI and both accounts in the SMI trust fund.

Note: Row sums may not exactly equal 100 percent due to rounding.

In 2012, general revenues (primarily those for SMI) represented 42 percent of total non-interest income to the Medicare program—becoming, for the fourth year in a row, the largest share of Medicare financing. HI payroll taxes were the next largest source of overall financing at 39 percent. Beneficiary premiums (again, primarily for SMI) were third, at 13 percent. Under current law, projected HI tax revenues fall short of projected HI expenditures for most future years. In contrast, SMI premium and general revenues will keep pace with SMI expenditure growth, and, once fully phased down,[89] State payments (on behalf of Medicare beneficiaries who also qualify for full Medicaid benefits) will grow with Part D expenditures. Under the Affordable Care Act, a new source of Part B financing, from fees on manufacturers and importers of brand-name prescription drugs, will increase from $2.5 billion in 2011 to $4.0 billion in 2018 but then decrease to $2.7 billion for 2019 and later. In the absence of legislation, HI tax income would represent a declining portion of total Medicare revenues. In 2026, for example, the projected year of depletion of the HI trust fund, currently scheduled HI payroll taxes would represent about 32 percent of total non-interest Medicare income. General revenues and beneficiary premiums would equal about 46 and 15 percent, respectively.

The Medicare Modernization Act requires an expanded analysis of the combined expenditures and dedicated revenues of the HI and SMI trust funds. In particular, the Act requires a determination as to

---

[89]State payments to Part D amounted to 90 percent of their projected foregone Medicaid prescription drug costs in 2006, with this percentage phasing down over a 10-year period to 75 percent in 2015.

whether projected annual "general revenue funding" exceeds 45 percent of total Medicare outlays within the next 7 fiscal years (2013-2019). For this purpose, the law defines general revenue funding as total Medicare outlays minus dedicated Medicare financing sources. Dedicated Medicare financing sources include HI payroll taxes; income from taxation of Social Security benefits; State transfers for the prescription drug benefit; premiums paid under Parts A, B, and D; fees on brand-name prescription drugs paid to Part B; fines and penalties collected as a result of program integrity efforts; and any gifts received by the Medicare trust funds. The test uses expenditures adjusted to avoid temporary distortions arising from the payment of Medicare Advantage capitation amounts in September when the normal October payment date is a Saturday or Sunday.

Lawmakers established the 45-percent test to help call attention to Medicare's impact on the Federal budget. The Trustees made determinations of "excess general revenue Medicare funding" in each of the reports for 2006 through 2012. Two consecutive such determinations trigger a "Medicare funding warning," which indicates that a trust fund's financing is inadequate or that the general revenues provided under current law are becoming unduly large. The 2007 through 2012 reports thus prompted "Medicare funding warnings." Such findings require the President to submit to Congress, within 15 days after the date of the Budget submission for the succeeding year, proposed legislation to respond to the warning. The law also requires Congress to consider the legislation proposed in response to "Medicare funding warnings" on an expedited basis. To date, elected officials have not enacted legislation responding to these funding warnings.

Figure V.B1 displays, on a calendar-year basis, the historical and projected ratio of the difference between total Medicare outlays and dedicated financing sources to total Medicare outlays. As indicated, this ratio exceeded 45 percent at the end of calendar years 2009 through 2012, and the Trustees estimate it to do so in 2013 (as a result of expected low payroll tax and benefit tax receipts caused by the continuing effects of the recent economic recession, together with a planned drawdown of excess Part B assets). Formal application of the test, however, is on a fiscal-year basis. In this year's report, the Trustees project that the difference will exceed 45 percent in fiscal year 2013. This is the seventh consecutive time that the ratio has exceeded the threshold within the first 7 years of the projection. Accordingly, a determination of "excess general revenue Medicare funding" is made again this year. With this eighth consecutive finding, another "Medicare funding warning" is triggered.[90] To reduce the ratio below 45 percent for 2013 would require revenue increases of at least $10 billion or benefit reductions of at least $18 billion, or some combination of revenue increases and benefit reductions.

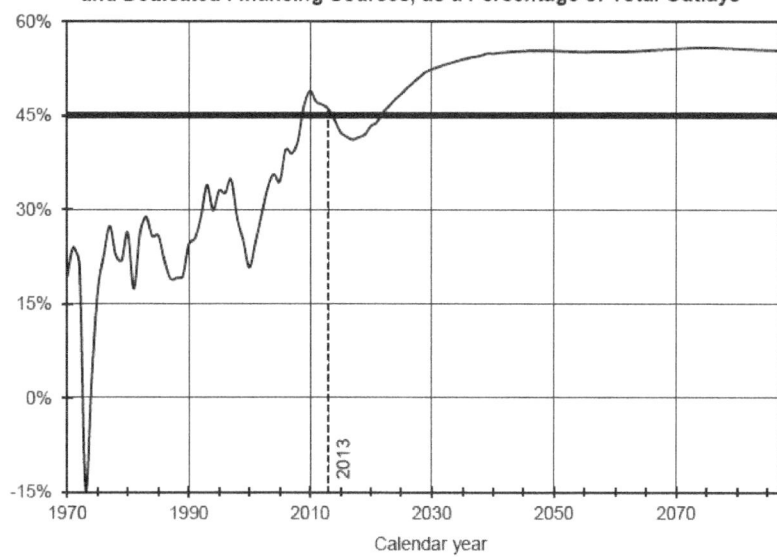

Figure V.B1.—Projected Difference between Total Medicare Outlays and Dedicated Financing Sources, as a Percentage of Total Outlays

As figure V.B1 also indicates, the Board projects that the difference between outlays and dedicated funding sources will reach 55 percent of outlays by 2038 and will remain at about that level throughout the remainder of the 75-year period. Although the law characterizes this difference as "general revenue funding," it is important to recognize that current law provides for general revenue transfers only for certain purposes related to Parts A, B, and D, as follows:

- Financing specified portions of SMI Part B and SMI Part D expenditures;

- Reimbursing the HI trust fund for the costs of certain uninsured beneficiaries;

- Paying interest on invested assets of the trust funds; and

---

[90]The Medicare Modernization Act directs the President to submit a legislative proposal responding to the funding warning within 15 days of the President's Fiscal Year 2015 Budget, which will be released in early February 2014.

• Redeeming the special Treasury securities held as assets by the trust funds.

The difference between outlays and dedicated funding sources, as shown in figure V.B1, will reflect all of these general revenue transfers, plus the imbalance between HI expenditures and dedicated revenues after HI asset depletion in 2026. There is no provision under current law to cover the shortfall. In particular, transfers from the general fund of the Treasury could not occur for the purpose of avoiding asset depletion without new legislation.

The Medicare Modernization Act also requires a comparison of projected growth in the difference between outlays and dedicated revenues with other health spending growth rates. Table V.B6 contains this comparison.

Table V.B6.—Comparative Growth Rates of Medicare, Private Health Insurance, National Health Expenditures, and GDP

	Average annual growth in:				
Calendar year	Incurred outlays minus dedicated revenues	Incurred Medicare outlays	GDP	National health expenditures[1]	Private health insurance[1]
2007	8 5%	7.6%	4.9%	6.2%	4.9%
2008	3.4	4.3	1.9	4.7	4.0
2009	24.2	8.7	−2.2	3.8	2.6
2010	10.8	4.0	3.8	3.9	2.4
2011	1 3	4.9	4.0	3.9	1.8
2012	4.1	4.9	4.1	4.2	2.8
2013	1.4	3.2	4.1	3.8	4.1
2014	−2 5	2.3	5.2	7.4	7.9
2015	2.1	5.6	6.1	5.7	6.3
2016	5 3	7.0	6.1	6.3	6.6
2017	6.6	7.4	5.8	5.9	5.4
2018	8 9	8.1	5.5	6.2	5.2
2019	8 5	7.4	5.0	6.5	6.1
2020	11.5	8.0	4.8	6.7	6.2
2021	9 5	7.9	4.7	6.5	5.9
2022	13.6	9.5	4.6	6.5	5.9
2023-2037	8 0	6.7	4.6	—	—
2038-2062	5 0	4.9	4.6	—	—
2063-2087	4 8	4.7	4.5	—	—

[1]Source: National health expenditure (NHE) projec ions article published in June, 2012 (*Health Affairs*; Vol. 31, No. 7). The findings presented in this article, along with the paper outlining its methodology, are available at http://www.cms.gov/Research-Statistics-Data-and-Systems/Statistics-Trends-and-Reports/ NationalHealthExpendData/NationalHealthAccountsProjected.html.

As shown in table V.B6, the gap between outlays and dedicated revenues increased substantially, as did Medicare outlays, in most historical years. In addition, this gap will increase faster than outlays in most years through 2037 since the dedicated sources of income to the HI trust fund will generally cover a decreasing percentage of HI outlays.

In addition to projected Medicare outlay growth, table V.B6 shows projected growth in GDP, total expenditures on health care in the U.S., and private health insurance expenditures. The Trustees expect each of the health expenditure categories to continue the longstanding trend of increasing more rapidly than GDP in most years. Private health insurance expenditures equal the total premiums earned by private health insurers, including benefits incurred and the net cost of insurance. The net cost of insurance includes administrative costs, additions to reserves, rate credits and dividends, premium taxes, and profits or losses.

Several factors affect comparisons between aggregate Medicare and private health insurance cost growth:

- The number of Medicare beneficiaries is currently increasing by about 3 percent per year, and this growth rate will continue as more of the post-World War II baby boom generation reaches eligibility age. The projected number of individuals with private health insurance is anticipated to be somewhat stable through 2013 as the economy works to recover from the recent recession. Thereafter, with the availability of Federal premium and cost-sharing subsidies for many individuals and families under the Affordable Care Act, the projected number of people with private health insurance increases significantly.

- Certain ACA provisions, such as the limitation on maximum out-of-pocket costs in 2014 and later and the 40-percent excise tax on high-cost employer-sponsored insurance plans in 2018 and later, will also affect the average actuarial value of private health insurance benefits.

- The use of health care services differs significantly between Medicare beneficiaries (who are generally over 65) and individuals with private health insurance (who are predominantly below age 65). The former group, for example, has a higher incidence of hospitalization, skilled nursing care, and home health care. For the latter group, physician services represent a greater proportion of their total health care needs. Different cost growth trends by type of service will affect overall growth rates and reflect the distribution of services for each category of people.

- There is some overlap between people with Medicare and those with private health insurance. For example, many Medicare beneficiaries have supplemental health insurance coverage through private "Medigap" insurance policies or employer-sponsored retiree health benefits, and private health insurance includes both of these categories. About 9 million Medicare beneficiaries receive supplemental coverage through the Medicaid program; neither the growth rates for Medicare nor those for private health insurance reflect the Medicaid costs for these "dual beneficiaries."

A number of research studies have attempted to control for some or all of these differences in comparing growth trends. Over long historical periods, average, demographically adjusted, per capita growth rates for common benefits have been somewhat lower for Medicare than for private health insurance. For shorter periods, however, the rates of growth have often diverged substantially, and the differential has been negative in some years and positive in others. More information on past and projected national and private health expenditures, and on comparisons to Medicare growth rates, is available in the sources cited in table V.B6.

C. ILLUSTRATIVE ALTERNATIVE PROJECTIONS

The Social Security Act requires the Trustees to evaluate the financial status of the Medicare trust funds. To comply with this mandate, the Trustees must assess whether the financing provided under current law is adequate to cover the benefit payments and other expenditures required under current law. Accordingly, the estimates shown in this report are based on all of the current statutory requirements, including (i) the sustainable growth rate (SGR) formula governing payments to physicians; (ii) the reductions in payment updates by the increase in economy-wide productivity for most other provider categories; and (iii) the operations of the Independent Payment Advisory Board.

As discussed in the Introduction, there is substantial uncertainty about the adequacy of future Medicare payment rates under current law. This appendix illustrates the higher Medicare outlays that would result if certain statutory Medicare payment provisions were not fully implemented in all future years.

Under current law, the SGR formula would reduce physician payments by an estimated 24.7 percent in 2014 and constrain growth in total physician expenditures to approximately the rate of increase in the GDP in subsequent years. Currently, the Medicare fees paid to physicians are about 80 percent of those paid by private health insurance. If continued implementation of the SGR requirements for Medicare did not affect the rate of growth of private payments, then Medicare physician payments would be less than 40 percent of the corresponding private health insurance prices within 20 years and, by the end of the 75-year period, would be only about 25 percent of private insurance levels. If lawmakers allowed such payment differentials to occur, Medicare beneficiaries would almost certainly face increasingly severe problems with access to physician services.

For all Part A services and most other (non-physician) Part B services, payment updates will be reduced in all future years by the increase in economy-wide multifactor productivity.[91] By the end of the long-range projection period, payment rates for affected providers would be about 55 percent lower than their level in the absence of

---

[91]In addition to the productivity adjustments, current law requires certain other reductions in payment updates for 2010 through 2019. For inpatient hospital services, the cumulative impact of these adjustments is a further reduction of 3.6 percent in payment levels. Also, Medicare payments to providers will be affected by an expected reduction of 2 percent in April 2013 through March 2022 under the Budget Control Act of 2011, as amended by the American Taxpayer Relief Act of 2012.

these reductions. Currently, the Medicare payment rates for inpatient hospital services are about 67 percent of those paid by private health insurance. If future improvements in productivity remain similar to what providers have achieved in the recent past (about 0.4 percent annually), then Medicare payment levels for inpatient hospital services at the end of the long-range projection period would be less than 40 percent of the corresponding level paid by private health insurance.[92] Absent other changes, the lower Medicare payment rates would result in an additional 15 percent of hospitals, skilled nursing facilities, and home health agencies experiencing negative total facility margins by 2019, and this percentage would reach roughly 25 percent in 2030 and 40 percent by 2050.

Over time, unless providers could alter their use of inputs to reduce their cost per service correspondingly, Medicare's payments for health services would fall increasingly below providers' costs. Providers could not sustain continuing negative margins and would have to withdraw from serving Medicare beneficiaries or (if total facility margins remained positive) shift substantial portions of Medicare costs to their non-Medicare, non-Medicaid payers. Under such circumstances, lawmakers might feel substantial pressure to override the productivity adjustments, much as they have done to prevent reductions in physician payment rates.

Under current law, the Independent Payment Advisory Board (IPAB) must submit proposals to the President for years in which the projected rate of growth in Medicare spending per beneficiary exceeds specified thresholds. For 2015 through 2019, the threshold rate of growth in Medicare spending per beneficiary is the average of the increases in the CPI for all items and in the CPI for Medical Care. Thereafter, the law requires IPAB proposals if the projected rate of growth in Medicare spending exceeds the estimated increase in the GDP plus 1.0 percentage point.[93] The IPAB's proposals will automatically take effect unless lawmakers enact an alternative measure that achieves the same level of savings. As a result of the other savings provisions incorporated into current law, the Trustees

---

[92]This comparison assumes that private payer rate increases would continue to be set through the same negotiation process used to date, independent of the Medicare reductions or other health system changes.

[93]The effects of the IPAB's proposals on Medicare expenditures are limited to 0.5 percentage point in 2015, 1.0 percentage point in 2016, 1.25 percentage points in 2017, and 1.5 percentage points in 2018 and subsequent years (or, if smaller, the amount by which the rate of growth in Medicare spending exceeds the threshold growth rate). A number of other provisions govern the operations of the IPAB; appendix V.A in the 2010 Medicare Trustees Report summarizes these additional provisions.

estimate that the IPAB provision will reduce Medicare growth rates for the first time in 2019, and by only 0.3 percent in that year. Rates are also projected to be reduced by similar small amounts in every second year starting in 2023 and ending in 2035. In the absence of these other ACA provisions, however, reducing cost growth rates to the degree required by the IPAB provision would be challenging. (See section V.B for more details about the IPAB determination.)

In view of these issues, it is important to note that the actual future costs for Medicare are likely to exceed those shown by the current-law projections in this report, possibly by substantial amounts. Use of alternative projections can illustrate the potential magnitude of this difference.

The physician fee reduction for 2014 is clearly unworkable, and lawmakers are almost certain to override it.[94] The productivity adjustments will affect other Medicare price levels much more gradually, but there is a strong likelihood that without very substantial and transformational changes in health care practices, payment rates would become inadequate in the long range. As a result, readers should not interpret the projections shown in this report for current law as the Trustees' expectation of actual Medicare financial operations in the future but rather as illustrations of the very favorable impact of permanently slower growth in health care costs, if such slower growth is achievable.

It is possible that health care providers could improve their productivity, reduce wasteful expenditures, and take other steps to keep their cost growth within the bounds imposed by the Medicare price limitations. For such efforts to be successful in the long range, however, providers would have to generate and sustain unprecedented levels of productivity gains—a very challenging and uncertain prospect.

A transformation of health care in the U.S., affecting both the means of delivery and the method of paying for care, is also a possibility. Current law supports important steps in this direction by initiating programs of research into innovative payment and service delivery models, such as accountable care organizations, patient-centered "medical homes," improvement in care coordination for individuals with multiple chronic health conditions, better coordination of post-acute care, payment bundling, "pay for performance," and assistance

---

[94]Lawmakers have overridden the SGR requirements every year for 2003 through 2013, replacing the reductions of 5 to 29 percent otherwise required with increases that averaged 0.8 percent per year during this period.

for individuals in making informed health choices. Such changes have the potential to reduce health care costs and cost growth rates and could, as a result, help lower Medicare cost growth rates to levels compatible with the lower price updates payable under current law.

The ability of new delivery and payment methods to lower cost growth rates is uncertain at this time, since specific changes have not yet been designed, tested, or evaluated. Hopes for success are high, but at this time there is insufficient evidence to support an assumption that improvements in efficiency can occur of the magnitude needed to align with the statutory Medicare price updates. Given these uncertainties, it will be important for policy makers to monitor the adequacy of Medicare payment rates over time to ensure beneficiary access to high-quality care.

To help illustrate and quantify the potential magnitude of the cost understatement under current law, the Trustees have asked the Office of the Actuary to prepare an illustrative set of Medicare trust fund projections under hypothetical alternatives to current law that assume that lawmakers override the physician fee reductions and that, starting in 2020, the economy-wide productivity adjustments gradually phase down to 0.4 percent.[95] Figure V.C1 compares the illustrative alternative projections with those based on current law.[96] Under current law and the intermediate set of assumptions, projected Medicare expenditures would increase from their current level of 3.6 percent of GDP to 5.8 percent in 2040 and more slowly thereafter to 6.5 percent at the end of the long-range projection period. The rapid increase in costs during 2018 through 2040 is primarily attributable to the baby boom generation's enrollment in Medicare and its subsequent attainment of older ages with increased use of medical services.

---

[95]The Trustees have used this approach since 2007 to address concerns with the SGR provision. The illustrative alternative projections included changes to the productivity adjustments starting with the 2010 annual report, following enactment of the Affordable Care Act.

[96]The 2010-2011 Medicare Technical Review Panel supported the continued use of illustrative alternative projections for this purpose. In addition, the Panel recommended a graphical comparison of the current-law and alternative projections within the Medicare annual report, highlighting the potential effects of both SGR and productivity adjustments. The *"Review of Assumptions and Methods of the Medicare Trustees' Financial Projections"* can be found at http://aspe.hhs.gov/health/reports/2013/MedicareTech/TechnicalPanelReport2010-2011.pdf. The text summarizes the specific assumptions chosen by the Trustees for the illustrative alternative projections.

Figure V.C1.—Medicare Expenditures as a Percentage of the Gross Domestic Product under Current Law and Illustrative Alternative Projections

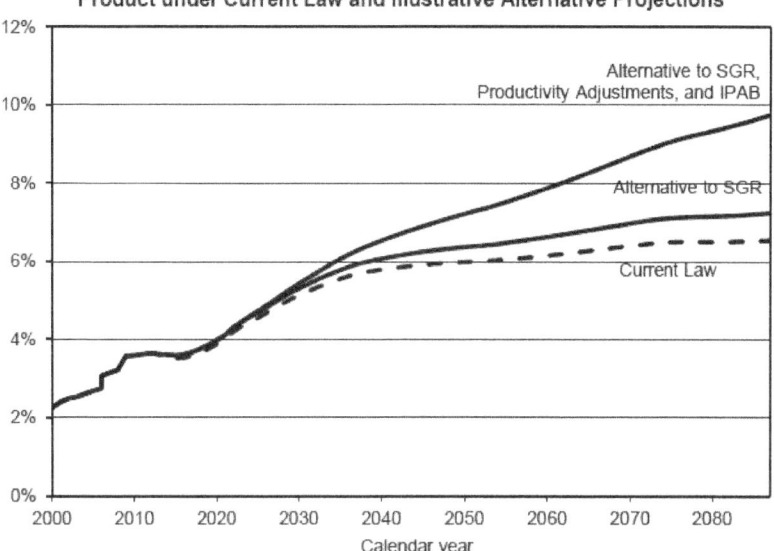

The middle projection in figure V.C1 illustrates the potential increase in Medicare expenditures resulting from further legislation to prevent large reductions in physician payment rates. This illustration assumes that the physician payment updates would be 0.7 percent per year through the short-run projection period, an increase which reflects the 10-year average Medicare physician fee schedule payment update that has occurred from 2004 through 2013, the most recent 10 years during which SGR reductions have been consistently overridden by legislative action. For 2023 through 2037, the illustration assumes that Medicare physician spending growth would gradually transition to the per capita increase in health spending in the U.S. overall and then equal that rate for the last 50 years of the projection.[97]

Overriding the 2014 physician payment reduction of approximately 25 percent would initially increase total Medicare expenditures by over 2 percent. This differential would increase to about 11 percent in 2087 as a result of the higher updates in subsequent years in the absence of the SGR provision. Under this illustration, total Medicare expenditures would represent 7.2 percent of GDP at the end of the long-range projection period.

---

[97]On average during this latter period, the growth rate for per capita national health spending is assumed to equal the per capita increase in GDP plus 1 percent. As described in section IV.D of this report, the year-by-year rates vary, declining from the per capita increase in GDP plus 1.2 percent in 2037 to per capita GDP growth plus 0.3 percent in 2087.

The top curve in figure V.C1 shows the cost levels that would result if the physician payment updates changed as described above and the productivity adjustments gradually phased down, starting in 2020, until the Medicare price updates equaled those assumed for private health plans in 2034.[98] The resulting Medicare payment rate updates are equivalent to assuming that roughly three-fourths of the statutory productivity adjustments would gradually phase out from 2020 through 2034. In addition, the projection assumes that the IPAB requirements would not be implemented. On average under this alternative, the long-range per beneficiary growth rate for all Medicare services would be similar to the long-range growth rate assumed for the overall health sector. These growth rates are very similar to the illustrative alternative projections referenced in the 2010-2012 reports. (See section V.B for more details about the IPAB determination.)

As indicated in figure V.C1, Medicare costs as a percentage of GDP would continue to increase rapidly throughout the projection period absent the statutory SGR impacts, full economy-wide productivity adjustments, and IPAB effects. The illustrative projection reaches 6.5 percent of GDP in 2040 and 9.8 percent in 2087, with the largest share of the increase relative to current law attributable to the reduced productivity adjustments.

Readers should consider higher expenditures from future SGR overrides as being quite likely, although it is possible that lawmakers would offset some of the higher costs through other Medicare savings provisions. In the SGR illustration, the additional Medicare expenditures in 2087 represent 0.7 percent of GDP. In contrast, higher costs from changes to the statutory productivity adjustments are more uncertain and would likely be less immediate, but the ultimate impact could be substantially greater—as much as 2.5 percent of GDP for the change illustrated here.

Difficult challenges lie ahead in making health care far more cost-efficient while ensuring its high quality, and awareness of these challenges must temper expectations. The sizable differences in projected Medicare cost levels between current law and the illustrative alternative projections highlight the critical importance of the new research authorized by the Affordable Care Act. It is necessary to expend every effort not only to bring Medicare costs—and health care costs in the U.S. generally—more in line with society's ability to afford them but also to improve health care outcomes.

---

[98]Section IV.D of this report describes the price component of health care cost increases for the overall health sector.

D. AVERAGE MEDICARE EXPENDITURES PER BENEFICIARY

Table V.D1 shows historical average per beneficiary expenditures for HI and SMI, as well as projected costs for calendar years 2013 through 2022 under the intermediate assumptions.

For both HI and SMI Part B, costs increased very rapidly in the early years, in part because the availability of Medicare coverage enabled many beneficiaries to obtain the full range of health services they needed. The rapid inflation of the 1970s and early 1980s also contributed to rapid Medicare expenditure increases, and the cost-based reimbursement mechanisms in place provided relatively little incentive for efficiency in the provision of health care. Growth in average HI expenditures moderated dramatically following the introduction of the inpatient hospital prospective payment system in fiscal year 1984, but accelerated again in the late 1980s and early 1990s due to rapid growth in skilled nursing and home health expenditures. During this same period, SMI Part B average costs generally continued to increase at relatively fast rates but slowed somewhat in the early 1990s with the implementation of physician fee reform legislation.

Expenditure growth moderated again during the late 1990s due to the effects of further legislation, including the Balanced Budget Act of 1997 (BBA), and efforts to control fraud and abuse. In addition, historically low levels of general and medical inflation helped reduce Medicare payment updates. HI per beneficiary costs actually decreased in 1998 and 1999, and slowed substantially in 2000, in part because of such BBA mandates as a reduction in payment updates to providers and a shift in home health benefits from HI to SMI Part B, and in part because of a decline in utilization of services. Growth rates returned to more typical levels during 2001-2004.

For 2005 through 2007, Part B grew substantially, reflecting increases in the volume and intensity of physician services and also an accounting error that occurred in these years, which resulted in certain Part A benefits being misallocated to Part B. This error was corrected in 2008, causing the unusual pattern of increases for both HI and Part B of SMI in 2008 and 2009.

Growth rates in 2010 slowed for both HI and Part B of SMI due to low provider payment updates caused by slow growth in wages and prices following the recent economic recession, the onset of Affordable Care Act provisions affecting HI, an adjustment for excess HI documentation and coding under the new MS-DRG classification system for inpatient admissions, unusually low volume and intensity growth for Part B services, and an adjustment to Medicare Advantage payment rates to compensate for excess growth in MA risk scores relative to fee-for-service beneficiaries.

Growth rates for 2011 rebounded somewhat for HI and Part B of SMI, and remained basically level for 2012.

Although SMI Part D began in 2004, full prescription drug coverage did not start until 2006. Accordingly, this discussion will include only the per beneficiary expenditures for 2006 and later. The initial open enrollment period for Part D ran through May 15, 2006. Beneficiaries who enrolled at the beginning of the year tended to have higher costs than did those who enrolled toward the end of the open enrollment period. As a result, the average per beneficiary costs in 2006 were relatively high. In addition, actual spending in 2006 was ultimately much less than the prospective amounts that were paid to the Part D plans based on their bids—a discrepancy that resulted in significant reconciliation payments from the plans to the Part D program. These reconciliation amounts reduced the total payments to the plans in 2007 and 2008, resulting in per capita drug cost growth rates that were lower than normal for those years. In contrast, actual drug spending exceeded the plan bids in 2008, resulting in more than $2 billion in additional outlays for 2009. The combination of reconciliation receipts in 2008 and additional reconciliation payments in 2009 caused the large rate of growth in the 2009 benefits. For 2010, Part D growth was negative due to the combined effects of a significant increase in the generic proportion of prescription drugs, reconciliation receipts in 2010, and reconciliation payments in 2009. The 2011 growth was higher, partially due to the slower recoupment of the advance payments from Part D under the brand-name drug discount program. Part D growth in 2012 was negative due to the delayed recoupment of 2011 advance payments, and the patent expiration of some high-cost drugs in 2012.

Table V.D1.—HI and SMI Average per Beneficiary Costs

Calendar year	Average per beneficiary costs				Average percent change[1]			
		SMI				SMI		
	HI	Part B	Part D	Total	HI	Part B	Part D	Total
Historical data:								
1970	$255	$101	—	$356	13.4%	14.8%	—	13.8%
1975	462	180	—	642	12.6	12.2	—	12.5
1980	895	390	—	1,285	14.1	16.7	—	14.9
1985	1,554	768	—	2,322	11.7	14.5	—	12.6
1990	1,963	1,304	—	3,267	4.8	11.2	—	7.1
1995	3,130	1,823	—	4,953	9.8	6.9	—	8.7
2000	3,272	2,381	—	5,653	0.9	5.5	—	2.7
2005	4,262	3,754	—	8,016	5.4	9.5	—	7.2
2006	4,388	4,111	$1,708	10,208	3.0	9.5	—	27.3
2007	4,548	4,293	1,556	10,397	3.6	4.4	-8.9%	1.9
2008	5,145	4,296	1,504	10,945	13.1	0.1	-3.3	5.3
2009	5,172	4,721	1,798	11,692	0.5	9.9	19.6	6.8
2010	5,161	4,779	1,775	11,715	-0.2	1.2	-1.3	0.2
2011	5,212	4,938	1,868	12,019	1.0	3.3	5.3	2.6
2012	5,227	5,097	1,779	12,103	0.3	3.2	-4.8	0.7
Intermediate es imates:								
2013	5,134	5,155	1,846	12,135	-1.8	1.1	3.8	0.3
2014	5,057	5,049	2,077	12,183	-1.5	-2.1	12.5	0.4
2015	5,048	5,184	2,165	12,396	-0.2	2.7	4.2	1.7
2016	5,202	5,401	2,267	12,870	3.1	4.2	4.7	3.8
2017	5,369	5,639	2,412	13,420	3.2	4.4	6.4	4.3
2018	5,621	5,932	2,562	14,115	4.7	5.2	6.2	5.2
2019	5,815	6,221	2,720	14,755	3.5	4.9	6.2	4.5
2020	6,045	6,553	2,904	15,502	4.0	5.3	6.7	5.1
2021	6,297	6,901	3,079	16,276	4.2	5.3	6.0	5.0
2022	6,643	7,392	3,287	17,322	5.5	7.1	6.8	6.4

[1]Percent changes for 1970 represent the average annual increases from 1967 (the first full year of trust fund operations) through 1970. Similarly, percent changes shown for 1975, 1980, 1985, 1990, 1995, 2000, and 2005 represent the average annual increase over the 5-year period ending in the indicated year.

On average, annual increases in per beneficiary costs have been greater for SMI Part B than for HI during the previous 4 decades—by approximately 1.0 percent, 4.7 percent, 1.0 percent, and 2.5 percent per year in the 1970s, 1980s, 1990s, and 2000s, respectively. The HI increase remains lower than the SMI Part B increase in 2013 and later (with the exception of 2014, which reflects the scheduled 2014 reduction in physician fees) due to the productivity adjustment and other payment rate adjustments affecting all of the HI providers but only some of the SMI Part B providers.

For 2014, the projected SMI Part B increase is almost certain to be substantially understated as a result of the large reduction in physician payments required under current law. Under the sustainable growth rate system (SGR), the physician payment update is projected to be −24.7 percent in 2014. Legislation to prevent or ameliorate such an outcome is highly likely. Note that the rapid growth rates in the 1970s and 1980s are not expected to recur for either HI or SMI Part B, due to more moderate inflation rates and the conversion of Medicare's remaining cost-based reimbursement mechanisms to prospective payment systems as part of the Balanced Budget Act of 1997, and due to the physician updates under the SGR. In addition, the reduction in Medicare price updates for most categories of providers will reduce growth rates by an average of 0.8 percent annually through 2022. The growth rates also reflect the impact of the mandatory sequestration process that is required under current law, per the Budget Control Act of 2011 as amended by the American Taxpayer Relief Act of 2012, which reduces Medicare expenditures by 2 percent per year. This results in a negative increase in 2013 for HI, followed by further negative increases in 2014 and 2015, due to enacted legislation. Specifically, the growth rates reflect a 2-percent reduction in inpatient hospital spending to recoup overpayments resulting from changes in documentation and coding during 2008-2010, per the American Taxpayer Relief Act of 2012; and further cuts to disproportionate share payments in 2015, required by the Affordable Care Act.

The reconciliation adjustments for Part D mentioned above, and the SGR penalties and bonuses for Part B, also distort the comparison of average annual increases from year to year. The average annual increases in Part D per beneficiary costs are expected to be somewhat greater than for HI or SMI Part B for the period 2013-2022, in part because the savings provisions of the Affordable Care Act affect Parts A and B only.

E. MEDICARE COST SHARING AND PREMIUM AMOUNTS

HI beneficiaries who use covered services may be subject to deductible and coinsurance requirements. A beneficiary is responsible for an inpatient hospital deductible amount, which is deducted from the amount payable by the HI trust fund to the hospital, for inpatient hospital services furnished in a spell of illness. When a beneficiary receives such services for more than 60 days during a spell of illness, he or she is responsible for a coinsurance amount equal to one-fourth of the inpatient hospital deductible for each of days 61-90 in the hospital. After 90 days in a spell of illness, each individual has 60 lifetime reserve days of coverage, for which the coinsurance amount is equal to one-half of the inpatient hospital deductible. A beneficiary is responsible for a coinsurance amount equal to one-eighth of the inpatient hospital deductible for each of days 21-100 of skilled nursing facility services furnished during a spell of illness. No cost sharing is required for home health or hospice services.

Most persons aged 65 and older and many disabled individuals under age 65 are insured for HI benefits without payment of any premium. The Social Security Act provides that certain aged and disabled persons who are not insured may voluntarily enroll, subject to the payment of a monthly premium. In addition, since 1994, voluntary enrollees may qualify for a reduced premium if they have at least 30 quarters of covered employment.

Table V.E1 shows the historical levels of the HI deductible, coinsurance amounts, and premiums, as well as projected values for future years based on the intermediate set of assumptions used in estimating the operations of the trust funds. Certain anomalies in these values resulted from specific trust fund features in particular years (for example, the effect of the Medicare Catastrophic Coverage Act of 1988 on 1989 values). The values listed in the table for future years are estimates, and the actual amounts are likely to be somewhat different as experience emerges.

Table V.E1.—HI Cost-Sharing and Premium Amounts

| Year | Inpatient hospital deductible[1] | Inpatient daily coinsurance[1] | | SNF daily coinsurance[1] | Monthly premium | |
		Days 61-90	Lifetime reserve days		Standard[2]	Reduced[1]
Historical data:						
1967	$40	$10	—	$5.00	—	—
1968	40	10	$20	5.00	—	—
1969	44	11	22	5.50	—	—
1970	52	13	26	6.50	—	—
1971	60	15	30	7.50	—	—
1972	68	17	34	8.50	—	—
1973	72	18	36	9.00	$33	—
1974	84	21	42	10.50	36	—
1975	92	23	46	11.50	40	—
1976	104	26	52	13.00	45	—
1977	124	31	62	15.50	54	—
1978	144	36	72	18.00	63	—
1979	160	40	80	20.00	69	—
1980	180	45	90	22.50	78	—
1981	204	51	102	25.50	89	—
1982	260	65	130	32.50	113	—
1983	304	76	152	38.00	113	—
1984	356	89	178	44.50	155	—
1985	400	100	200	50.00	174	—
1986	492	123	246	61.50	214	—
1987	520	130	260	65.00	226	—
1988	540	135	270	67.50	234	—
1989[3]	560	—	—	25.50	156	—
1990	592	148	296	74.00	175	—
1991	628	157	314	78.50	177	—
1992	652	163	326	81.50	192	—
1993	676	169	338	84.50	221	—
1994	696	174	348	87.00	245	$184
1995	716	179	358	89.50	261	183
1996	736	184	368	92.00	289	188
1997	760	190	380	95.00	311	187
1998	764	191	382	95.50	309	170
1999	768	192	384	96.00	309	170
2000	776	194	388	97.00	301	166
2001	792	198	396	99.00	300	165
2002	812	203	406	101.50	319	175
2003	840	210	420	105.00	316	174
2004	876	219	438	109.50	343	189
2005	912	228	456	114.00	375	206
2006	952	238	476	119.00	393	216
2007	992	248	496	124.00	410	226
2008	1,024	256	512	128.00	423	233
2009	1,068	267	534	133.50	443	244
2010	1,100	275	550	137.50	461	254
2011	1,132	283	566	141.50	450	248
2012	1,156	289	578	144.50	451	248
2013	1,184	296	592	148.00	441	243
Intermediate estimates:						
2014	1,220	305	610	152.50	421	232
2015	1,268	317	634	158.50	422	232
2016	1,320	330	660	165.00	435	239
2017	1,364	341	682	170.50	451	248
2018	1,408	352	704	176.00	471	259
2019	1,448	362	724	181.00	487	268
2020	1,500	375	750	187.50	506	278
2021	1,556	389	778	194.50	527	290
2022	1,608	402	804	201.00	558	307

[1]Amounts shown are effective for calendar years.

[2]Amounts shown for 1967-1982 are for the 12-month periods ending June 30; amounts shown for 1983 are for the period July 1, 1982 through December 31, 1983; amounts shown for 1984 and later are for calendar years.
[3]Anomalies in the 1989 values are due to the Medicare Catastrophic Coverage Act of 1988. Most of the provisions of the Act were repealed the following year.

The *Federal Register* notice announcing the HI deductible and coinsurance amounts for 2013 included an estimate of the aggregate cost to HI beneficiaries for the changes in the deductible and coinsurance amounts from 2012 to 2013. At the time of the notice's publication, it was estimated that in 2013 there would be 8.44 million inpatient deductibles paid at $1,184 each, 2.17 million inpatient days subject to coinsurance at $296 per day (for hospital days 61 through 90), 1.08 million lifetime reserve days subject to coinsurance at $592 per day, and 45.72 million extended care days subject to coinsurance at $148.00 per day. Similarly, it was estimated that in 2012 there would be 8.19 million deductibles paid at $1,156 each, 2.11 million days subject to coinsurance at $289 per day (for hospital days 61 through 90), 1.04 million lifetime reserve days subject to coinsurance at $578 per day, and 45.72 million extended care days subject to coinsurance at $144.50 per day. The total increase in cost to beneficiaries was estimated to be $1,031 million due to (i) the increase in the inpatient deductible and coinsurance amounts; and (ii) the change in the number of deductibles and daily coinsurance amounts paid.

Table V.E2 displays the SMI cost-sharing and premium amounts for Parts B and D. The projected values for future years are based on the intermediate set of assumptions used in estimating the operations of the Part B and Part D accounts. As a result, these values are estimates, and the actual amounts are likely to be somewhat different as experience emerges. The Part B premiums include a margin for the likely legislative override of the scheduled reduction in physician payment rates for 2014 under the sustainable growth rate system. Legislation has overridden physician payment reductions otherwise required for each of the past 11 years.

The premiums shown in table V.E2 include an above-average contingency margin in recognition of the strong likelihood of legislation that would increase Part B costs after financing for a year had been established. The premiums for 2010 and 2011 also reflect significant additional increases designed to offset the loss of revenues attributable to the "hold-harmless" provision, as described in section III.C and later in this appendix.

Table V.E2.—SMI Cost-Sharing and Premium Amounts

| Calendar year | Part B | | Part D | | | |
	Standard monthly premium[1]	Annual deductible[2]	Base beneficiary premium	Deductible	Initial benefit limit	Catastrophic threshold
Historical data:						
1967	$3.00	$50	—	—	—	—
1968	4.00	50	—	—	—	—
1969	4.00	50	—	—	—	—
1970	4.00	50	—	—	—	—
1971	5.30	50	—	—	—	—
1972	5.60	50	—	—	—	—
1973	5.80	60	—	—	—	—
1974	6.30[3]	60	—	—	—	—
1975	6.70	60	—	—	—	—
1976	6.70	60	—	—	—	—
1977	7.20	60	—	—	—	—
1978	7.70	60	—	—	—	—
1979	8.20	60	—	—	—	—
1980	8.70	60	—	—	—	—
1981	9.60	60	—	—	—	—
1982	11.00	75	—	—	—	—
1983	12.20	75	—	—	—	—
1984	14.60	75	—	—	—	—
1985	15.50	75	—	—	—	—
1986	15.50	75	—	—	—	—
1987	17.90	75	—	—	—	—
1988	24.80	75	—	—	—	—
1989[4]	31.90	75	—	—	—	—
1990	28.60	75	—	—	—	—
1991	29.90	100	—	—	—	—
1992	31.80	100	—	—	—	—
1993	36.60	100	—	—	—	—
1994	41.10	100	—	—	—	—
1995	46.10	100	—	—	—	—
1996	42.50	100	—	—	—	—
1997	43.80	100	—	—	—	—
1998	43.80	100	—	—	—	—
1999	45.50	100	—	—	—	—
2000	45.50	100	—	—	—	—
2001	50.00	100	—	—	—	—
2002	54.00	100	—	—	—	—
2003	58.70	100	—	—	—	—
2004	66.60	100	—	—	—	—
2005	78.20	110	—	—	—	—
2006	88.50	124	$32.20	$250	$2,250	$3,600
2007	93.50	131	27.35	265	2,400	3,850
2008	96.40	135	27.93	275	2,510	4,050
2009	96.40	135	30.36	295	2,700	4,350
2010	110.50	155	31.94	310	2,830	4,550
2011	115.40	162	32.34	310	2,840	4,550
2012	99.90	140	31.08	320	2,930	4,700
2013	104.90	147	31.17	325	2,970	4,750
Intermediate estimates:						
2014	104.90	147	33.93	310[5]	2,850[5]	4,550[5]
2015	110.70	155	36.68	320	2,920	4,650
2016	115.40	162	38.66	335	3,050	4,850
2017	120.90	170	41.28	350	3,190	5,100
2018	127.40	179	43.99	370	3,360	5,350
2019	134.40	189	46.99	390	3,560	5,600
2020	141.80	199	50.18	415	3,780	6,000
2021	150.00	210	53.28	440	4,010	6,350
2022	160.50	225	56.59	470	4,260	6,750

[1]Amounts shown for 1967-1982 are for the 12-month periods ending June 30; amounts shown for 1983 are for the period July 1, 1982 through December 31, 1983; amounts shown for 1984 and later are for calendar years.
[2]Prior to the Medicare Modernization Act, the Part B deductible was fixed by statute and had only occasionally been adjusted. The Medicare Modernization Act raised the deductible to $110 in 2005 and specified that it be indexed by average per beneficiary Part B expenditures thereafter.
[3]In accordance with limitations on the costs of health care imposed under Phase III of the Economic Stabilization program, the standard premium rates for July and August 1973 were set at $5.80 and $6.10, respectively. Effective September 1973, the rate increased to $6.30.
[4]Anomalies in the 1989 values are due to the Medicare Catastrophic Coverage Act of 1988. Most of the provisions of the Act were repealed the following year.
[5]These amounts have already been determined.

The Part B monthly premiums displayed in table V.E2 are the standard premium rates paid by most Part B enrollees. However, there are three provisions that alter the premium rate for certain Part B enrollees. First, there is a premium surcharge for those beneficiaries who enroll after their initial enrollment period. Second, beginning in 2007, there is a higher "income-related" premium for those individuals whose modified adjusted gross income exceeds a specified threshold. Table V.E3 displays these Part B income-related premium amounts for 2007-2022, based on the intermediate set of assumptions.

Table V.E3.—Part B Income-Related Premium Amounts[1]

| Calendar year | Ul imate percentage of program costs represented by premium | | | |
	35%	50%	65%	80%
Historical data:				
2007	$105.80	$124.40	$142.90	$161.40
2008	122.20	160.90	199.70	238.40
2009	134.90	192.70	250 50	308.30
2010	154.70	221.00	287 30	353.60
2011	161.50	230.70	299 90	369.10
2012	139.90	199.80	259.70	319.70
2013	146.90	209.80	272.70	335.70
Intermediate es imates:				
2014	146.90	209.80	272.70	335.70
2015	154.90	221.30	287.70	354.10
2016	161.60	230.80	300 00	369.30
2017	169.20	241.70	314 20	386.70
2018	178.30	254.70	331.10	407.50
2019	188.20	268.80	349.40	430.10
2020	198.50	283.60	368.70	453.80
2021	209.90	299.90	389 90	479.80
2022	224.70	321.00	417 30	513.60

[1]Includes the impact of the 3-year transition in 2007 and 2008.

In 2012 the initial threshold is $85,000 for an individual tax return and $170,000 for a joint return. The thresholds are not indexed to inflation in the years 2011-2019 but are thereafter. Individuals exceeding the threshold will pay premiums covering 35, 50, 65, or 80 percent of the average program cost for aged beneficiaries, depending on their income level, compared to the standard premium covering 25 percent.

Lastly, Part B premiums may also vary from the standard rate because a "hold-harmless" provision can lower the premium rate for individuals who have their premiums deducted from their Social Security benefits. On an individual basis, this provision limits the dollar increase in the Part B premium to the dollar increase in the individual's Social Security benefit. As a result, the person affected pays a lower Part B premium, and the net amount of the individual's Social Security benefit does not decrease despite the greater increase in the premium.

Most services under Part B are subject to an annual deductible and coinsurance. The annual deductible was set by statute through 2005. Thereafter, it increases with the increase in the Part B aged actuarial rate to approximate the growth in per capita Part B expenditures.[99] After meeting the deductible, the beneficiary pays an amount equal to the product of the coinsurance percentage and the remaining allowed charges. The coinsurance percentage is 20 percent for most services For those services not subject to the deductible or coinsurance (clinical lab tests, home health agency services, and most preventive care services), the beneficiary pays nothing.

The Part D average premiums displayed in table V.E2 are the estimated base beneficiary premiums. For 2006, the base beneficiary premium was calculated based on a national average plan bid that gave each bid an equal weight. The actual premium that a beneficiary pays varies according to the plan in which the beneficiary enrolls. Some pay lower premiums than those displayed in table V.E2, and others pay more. The average premium rate that beneficiaries paid in 2006 was roughly $23. In 2007 and 2008, the national average was calculated under a transitional demonstration program using 80 percent and then 40 percent of the equally weighted bids and 20 percent and then 60 percent of the enrollment-weighted average bid. As a result of this calculation, the average premium rate paid by beneficiaries fell to about $22 in 2007 and increased to $24 in 2008. Starting in 2009, the national average plan bid is based on the enrollment-weighted average. The average premiums paid in 2009

---

[99]The current mechanism to index the Part B deductible has technical computational issues mainly due to the timing of the calculation. Under current law, the Part B deductible for any given year is indexed by the increase in the monthly aged actuarial rate for that same year, which represents estimated monthly per capita expenditures. However, these expenditures are dependent on the Part B deductible, which isn't known until the actuarial rate is determined. The result is circularity in the modeling process. A possible alternative approach is to index the Part B deductible using the increase in the actuarial rate from the prior year, which is already known when the determination is made, thereby removing any circularity.

and 2010 were around $28 and $30, respectively. The average premium for 2011 was approximately $31 and fell to about $30 in both 2012 and 2013 primarily due to the patent expiration of several high-volume prescription drugs, and a lower projected trend for 2013. Since beneficiaries may switch plans each year once the premium rates become known, it is assumed that the estimated average premium rate paid by beneficiaries will continue to be slightly less than the base beneficiary premium in future years.

Similar to Part B, there are two provisions that affect the premium rate for certain Part D beneficiaries. First, there is a Part D late enrollment penalty for those beneficiaries enrolling after their initial enrollment period. Second, starting in 2011, individuals whose modified adjusted gross income exceeds the same thresholds applicable to the Part B premium, pay an "income-related" premium in addition to the premium charged by the plan in which the individual enrolled. The amount of the "income-related" premium adjustment is dependent on the individual's income level, and the extra premium amount is the difference between 35, 50, 65, or 80 percent and 25.5 percent, applied to the National Average Monthly Bid Amount adjusted for reinsurance. Table V.E4 displays the historical and projected Part D income-related premium adjustment amounts for 2011-2022, based on the intermediate set of assumptions.

Table V.E4.—Part D Income-Related Premium Adjustment Amounts

Calendar year	Percentage of program costs represented by premium			
	35%	50%	65%	80%
Historical data:				
2011	$12.00	$31.10	$50.10	$69.10
2012	11.60	29.90	48.10	66.40
2013	11.60	29.90	48.30	66.60
Intermediate es imates:				
2014	12.60	32.60	52.60	72.50
2015	13.70	35.20	56.80	78.40
2016	14.40	37.10	59.90	82.60
2017	15.40	39.70	63.90	88.20
2018	16.40	42.30	68.10	94.00
2019	17.50	45.20	72.80	100.40
2020	18.70	48.20	77.70	107.20
2021	19.80	51.20	82.50	113.90
2022	21.10	54.40	87.70	120.90

In addition, there are premium and cost-sharing subsidies for those beneficiaries with incomes less than 150 percent of the Federal poverty level and with assets in 2013 less than $13,300 for an individual and $26,580 for a couple. The asset thresholds are indexed in subsequent years by the Consumer Price Index (CPI). Under the current statutory adjustment formula, the asset figures for 2013 increase for both an individual and a couple as a result of increases in the CPI.

Under standard Part D coverage, there is an initial deductible. After meeting the deductible, the beneficiary pays 25 percent of the remaining costs up to the initial benefit limit. Beyond this limit, prior to 2011, the beneficiary paid all the drug costs until his or her total out-of-pocket expenditures reached the catastrophic threshold. (This total includes the deductible and coinsurance payments for expenses up to the initial benefit limit.) The ACA will gradually fill in the coverage gap from 2011 until 2020, when beneficiaries will pay 25 percent of the drug costs between the deductible and the catastrophic threshold under the standard coverage. In 2013, after reaching the catastrophic threshold, the beneficiary pays the greater of (i) 5 percent of the drug cost; or (ii) $2.65 for generic or preferred multiple-source drugs or $6.60 for preferred single-source drugs. The latter copayment amounts from 2013 are indexed annually by per enrollee Part D average costs. Beneficiaries qualifying for the Part D low-income subsidy pay substantially reduced premium and cost-sharing amounts. Many Part D plans offer alternative coverage that differs from the standard coverage described above. The majority of beneficiaries have not enrolled in the standard benefit design but rather in plans with low or no deductibles, flat copayments for covered drugs, and, in some cases, partial coverage in the coverage gap.

F. MEDICARE AND SOCIAL SECURITY TRUST FUNDS AND THE FEDERAL BUDGET

One can view the financial operations of Medicare and Social Security in the context of the programs' trust funds or in the context of the overall Federal budget. The financial status of the trust funds differs fundamentally from the impact of these programs on the budget, and people often misunderstand the relationship between these two perspectives. Each perspective is appropriate and important for its intended purpose; this appendix attempts to clarify their roles and relationship.

By law, the annual reports of the Medicare and Social Security Boards of Trustees to Congress focus on the financial status of the programs' trust funds—that is, whether these funds have sufficient revenues and assets to enable the payment of benefits and administrative expenses. This "trust fund perspective" is important because the existence of trust fund assets provides the statutory authority to make such payments without the need for an appropriation from Congress. Medicare and Social Security benefits can be paid only if the relevant trust fund has sufficient income or assets.

The trust fund perspective does not encompass the interrelationship between the Medicare and Social Security trust funds and the overall Federal budget. The budget is a comprehensive display of all Federal activities, whether financed through trust funds or from the general fund of the Treasury. This broader focus may appropriately be termed the "budget perspective" or "government-wide perspective" and is officially presented in the *Budget of the United States Government* and in the *Financial Report of the United States Government*.

Payroll taxes, income taxes on Social Security benefits, Medicare premiums, and special State payments to Medicare finance the majority of Medicare and Social Security costs. In addition to these "earmarked" receipts from workers, employers, beneficiaries, and States, Medicare and Social Security rely on Federal general fund revenues for some of their financing (principally for the SMI trust fund), and the trust funds are credited with interest payments on their accumulated assets as well. The financial status of a trust fund appropriately considers all sources of financing provided under current law for that fund, including the availability of trust fund assets that Medicare or Social Security can use to meet program expenditures. From a budget perspective, however, general fund transfers, interest payments to the trust funds, and asset redemptions represent a draw on other Federal resources for which there is no earmarked source of revenue from the public.

In the past, general fund and interest payments for Medicare and Social Security were relatively small. These amounts have increased substantially over the last 2 decades, however, and the expected rapid future growth of Medicare and Social Security will make their interaction with the Federal budget increasingly important. As the difference between earmarked and total trust fund revenues grows, the financial operations of Social Security and Medicare can appear markedly different depending on which of the two perspectives one uses.[100]

Illustration with Actual Data for 2012

Table V.F1 illustrates the trust fund and budget perspectives using actual data on Federal financial operations for fiscal year (FY) 2012. The first three columns show revenues and expenditures for HI, SMI, and OASDI, respectively, and the fourth column is the sum of these three columns. The fifth column shows total revenues and expenditures for all other government programs (including the general fund account of the Treasury), and the final column is the sum of the "Combined" and "Other Government" columns. The table shows earmarked revenues from the public separately from revenues from other government accounts (general revenue transfers and interest credits). Note that the transfers and interest credits received by the trust funds appear in total as negative entries under the "Other Government" column and are thus offsetting when summed for the total budget in the final column. These two intragovernmental transactions are key to the differences between the two perspectives.

---

[100]A more complete treatment of this topic appears in the *2012 Financial Report of the United States Government* at www.fms.treas.gov/fr/ and in a May 2009 Treasury report titled "Social Security and Medicare Trust Funds and the Federal Budget" at http://www.treasury.gov/resource-center/economic-policy/ss-medicare/Documents/budget_trust_fund_perspectives_2009.pdf. Additional information is available in a Health Care Financing Review article titled "Medicare Financial Status, Budget Impact, and Sustainability: Which Concept Is Which?", at http://www.cms.gov/Research-Statistics-Data-and-Systems/Research/HealthCareFinancingReview/Downloads/05-06Winpg127.pdf.

Table V.F1.—Annual Revenues and Expenditures
for Medicare and Social Security Trust Funds and the Total Federal Budget,
Fiscal Year 2012
(In billions)

Revenue and expenditures categories	Trust funds				Other government	Total[1]
	HI	SMI	OASDI	Combined		
Revenues from public:						
Payroll and benefit taxes	$223.4	—	$613.3	$836.7	—	$836.7
Premiums[2]	6.2	$66.3	—	72.4	—	72.4
Other taxes, fees, and payments[3]	—	11.1	—	11.1	$1,529.9	1,541.1
Total	229.6	77.4	613.3	920.2	1,529.9	2,450.2
Total expenditures to public[4]	258.2	291.9	773.2	1,323.3	2,213.8	3,537.1
Net Results for Budget Perspective	**−28.6**	**−214.5**	**−160.0**	**−403.1**	**−683.9**	**−1,087.0**
Revenues from other government accounts:						
Transfers	0.9	210.5	112.2	323.6	−323.6	—
Interest credits	11.3	2.9	112.4	126.6	−126.6	—
Total	12.2	213.5	224.6	450.2	−450.2	—
Net Results for Trust Fund Perspective	**−16.4**	**−1.0**	**64.6**	**47.1**	**n/a**	**n/a**

[1]This column is the sum of the preceding two columns and shows data for the total Federal budget. The figure $1,087.0 billion was he total Federal budget deficit for fiscal year 2012.
[2]Includes Part D premiums paid directly to plans, which are not displayed on Treasury statements and are estimated.
[3]Includes Part D State transfers.
[4]The OASDI figure includes $4.7 billion transferred to the Railroad Retirement Board.

Notes: 1. For comparison, HI taxable payroll, OASDI taxable payroll, and GDP were $7,097 billion, $5,697 billion, and $15,700 billion, respectively, in 2012.
2. Totals do not necessarily equal the sums of rounded components.
3. "n/a" indicates not applicable.

The trust fund perspective reflects both categories of revenues for each trust fund. For HI, revenues from the public plus transfers/credits from other government accounts were $16.4 billion less than total expenditures in FY 2012, as shown at the bottom of the first column.[101] For the SMI trust fund, the statutory revenues from beneficiary premiums, State transfers, general revenue transfers, and interest earnings collectively were $1.0 billion less than expenditures in FY 2012. Note that it is appropriate to view the general revenue transfers from other government accounts as financial resources from the trust fund perspective since they are available under current law to help meet trust fund outlays. For OASDI, total trust fund revenues from all sources (including $112.4 billion in interest payments and $112.2 billion in general fund reimbursements) exceeded total expenditures by $64.6 billion.

---

[101]The Department of Treasury invests surplus revenues from the public over expenditures to the public in special Treasury securities and thereby represent a loan from the trust funds to the general fund of the Federal Government. These loans reduce the amount that the general fund has to borrow from the public to finance a deficit (or likewise increase the amount of debt paid off if there is a surplus). Interest is credited to the trust funds while the securities are being held. Trust fund securities can be redeemed at any time if needed to help meet program expenditures. Thus, the accumulation of fund assets creates budget commitments for future years when interest earnings and asset redemptions are used to meet expenditures.

From the government-wide or budget perspective, only earmarked revenues received from the public—principally taxes on payroll and benefits, plus premiums—and expenditures made to the public are important for the final balance.[102] For HI, the difference between such revenues ($229.6 billion) and total expenditures made to the public ($258.2 billion) was $28.6 billion in FY 2012, indicating that HI had a negative effect on the overall budget in FY 2012. For SMI, beneficiary premiums, fees on brand-name prescription drugs to Part B, and State payments to Part D of Medicare were the only sources of revenues from the public in FY 2012 and represented only about 26 percent of total expenditures. The remaining $214.5 billion in FY 2012 outlays represented a substantial net draw on the Federal budget in that year.[103] For OASDI, the difference between revenues from the public ($613.3 billion) and total expenditures ($773.2 billion) was $160.0 billion, indicating that OASDI also had a negative effect on the overall budget last year.

Thus, from the trust fund perspective, OASDI had an annual surplus in FY 2012, and HI and SMI had deficits. From the budget perspective, HI, SMI, and OASDI each required a net draw on the budget. HI, SMI, and OASDI collectively had a trust fund surplus of $47.1 billion in FY 2012 but a net draw of $403.1 billion on the budget.

It is important to recognize that each viewpoint is appropriate for its intended purpose but that one perspective cannot be used to answer questions related to the other. In the case of SMI, under current-law financing the trust fund will always be in balance and there will always be a net draw on the Federal budget. In the case of HI, trust fund surpluses in a given year may occur with either a positive or negative direct impact on the budget for that year. Conversely, a positive or negative budget impact from HI offers minimal insight into whether its trust fund has sufficient total revenues and assets to permit payment of benefits.

The next section illustrates the magnitude of the long-range difference between projected expenditures and revenues for Medicare and Social Security from both the trust fund and budget perspectives.

---

[102]For this purpose, "the public" includes State governments since they are outside of the Federal Government.

[103]Three types of trust fund transactions constituted this net budget obligation: $210.5 billion was drawn in the form of general revenue transfers, and another $2.9 billion in interest payments, while $1.0 billion was transferred to the trust fund from the general fund through the redemption of special-issue Treasury securities in an amount equal to the trust fund deficit for the year.

Future Obligations of the Trust Funds and the Budget

Table V.F2 collects from the Medicare and OASDI Trustees Reports the present values of projected future revenues and expenditures over the next 75 years under current law. For HI and OASDI, tax revenues from the public are projected to fall short of statutory expenditures by $4.8 trillion and $12.3 trillion, respectively, in present value terms.[104]

Table V.F2.—Present Values of Projected Revenue and Cost Components
of 75-Year Open-Group Obligations for HI, SMI, and OASDI
(In trillions, as of January 1, 2013)

Revenue and expenditure categories	HI	SMI	OASDI	Combined
Revenues from public:				
Payroll and benefit taxes	$16.2	—	$48.9	$65.1
Premiums	0.0	$7.1	—	7.1
Other taxes and fees[1]	—	0.9	—	0.9
Total	16.2	8.1	48.9	73.2
Total expenditures to public	21.0	30.6	61.2	112.8
Net Results for Budget Perspective	**−4.8**	**−22.5**	**−12.3**	**−39.6**
Revenues from other government accounts:				
Transfers	0.0	22.4	0.0	22.4
Interest credits	n/a	n/a	n/a	n/a
Total	0.0	22.4	0.0	22.4
Trust fund assets on January 1, 2013	0.2	0.1	2.7	3.0
Net Results for Trust Fund Perspective	**−4.6**	**0.0**	**−9.6**	**−14.2**

[1]Includes Part B revenues from fees on manufacturers and importers of brand-name prescription drugs and Part D State transfers.

Notes: 1. For comparison, the present values of HI taxable payroll, OASDI taxable payroll, and GDP are $428.2 trillion, $372.2 trillion, and $944.2 trillion, respectively, over the next 75 years. This present value of GDP is calculated using HI-specific interest discount factors and differs slightly from the corresponding amount shown in the OASDI Trustees Report.
    2. Medicare present values are calculated using HI-specific discount factors, while OASDI amounts use OASDI-specific discount factors.
    3. Totals do not necessarily equal the sums of rounded components.
    4. "n/a" indicates not applicable.
    5. "0.0" indicates an amount of less than $50 billion.

From the budget perspective, these are the additional amounts that would be necessary in order to pay HI and OASDI benefits and other costs at the level scheduled under current law over the next 75 years. From the trust fund perspective, the amounts needed are smaller by the value of the accumulated assets in the respective trust funds— $0.2 trillion for HI and $2.7 trillion for OASDI—that could be drawn down to cover a part of the projected shortfall in tax revenues. Two points about this comparison are important to note:

---

[104]Interest income is not a factor in this table, as dollar amounts are in present value terms.

- Other than asset redemptions and interest payments, no provision exists under current law to address the projected HI and OASDI financial imbalances. Once assets are depleted, expenditures cannot be made except to the extent covered by ongoing tax receipts.

- From a trust fund perspective, the long-range HI and OASDI deficits reflect the net imbalance after redemption of trust fund assets. From a government-wide perspective, the deficits represent the cost of redeeming those assets plus the additional legislative authorization that would be necessary to fully satisfy future scheduled benefit payments. [105]

The situation for SMI is somewhat different. SMI expenditures for Part B and Part D are projected to exceed premium and other dedicated revenues by $22.5 trillion. To keep the SMI trust fund solvent for the next 75 years will require general fund transfers of this amount, and these transfers represent a formal budget requirement under current law. From the trust fund perspective, the present value of projected total premiums and general revenues is about equal to the present value of future expenditures.

From the 75-year budget perspective, the present value of the additional resources that would be necessary to meet projected expenditures, at current-law levels for the three programs combined, is $39.6 trillion. [106] To put this very large figure in perspective, it would represent 4.2 percent of the present value of projected GDP over the same period ($944 trillion). The components of the $39.6-trillion total are as follows:

---

[105]In practice, the long-range HI and OASDI deficits could be addressed by reducing expenditures, increasing payroll or other earmarked tax revenues, implementing a general revenue subsidy, or some combination of such measures. For Medicare, in particular, lawmakers have frequently enacted legislation to slow the growth of expenditures.

[106]As noted previously, the long-range HI and OASDI financial imbalances could instead be partially addressed by expenditure reductions, thereby reducing the need for additional revenues. Similarly, SMI expenditure reductions would reduce the need for general fund transfers.

Unfunded Medicare and OASDI obligations
(trust fund perspective)[107] .... $14.2 trillion (1.5% of GDP)
HI, SMI, and OASDI asset redemptions.............. $3.0 trillion (0.3% of GDP)
SMI and OASDI general revenue financing .... $22.4 trillion (2.4% of GDP)

These resource needs would be in addition to the payroll taxes, benefit taxes, and premium payments scheduled under current law. As noted, the asset redemptions and SMI general revenue transfers represent formal budget commitments under current law, but no provision exists for covering the HI and OASDI trust fund deficits once assets are depleted.

As discussed elsewhere in this report, there is a significant likelihood that the projected HI and SMI expenditures are substantially understated as a result of potentially unsustainable elements of current law. Although this issue does not affect the nature of the budget and trust fund perspectives described in this appendix, it is important to note that actual long-range present values for HI expenditures and SMI expenditures and revenues are likely to exceed the amounts shown in table V.F2 by a substantial margin.

---

[107]Additional revenues and/or expenditure reductions totaling $14.2 trillion, together with $3.0 trillion in asset redemptions, would cover the projected financial imbalance but would leave the HI and OASDI trust funds depleted at the end of the 75-year period. The long-range actuarial deficits for HI and OASDI include a cost factor to allow for a normal level of fund assets. See section III.B3 in this report, and section IV.B4 in the OASDI Trustees Report, for the numerical relationship between the actuarial deficit and the "unfunded obligations" of each program.

G. INFINITE HORIZON PROJECTIONS

Consistent with the practice of previous reports, this report focuses on the 75-year period from 2013 to 2087 for the evaluation of the long-run financial status of the Medicare program. The estimates are for the "open-group" population—all persons who will participate during the period as either taxpayers or beneficiaries, or both—and consist of payments from, and on behalf of, employees now in the workforce, as well as those who will enter the workforce over the next 75 years.

Experts have noted that limiting the projections to 75 years understates the magnitude of the long-range unfunded obligations because summary measures (such as the actuarial balance and open-group unfunded obligations) reflect the full amount of taxes paid by the next two or three generations of workers, but not the full amount of their benefits. One approach to addressing the limitations of 75-year summary measures is to extend the projection horizon indefinitely, so that the overall results reflect the projected costs and revenues after the first 75 years.[108] Such extended projections can also help indicate whether the financial imbalance would be improving or continuing to worsen beyond the normal 75-year period.

Table V.G1 presents estimates of HI unfunded obligations that extend to the infinite horizon. The extension assumes that the current-law HI program and the demographic and economic trends used for the 75-year projection continue indefinitely except that average HI expenditures per beneficiary increase at the same rate as GDP per capita less the productivity adjustments beginning in 2087. If the slower HI price updates under the ACA can continue indefinitely then the HI financial imbalance would actually improve beyond the 75-year period. Specifically, under these assumptions, extending the calculations beyond 2087 *subtracts* $1.1 trillion in unfunded obligations from the amount estimated through 2087. Over the infinite horizon, the HI program thus has a projected deficit of $3.5 trillion. This amount represents 0.6 percent of the present value of future HI taxable payroll over the infinite horizon, or 0.2 percent of GDP.

---

[108]The calculation of present values, in effect, applies successively less weight to future amounts over time, through the process of interest discounting. For example, the weights associated with the 25th, 75th, and 200th years of the projection would be about 29 percent, 2 percent, and 0.0015 percent, respectively, of the weight for the first year. In this way, it is possible to calculate a finite summary measure for an infinite projection period.

**Table V.G1.—Unfunded HI Obligations from Program Inception
through the Infinite Horizon**
[Present values as of January 1, 2013; dollar amounts in trillions]

	Present value	As a percentage of:	
		HI taxable payroll	GDP
Unfunded obliga ions through the infinite horizon[1]	$3.5	0.6%	0.2%
Unfunded obliga ions from program inception through 2087[1]	4.6	1.1	0.5

[1]Present value of future expenditures less income, reduced by the amount of trust fund assets at the beginning of the period.

Notes: 1. The present values of future HI taxable payroll for 2013-2087 and for 2013 through the infinite horizon are $428.2 trillion and $664.1 trillion, respectively.
2. The present values of GDP for 2013-2087 and for 2013 through the infinite horizon are $944 2 trillion and $1,559.1 trillion, respectively. (These present values differ slightly from the corresponding amounts shown in he OASDI Trustees Report due to the use of HI-specific interest discount factors.)
3. Totals do not necessarily equal the sums of rounded components.

It is possible to separate the projected HI unfunded obligation over the infinite horizon into the portions associated with current participants versus future participants. The first line of table V.G2 shows the present value of future expenditures less future taxes for current participants, including both beneficiaries and covered workers. Subtracting the current value of the HI trust fund (the accumulated value of past HI taxes less outlays) results in a "closed group" unfunded obligation of $9.4 trillion. In contrast, the projected difference between taxes and expenditures for future participants under current law is a surplus of $5.9 trillion.

The year-by-year HI deficits described in section III.B have shown that HI taxes will not be adequate to finance the program on a "pay-as-you-go" basis (whereby payroll taxes from today's workers provide benefits to today's beneficiaries).[109] The unfunded obligations shown in table V.G2 for current participants further indicate that their HI taxes are not adequate to cover their own future costs when they become eligible for HI benefits—and that this situation has also occurred for workers in the past. For future workers under current law, however, the compounding effects of the lower HI price updates would, if they can continue indefinitely, lower costs to the point that scheduled HI taxes would be more than sufficient. In practice, lawmakers could address the projected aggregate HI deficits by raising additional revenue or reducing benefits (or some combination of these actions). The impact of such changes on the unfunded obligation amounts for current versus future participants would depend on the specific policies selected.

---

[109]As noted previously, the HI trust fund also receives small amounts of income in the form of income taxes on OASDI benefits, interest, and general revenue reimbursements for certain uninsured beneficiaries.

**Table V.G2.—Unfunded HI Obligations for Current and Future Program Participants
through the Infinite Horizon**

[Present values as of January 1, 2013; dollar amounts in trillions]

		As a percentage of:	
	Present value	HI taxable payroll	GDP
Future expenditures less income for current participants............................	$9.6	1.4%	0.6%
Less current trust fund (income minus expenditures to date for past and current participants)......	0.2	0.0	0 0
Equals unfunded obligations for past and current participants[1]	9.4	1.4	0.6
Plus expenditures less income for future participants for the infinite horizon	−5.9	−0.9	−0.4
Equals unfunded obligations for all participants for the infinite future............	3.5	0.5	0 2

[1]This concept is also referred to as the closed-group unfunded obligation.

Notes: 1. The es imated present value of future HI taxable payroll for 2013 through the infinite horizon is $664.1 trillion.
2. The es imated present value of GDP for 2013 through the infinite horizon is $1,559.1 trillion. See note 2 in table V.G1.
3. Totals do not necessarily equal the sums of rounded components.

Tables V.G3 and V.G4 show the infinite horizon estimates for Part B. The extension assumes that the demographic and economic trends used for the 75-year projection continue indefinitely and that, similarly, the provisions of current law remain unchanged, including the sustainable growth rate formula for physician payments and the productivity adjustments to payment updates for most other providers. To simplify and stabilize the modeling for the infinite horizon, the Trustees project that average Part B expenditures per beneficiary will increase at about the same rate as GDP per capita minus 0.5 percentage point in every year, reflecting the mix of costs by provider category in 2087 and the payment rate updates applicable to each category.

Table V.G3 shows an estimated present value of Part B expenditures through the infinite horizon of $34.2 trillion, of which $21.4 trillion would occur during the first 75 years. Because such amounts, calculated over extremely long horizons, can be difficult to interpret, they are also shown as percentages of the present value of future GDP. So expressed, the corresponding figures are 2.2 percent and 2.3 percent, respectively. The table also indicates that beneficiary premiums will finance approximately 26 percent of expenditures for each time period and that fees collected related to brand-name prescription drugs will finance less than 0.2 percent. General revenues pay for the remaining 73 percent, as mandated by current law.

Table V.G3.—Unfunded Part B Obligations from Program Inception through the Infinite Horizon
[Present values as of January 1, 2013; dollar amounts in trillions]

	Present value	As a percentage of GDP
Unfunded obligations hrough the infinite horizon[1]	$0.0	0.0%
Expenditures	34.2	2.2
Income	34.2	2.2
Beneficiary premiums	9.1	0.6
General revenue contributions	25.0	1.6
Fees related to brand-name prescription drugs	0.1	0.0
Unfunded obligations from program incep ion through 2087[1]	0.0	0.0
Expenditures	21.4	2.3
Income	21.4	2.3
Beneficiary premiums	5.7	0.6
General revenue contributions	15.7	1.7
Fees related to brand-name prescription drugs	0.1	0.0

[1]Present value of future expenditures less income, reduced by the amount of trust fund assets at the beginning of the period.

Notes: 1. The present values of GDP for 2013-2087 and for 2013 through the infinite horizon are $944 2 trillion and $1,559.1 trillion, respectively. See note 2 of table V.G1.
2. Totals do not necessarily equal the sums of rounded components.

Table V.G4 shows corresponding present values separately for current versus future beneficiaries. As indicated, about 53 percent of the projected total, infinite-horizon cost is attributable to current beneficiaries, with the remaining 47 percent attributable to beneficiaries becoming eligible for Part B benefits after January 1, 2013.

Table V.G4.—Unfunded Part B Obligations
for Current and Future Program Participants through the Infinite Horizon
[Present values as of January 1, 2013; dollar amounts in trillions]

	Present value	As a percentage of GDP
Future expenditures less income for current participants	$0.1	0.0%
Expenditures	18.0	1.2
Income	17.8	1.1
Beneficiary premiums	4 8	0.3
General revenue contributions	13.1	0.8
Fees related to brand-name prescription drugs	0 0	0.0
Less current trust fund (Income minus expenditures to date for past and current participants)	0.1	0.0
Equals unfunded obligations for past and current participants[1]	0 0	0.0
Expenditures	17.9	1.1
Income	17.8	1.1
Beneficiary premiums	4.7	0.3
General revenue contributions	13.0	0.8
Fees related to brand-name prescription drugs	0 0	0.0
Plus expenditures less income for future participants for the infinite horizon	−0.1	0.0
Expenditures	16.2	1.0
Income	16.3	1.0
Beneficiary premiums	4.4	0.3
General revenue contributions	12.0	0.8
Fees related to brand-name prescription drugs	0 0	0.0
Equals unfunded obligations for all participants for the infinite future	−0.1	0.0
Expenditures	34.1	2.2
Income	34.1	2.2
Beneficiary premiums	9 0	0.6
General revenue contributions	24.9	1.6
Fees related to brand-name prescription drugs	0 0	0.0

[1] This concept is also referred to as the closed-group unfunded obligation.

Notes: 1. The es imated present value of GDP for 2013 through the infinite horizon is $1,559.1 trillion. See note 2 of table V.G1.
2 Totals do not necessarily equal the sums of rounded components.

Tables V.G5 and V.G6 present revenue and expenditures estimates for Part D that extend to the infinite horizon. The extension assumes no change to current law, and the demographic and economic trends used for the 75-year projection continue indefinitely except that average Part D expenditures per beneficiary would increase at the same rate as GDP per capita beginning in about 2087.

Table V.G5 shows an estimated present value of Part D expenditures through the infinite horizon of $19.3 trillion, of which $9.2 trillion would occur during the first 75 years. To put the estimates in perspective, they are also shown as percentages of the present value of future GDP. Expressed in this way, the corresponding figures are 1.2 percent and 1.0 percent of GDP, respectively. The table also indicates that, for each time period, beneficiary premiums would finance approximately 16 percent of expenditures and State transfers would finance 9 percent, with general revenues paying for the remaining 75 percent, as mandated by current law.

Table V.G5.—Unfunded Part D Obligations from Program Inception through the Infinite Horizon

[Present values as of January 1, 2013; dollar amounts in trillions]

	Present value	As a percentage of GDP
Unfunded obligations hrough the infinite horizon[1]	$0.0	0.0%
Expenditures	19.3	1.2
Income	19.3	1.2
Beneficiary premiums	3.1	0.2
State transfers	1.8	0.1
General revenue contributions	14.4	0.9
Unfunded obligations from program incep ion through 2087[1]	0.0	0.0
Expenditures	9.2	1.0
Income	9.2	1.0
Beneficiary premiums	1.5	0.2
State transfers	0.9	0.1
General revenue contributions	6.9	0.7

[1]Present value of future expenditures less income, reduced by the amount of trust fund assets at the beginning of the period.

Notes: 1. The present values of GDP for 2013-2087 and for 2013 through the infinite horizon are $944 2 trillion and $1,559.1 trillion, respectively. See note 2 of table V.G1.
2 Totals do not necessarily equal the sums of rounded components.

Table V.G6 shows corresponding projections separately for current versus future beneficiaries. As indicated, about 34 percent of the projected total, infinite-horizon cost is attributable to current beneficiaries, with the remaining 66 percent attributable to beneficiaries becoming eligible for Part D benefits after January 1, 2013.

Table V.G6.—Unfunded Part D Obligations
for Current and Future Program Participants through the Infinite Horizon
[Present values as of January 1, 2013; dollar amounts in trillions]

	Present value	As a percentage of GDP
Future expenditures less income for current participants	$0.0	0.0%
Expenditures	6.6	0.4
Income	6.6	0.4
Beneficiary premiums	1.1	0.1
State transfers	0.6	0.0
General revenue contributions	4.9	0.3
Less current trust fund (Income minus expenditures to date for past and current participants)	0.0	0.0
Equals unfunded obligations for past and current participants[1]	0.0	0.0
Expenditures	6.6	0.4
Income	6.6	0.4
Beneficiary premiums	1.1	0.1
State transfers	0.6	0.0
General revenue contributions	4.9	0.3
Plus expenditures less income for future participants for the infinite horizon	0.0	0.0
Expenditures	12.7	0.8
Income	12.7	0.8
Beneficiary premiums	2.0	0.1
State transfers	1.2	0.1
General revenue contributions	9.5	0.6
Equals unfunded obligations for all participants for the infinite future	0.0	0.0
Expenditures	19.3	1.2
Income	19.3	1.2
Beneficiary premiums	3.1	0.2
State transfers	1.8	0.1
General revenue contributions	14.4	0.9

[1]This concept is also referred to as the closed-group unfunded obligation.

Notes: 1. The es imated present value of GDP for 2013 through the infinite horizon is $1,559.1 trillion. See note 2 of table V.G1.
2. Totals do not necessarily equal the sums of rounded components.

H. FISCAL YEAR HISTORICAL DATA AND PROJECTIONS THROUGH 2022

Tables V.H1, V.H2, and V.H3 present detailed operations of the HI trust fund, along with Part B and Part D of the SMI trust fund, for fiscal year 2012. These tables are similar to the calendar-year operation tables displayed in sections III.B, III.C, and III.D.

Table V.H1.—Statement of Operations of the HI Trust Fund during Fiscal Year 2012
[In thousands]

Total assets of the trust fund, beginning of period	$245,797,302
Revenue:	
Payroll taxes	$204,751,782
Income from taxation of OASDI benefits	18,643,000
Interest on investments	11,268,941
Premiums collected from voluntary participants	3,400,056
Premiums collected from Medicare Advantage participants	234,406
Transfer from Railroad Retirement account	483,900
Reimbursement, transitional uninsured coverage	262,000
Reimbursement, program management general fund	226,337
Interfund interest payments[1]	1,203
Interest on reimbursements, Railroad Retirement	26,978
Other	2,726
Reimbursement, Union activity	1,214
Fraud and abuse control receipts:	
Criminal fines	1,389,127
Civil monetary penalties	15,766
Civil penalties and damages, CMS	2,294
Civil penalties and damages, Department of Justice	581,770
Asset Forfeitures, Department of Justice	20,371
3% administrative expense reimbursement, Department of Justice	18,094
3% administrative expense reimbursement, CMS	114
General fund transfer, Small Jobs Act	100,000
General fund transfer, Discretionary	167,736
Fraud and abuse appropriation for FBI	131,872
Total revenue	$241,729,685
Expenditures:	
Net benefit payments	$254,458,992
Administrative expenses:	
Treasury administrative expenses	145,962
Salaries and expenses, SSA[2]	912,880
Salaries and expenses, CMS[3]	1,027,685
Salaries and expenses, Office of the Secretary, HHS	36,005
Payment Assessment Commission, HHS	7,067
AOA MIPPA funding	11,924
CMS program management – Patient Protection and Affordable Care Act	1,201
Fraud and abuse control expenses:	
HHS Medicare integrity program	701,994
HHS Office of Inspector General	373,760
Department of Justice	52,114
FBI	126,258
HCFAC discretionary, CMS	215,379
HCFAC other HHS discretionary, CMS	4,100
HCFAC Department of Justice discretionary, CMS	35,871
HCFAC Department of Inspector General discretionary, CMS	43,860
Total administrative expenses	3,696,062
Total expenditures	$258,155,054
Net addition to the trust fund	−16,425,368
Total assets of the trust fund, end of period	$229,371,934

[1]Reflects interest adjustments on the reallocation of administrative expenses between the Medicare trust funds, the OASDI trust funds, and the general fund of the Treasury. Estimated payments are made from the trust funds, and then reconciled, with interest, the next year when the actual costs are known. A positive figure represents a transfer to the HI trust fund from the other trust funds. A negative figure represents a transfer from the HI trust fund to the other funds.

[2]For facilities, goods, and services provided by SSA.

[3]Includes administrative expenses of the intermediaries.

Note: Totals do not necessarily equal the sums of rounded components.

Table V.H2.—Statement of Operations of the Part B Account
in the SMI Trust Fund during Fiscal Year 2012
[In thousands]

Total assets of the Part B account in the trust fund, beginning of period		$72,795,521
Revenue:		
Premiums from enrollees:		
Enrollees aged 65 and over	$48,297,299	
Disabled enrollees under age 65	9,591,759	
Total premiums		57,889,058
Premiums collected from Medicare Advantage participants		207,869
Government contributions:		
Enrollees aged 65 and over	136,099,541	
Disabled enrollees under age 65	29,154,439	
Total government contributions		165,253,981
Other		2,516
Interest on investments		2,942,613
Interfund interest receipts[1]		−1,516
Annual fees – branded Rx manufacturers and importers		2,807,805
Total revenue		$229,102,326
Expenditures:		
Net Part B benefit payments		$227,198,388
Administrative expenses:		
Transfer to Medicaid[2]	602,303	
Treasury administrative expenses	504	
Salaries and expenses, CMS[3]	2,084,400	
Salaries and expenses, Office of the Secretary, HHS	36,005	
Salaries and expenses, SSA	999,531	
Medicare Payment Advisory Commission	4,711	
Railroad Re irement administrative expenses	10,247	
AOA MIPPA Funding	10,507	
CMS program management – ACA	1,930	
Total administrative expenses		3,750,138
Total expenditures		$230,948,527
Net addition to the trust fund		−1,846,201
Total assets of the Part B account in the trust fund, end of period		$70,949,320

[1]Reflects interest adjustments on the reallocation of administrative expenses between the Medicare trust funds, the OASDI trust funds, and the general fund of the Treasury. Estimated payments are made from he trust funds, and then reconciled, with interest, the next year when the actual costs are known. A positive figure represents a transfer to the Part B account in the SMI trust fund from the other trust funds. A negative figure represents a transfer from the Part B account in the SMI trust fund to the other funds.
[2]Represents amount transferred from the Part B account in the SMI trust fund to Medicaid to pay the Part B premium for certain qualified individuals, as legislated by the Balanced Budget Act of 1997.
[3]Includes administrative expenses of the carriers and intermediaries.

Note: Totals do not necessarily equal the sums of rounded components.

**Table V.H3—Statement of Operations of the Part D Account
in the SMI Trust Fund during Fiscal Year 2012**

[In thousands]

Total assets of the Part D account in the trust fund, beginning of period		$31,061
Revenue:		
Premiums from enrollees		
Premiums deducted from Social Security benefits	$2,955,214	
Premiums paid directly to plans[1]	5,208,640	
Total premiums		8,163,854
Government contributions:		
Prescription drug benefits	44,874,408	
Prescription drug administrative expenses	379,536	
Total government contributions		45,253,944
Payments from States		8,324,149
Interest on investments		5,718
Total revenue		$61,747,665
Expenditures:		
Part D benefit payments[1]		$60,564,994
Part D administrative expenses		379,714
Total expenditures		$60,944,708
Net addition to the trust fund		802,957
Total assets of the Part D account in the trust fund, end of period		$834,018

[1]Premiums paid directly to plans are not displayed on Treasury statements and are estimated. These premiums have been added to the benefit payments reported on the Treasury statement to obtain an estimate of total Part D benefits. Direct data on such benefit amounts are not yet available.

Note: Totals do not necessarily equal the sums of rounded components.

Tables V.H4, V.H5, V.H6, V.H7, and V.H8 present estimates of the fiscal year operations of total Medicare, the HI trust fund, the SMI trust fund, the Part B account in the SMI trust fund, and the Part D account in the SMI trust fund, respectively. These tables correspond to the calendar-year trust fund operation tables shown in section V.B and in section III.

Table V.H4.—Total Medicare Income, Expenditures, and Trust Fund Assets during Fiscal Years 1970-2022

[In billions]

Fiscal year	Total income	Total expenditures	Net change in assets	Assets at end of year
Historical data:				
1970	$7.5	$7.1	$0.3	$2.7
1975	16.9	14.8	2.1	11.3
1980	35.7	35.0	0.7	19.0
1985	75.5	71.4	4.1	31.9
1990	125.7	109.7	16.0	110.2
1995	173.0	180.1	−7.1	143.4
2000	248.9	219.3	29.6	214.0
2005	349.4	336.9	12.5	294.6
2006	422.3	380.5	41.8	336.4
2007	457.1	434.8	22.2	358.7
2008	474.6	455.1	19.5	378.1
2009	491.5	498.3	−6.8	371.4
2010	500.7	521.2	−20.5	350.9
2011	528.0	560.3	−32.3	318.6
2012	532.6	550.0	−17.5	301.2
Intermediate es imates:				
2013	561.2	589.2	−27.9	273.2
2014	602.2	607.2	−5.0	268.2
2015	654.0	634.5	19.5	287.7
2016	710.7	693.3	17.4	305.1
2017	758.6	721.6	37.0	342.1
2018	810.9	760.2	50.7	392.9
2019	879.0	838.5	40.5	433.4
2020	943.1	904.7	38.4	471.8
2021	1,015.9	976.6	39.3	511.1
2022	1,105.4	1,092.1	13.3	524.4

Note: Totals do not necessarily equal the sums of rounded components.

Table V.H5.—Operations of the HI Trust Fund during Fiscal Years 1970-2022

[In billions]

Fiscal year[1]	Income								Expenditures			Trust fund	
	Payroll taxes	Income from taxation of benefits	Railroad Retirement account transfers	Reimbursement for uninsured persons	Premiums from voluntary enrollees	Payments for military wage credits	Interest and other[2,3]	Total	Benefit payments[3,4]	Administrative expenses[5]	Total	Net change	Balance at end of year
Historical data:													
1970	$4.8	—	$0.1	$0.6	—	$0.0	$0.1	$5.6	$4.8	$0.1	$5.0	$0.7	$2.7
1975	11.3	—	0.1	0.5	$0.0	0.0	0.6	12.6	10.4	0.3	10.6	2.0	9.9
1980	23.2	—	0.2	0.7	0.0	0.1	1.1	25.4	23.8	0.5	24.3	1.1	14.5
1985	46.5	—	0.4	0.8	0.1	0.1	3.2	50.9	47.8	0.8	48.7	4.1[6]	21.3
1990	70.7	—	0.4	0.4	0.1	0.1	7.9	79.6	65.9	0.8	66.7	12.9	95.6
1995	98.1	$3.9	0.4	0.5	1.0	0.1	11.0	114.8	113.6	1.3	114.9	-0.0	129.5
2000	137.7	8.8	0.5	0.5	1.4	0.0	10.8	159.7	127.9[7]	2.4	130.3	29.4	168.1
2005	169.0	8.8	0.4	0.3	2.3	0.0	16.2	196.9	181.3	2.9	184.1	12.8	277.7
2006	180.4	10.3	0.5	0.4	2.6	0.0	16.1	210.3	181.8	3.1	184.9	25.4	303.1
2007	188.0	10.6	0.5	0.5	2.8	0.0	16.9	219.2	200.2	2.6	202.8	16.4	319.5
2008	197.2	11.7	0.5	0.5	2.9	0.0	16.9	229.7	227.0[8]	3.2	230.2	-0.5	319.0
2009	194.1	12.4	0.5	0.6	2.8	1.0[9]	17.5	228.9	234.7	3.3	238.0	-9.1	309.9
2010	183.6	13.8	0.5	-0.1	3.3	0.0	16.9	218.0	245.6	3.3	249.0	-31.0	278.9
2011	192.1	15.1	0.5	0.3	3.3	0.0	15.3	226.5	255.7	3.9	259.6	-33.1	245.8
2012	204.8	18.6	0.5	0.3	3.4	0.0	14.2	241.7	254.5	3.7	258.2	-16.4	229.4
Intermediate estimates:													
2013	211.6	14.7	0.5	0.2	3.5	0.0	13.3	243.8	265.1	3.9	269.0	-25.2	204.2
2014	224.8	18.2	0.5	0.2	3.5	0.0	12.6	259.8	270.4	4.1	274.4	-14.6	189.6
2015	243.2	21.0	0.6	0.2	3.5	0.0	12.5	281.0	276.4	4.5	280.9	0.1	189.7
2016	263.2	23.6	0.6	0.2	3.7	0.0	13.3	304.5	297.5	5.0	302.5	2.0	191.7
2017	280.4	26.1	0.6	0.2	3.9	0.0	14.2	325.3	309.5	5.6	315.1	10.2	201.9
2018	298.7	28.7	0.6	0.2	4.1	0.0	15.4	347.7	328.0	6.1	334.1	13.6	215.4
2019	315.6	32.4	0.7	0.2	4.4	0.0	16.6	369.8	355.6	6.6	362.1	7.7	223.1
2020	330.0	35.1	0.7	0.2	4.6	0.0	17.5	388.1	380.0	7.0	387.0	1.0	224.2
2021	348.4	39.2	0.7	0.2	4.9	0.0	18.1	411.5	407.2	7.6	414.7	-3.3	220.9
2022	365.6	42.4	0.7	0.1	5.3	0.0	18.0	432.2	447.7	8.3	456.0	-23.8	197.0

[1] Fiscal years 1970 and 1975 consist of the 12 months ending on June 30 of each year; fiscal years 1980 and later consist of the 12 months ending on September 30 of each year.

[2] Other income includes recoveries of amounts reimbursed from the trust fund that are not obligations of the trust fund, receipts from the fraud and abuse control program, and a small amount of miscellaneous income. In 2008, includes an adjustment of –$0.9 billion for interest inadvertently earned as a result of Part A hospice costs that were misallocated to the Part B trust fund account.

[3] See footnote 2 of table III.B4.

[4] Includes costs of Peer Review Organizations from 1983 through 2001 (beginning with the implementation of the prospective payment system on October 1, 1983) and costs of Quality Improvement Organizations beginning in 2002.

[5] Includes costs of experiments and demonstration projects. Beginning in 1997, includes fraud and abuse control expenses, as provided for by the Health Insurance Portability and Accountability Act of 1996 (Public Law 104-191).

[6] Includes repayment of loan principal, from the OASI trust fund, of $1.8 billion.

[7] For 1998 to 2003, includes monies transferred to the SMI trust fund for home health agency costs, as provided for by the Balanced Budget Act of 1997 (Public Law 105-33).

[8] Includes the $8.5 billion transferred to the general fund of the Treasury for Part A hospice costs that were previously misallocated to the Part B trust fund account.

[9] Includes he lump-sum general revenue adjustment of $1.0 billion, as provided for by section 151 of the Social Security Amendments of 1983 (Public Law 98-21).

Note: Totals do not necessarily equal the sums of rounded components.

Table V.H6.—Operations of the SMI Trust Fund (Cash Basis) during Fiscal Years 1970-2022

[In billions]

		Income					Expenditures			Trust fund	
Fiscal year[1]	Premium income	General revenue[2]	Transfers from States	Interest and other[3,4]	Total	Benefit payments[4,5]	Adminis-trative expense	Total	Net change	Balance at end of year[6]
Historical data:											
1970	$0.9	$0.9	—	$0.0	$1.9	$2.0	$0.2	$2.2	−$0.3	$0.1
1975	1.9	2.3	—	0.1	4.3	3.8	0.4	4.2	0.2	1.4
1980	2.9	6.9	—	0.4	10.3	10.1	0.6	10.7	−0.5	4.5
1985	5.5	17.9	—	1.2	24.6	21.8	0.9	22.7	1.8	10.6
1990	11.5[7]	33.2	—	1.4[7]	46.1[7]	41.5	1.5[7]	43.0[7]	3.1[7]	14.5[7]
1995	19.2	37.0	—	1.9	58.2	63.5	1.7	65.2	−7.0	13.9
2000	20.5	65.6	—	3.2	89.2	87.2[8]	1.8	89.0	0.2	45.9
2005	35.9	115.2	—	1.4	152.5	149.8	2.9	152.7	−0.2	16.9
2006	44.2	162.6	$3.6	1.5	212.0	192.1	3.5	195.6	16.4	33.3
2007	49.7	179.2	7.0	2.1	237.9	228.6	3.4	232.0	5.9	39.1
2008	54.2	180.4	7.0	3.2	244.9	221.4[9]	3.4	224.9	20.0	59.1
2009	57.7	194.3	7.5	3.1	262.6	256.9	3.3	260.3	2.3	61.5
2010	61.4	213.7	4.5	3.2	282.7	268.7	3.5	272.2	10.5	72.0
2011	64.5	225.2	6.5	5.3	301.5	296.8	3.8	300.7	0.9	72.8
2012	66.1	210.5	8.3	6.0	290.8	287.8	4.1	291.9	−1.0	71.8
Intermediate es imates:											
2013	72.3	231.0	8.6	5.6	317.4	316.5	3.6	320.1	−2.7	69.0
2014	75.5	252.2	8.7	5.9	342.3	328.9	3.8	332.7	9.6	78.7
2015	81.8	275.5	8.9	6.7	373.0	349.4	4.2	353.6	19.4	98.0
2016	89.8	299.0	9.5	7.9	406.3	386.2	4.6	390.8	15.4	113.4
2017	99.2	313.5	10.1	10.4	433.3	401.3	5.1	406.5	26.8	140.2
2018	109.4	330.7	10.9	12.2	463.2	420.4	5.6	426.0	37.2	177.4
2019	119.9	364.7	11.7	12.9	509.2	470.3	6.0	476.3	32.9	210.3
2020	128.6	398.6	12.7	15.0	555.0	511.2	6.5	517.6	37.4	247.7
2021	139.4	433.7	13.9	17.4	604.4	555.0	6.9	561.8	42.6	290.2
2022	153.1	485.0	15.2	20.1	673.3	628.4	7.6	636.1	37.2	327.4

[1]Fiscal years 1970 and 1975 consist of the 12 mon hs ending on June 30 of each year; fiscal years 1980 and later consist of the 12 months ending on September 30 of each year.

[2]Includes Part B general fund matching payments, Part D subsidy costs, and certain interest-adjustment items.

[3]Other income includes recoveries of amounts reimbursed from the trust fund that are not obliga ions of he trust fund and other miscellaneous income. In 2008, includes an adjustment of $0.8 billion for interest inadvertently earned as a result of Part A hospice costs that were misallocated to the Part B trust fund account.

[4]See footnote 2 of table III.B4.

[5]See footnote 3 of table III.B4.

[6]The financial status of SMI depends on both the assets and the liabilities of the trust fund (see table III.C8).

[7]Includes the impact of the Medicare Catastrophic Coverage Act of 1988 (Public Law 100-360).

[8]Benefit payments less monies transferred from the HI trust fund for home health agency costs, as provided for by the Balanced Budget Act of 1997.

[9]Benefits shown for 2008 are lower by the $8.5 billion transferred from the general fund of the Treasury to reimburse Part B for Part A hospice costs hat were previously misallocated to the Part B trust fund account.

Note: Totals do not necessarily equal the sums of rounded components.

Table V.H7.—Operations of the Part B Account in the SMI Trust Fund (Cash Basis) during Fiscal Years 1970-2022

[In billions]

Fiscal year[1]	Income Premium income	Income General revenue[2]	Income Interest and o her[3,4]	Income Total	Expenditures Benefit payments[4,5]	Expenditures Adminis- trative expense	Expenditures Total	Account Net change	Account Balance at end of year[6]
Historical data:									
1970	$0.9	$0.9	$0.0	$1.9	$2.0	$0.2	$2.2	−$0.3	$0.1
1975	1.9	2.3	0.1	4.3	3.8	0.4	4.2	0.2	1.4
1980	2.9	6.9	0.4	10.3	10.1	0.6	10.7	−0.5	4.5
1985	5.5	17.9	1.2	24.6	21.8	0.9	22.7	1.8	10.6
1990	11.5[	33.2	1.4[	46.1[	41.5	1.5[	43.0[	3.1[	14.5[
1995	19.2	37.0	1.9	58.2	63.5	1.7	65.2	−7.0	13.9
2000	20.5	65.6	3.2	89.2	87.2[8]	1.8	89.0	0.2	45.9
2005	35.9	114.0	1.4	151.3	148.6	2.9	151.5	−0.2	16.9
2006	41.6	134.3	1.5	177.4	158.3	3.3	161.6	15.7	32.6
2007	45.7	137.8	2.0	185.6	177.2	2.4	179.7	6.0	38.6
2008	49.4	144.9	3.2	197.5	174.7[9]	3.0	177.7	19.8	58.3
2009	51.9	150.7	3.1	205.7	200.3	3.1	203.4	2.3	60.6
2010	54.8	161.1	3.2	219.0	205.1	3.3	208.4	10.7	71.3
2011	57.0	168.8	5.3	231.2	226.2	3.4	229.6	1.5	72.8
2012	57.9	165.3	6.0	229.1	227.2	3.8	230.9	−1.8	70.9
Intermediate es imates:									
2013	62.8	179.6	5.6	247.9	247.3	3.3	250.6	−2.6	68.3
2014	64.4	192.4	5.9	262.7	249.6	3.5	253.1	9.6	77.9
2015	69.0	207.4	6.7	283.1	260.0	3.8	263.8	19.3	97.3
2016	75.4	222.0	7.9	305.3	284.9	4.2	289.1	16.2	113.4
2017	83.1	236.2	10.4	329.7	298.2	4.7	302.9	26.8	140.2
2018	91.5	253.2	12.2	356.9	315.6	5.1	320.7	36.2	176.5
2019	100.2	273.2	12.8	386.2	347.9	5.5	353.4	32.8	209.3
2020	107.0	297.9	15.0	419.8	376.6	5.9	382.6	37.3	246.5
2021	115.7	323.8	17.3	456.9	408.1	6.3	414.4	42.5	289.0
2022	127.1	354.6	20.0	501.8	456.4	7.1	463.4	38.4	327.4

[1]Fiscal years 1970 and 1975 consist of the 12 mon hs ending on June 30 of each year; fiscal years 1980 and later consist of the 12 months ending on September 30 of each year.
[2]General fund matching payments, plus certain interest-adjustment items.
[3]Other income includes recoveries of amounts reimbursed from the trust fund that are not obliga ions of he trust fund and other miscellaneous income. In 2008, includes an adjustment of $0.8 billion for interest earned as a result of Part A hospice costs that were misallocated to the Part B trust fund account.
[4]See footnote 2 of table III.B4.
[5]See footnote 3 of table III.B4.
[6]The financial status of Part B depends on both the assets and the liabilities of the trust fund (see table III.C8).
[7]Includes the impact of the Medicare Catastrophic Coverage Act of 1988 (Public Law 100-360).
[8]Benefit payments less monies transferred from the HI trust fund for home health agency costs, as provided for by the Balanced Budget Act of 1997.
[9]Benefits shown for 2008 are lower by the $8.5 billion transferred from the general fund of the Treasury to reimburse Part B for Part A hospice costs hat were previously misallocated to the Part B trust fund account.

Note: Totals do not necessarily equal the sums of rounded components.

**Table V.H8.—Operations of the Part D Account in the SMI Trust Fund (Cash Basis)
during Fiscal Years 2004-2022**

[In billions]

Fiscal year	Premium income	General revenue[1]	Transfers from States[2]	Interest and other	Total	Benefit payments[3]	Administrative expense	Total	Net change	Balance at end of year
			Income			Expenditures			Account	
Historical data:										
2004	—	$0.2	—	—	$0.2	$0.2	—	$0.2	—	—
2005	—	1 2	—	—	1.2	1.2	—	1.2	—	—
2006	$2.6	28.3	$3.6	$0.0	34.6	33.7	$0.2	33.9	$0.7	$0.7
2007	3.9	41.4	7.0	0.0	52.3	51.4	1.0	52.4	-0.1	0.6
2008	4.8	35.5	7.0	0.0	47.4	46.8	0.4	47.2	0.2	0.8
2009	5.8	43.5	7.5	0.0	56.9	56.6	0.2	56.8	0.0	0.9
2010	6.6	52.6	4.5	0.0	63.7	63.6	0.3	63.8	-0.2	0.7
2011	7.5	56.3	6.5	0.0	70.4	70.6	0.4	71.0	-0.7	0.0
2012	8.2	45.3	8.3	0.0	61.7	60.6	0.4	60.9	0.8	0.8
Intermediate es imates:										
2013	9.5	51.4	8.6	0.0	69.5	69.2	0.4	69.6	-0.1	0.7
2014	11.1	59.8	8.7	0.0	79.7	79.3	0.4	79.7	0.0	0.7
2015	12.8	68.1	8.9	0.0	89.9	89.5	0.4	89.9	0.0	0.8
2016	14.4	77.0	9.5	0.0	100.9	101.3	0.4	101.7	-0.8	0.0
2017	16.1	77.3	10.1	0.0	103.5	103.1	0.5	103.5	0.0	0.0
2018	17.9	77.5	10.9	0.0	106.3	104.9	0.5	105.3	0.9	0.9
2019	19.8	91.5	11.7	0.0	123.0	122.4	0.5	122.9	0.1	1.0
2020	21.7	100.7	12.7	0.0	135.2	134.6	0.5	135.1	0.1	1.1
2021	23.7	109 9	13.9	0.0	147.5	146.8	0.5	147.4	0.1	1.2
2022	26.0	130 3	15.2	0.0	171.5	172.1	0.6	172.7	-1.2	—

[1]Includes all government transfers including amounts for the general subsidy, reinsurance, employer drug subsidy, low-income subsidy, administrative expenses, risk sharing, and State expenses for making low-income eligibility determinations. Includes amounts for the Transitional Assistance program of $0.2, $1.1, and $0.2 billion in 2004-2006, respectively.

[2]See footnote 3 of table III.D3.

[3]Includes payments to plans, subsidies to employer re iree prescription drug plans, payments to States for making low-income eligibility determina ions, and Part D drug premiums collected from beneficiaries and transferred to Medicare Advantage plans and private drug plans. Includes amounts for the Transitional Assistance program of $0.2, $1.1, and $0.2 billion in 2004-2006, respectively.

Note: Totals do not necessarily equal the sums of rounded components.

Table V.H9 shows the total assets of the HI trust fund and their distribution by interest rate and maturity date at the end of fiscal years 2011 and 2012. The assets at the end of fiscal year 2012 totaled $244.2 billion: $228.3 billion in the form of U.S. Government obligations and an undisbursed balance of $15.9 billion.

Table V.H9.—Assets of the HI Trust Fund, by Type, at the End of Fiscal Years 2011 and 2012[1]

	September 30, 2011	September 30, 2012
Investments in public-debt obligations sold only to the trust funds (special issues):		
Certificates of indebtedness:		
1.375-percent, 2012	—	8,098,001,000.00
1.875-percent, 2012	1,145,114,000.00	—
Bonds:		
3.250-percent, 2023-2024	18,380,800,000.00	18,380,800,000.00
3.500-percent, 2014	1,491,940,000.00	—
3.500-percent, 2015-2018	21,493,628,000.00	21,493,628,000.00
4.000-percent, 2014	1,201,235,000.00	—
4.000-percent, 2015-2023	31,498,599,000.00	31,498,599,000.00
4.125-percent, 2014	986,225,000.00	—
4.125-percent, 2014-2020	23,735,345,000.00	23,735,345,000.00
4.625-percent, 2014	977,469,000.00	—
4.625-percent, 2015-2019	21,727,836,000.00	21,727,836,000.00
5.000-percent, 2014	979,723,000.00	—
5.000-percent, 2015-2022	27,545,546,000.00	27,545,546,000.00
5.125-percent, 2014	903,572,000.00	—
5.125-percent, 2015-2021	25,129,164,000.00	25,129,164,000.00
5.250-percent, 2014	2,028,429,000.00	—
5.250-percent, 2015-2017	19,228,105,000.00	19,228,105,000.00
5.625-percent, 2014	2,537,725,000.00	—
5.625-percent, 2015-2016	15,857,854,000.00	15,857,854,000.00
6.000-percent, 2013	5,781,094,000.00	—
6.000-percent, 2014	7,775,380,000.00	1,807,985,000.00
6.500-percent, 2013	1,745,156,000.00	—
6.500-percent, 2014-2015	13,789,424,000.00	13,789,424,000.00
Total investments	$245,939,363,000.00	$228,292,287,000.00
Undisbursed balance[2]	−142,061,093.98	15,897,108,653.58
Total assets	$245,797,301,906.02	$244,189,395,653.58

[1]Certificates of indebtedness and bonds are carried at par value, which is the same as book value.
[2]Nega ive figures represent an extension of credit against securities to be redeemed within he following few days.

The effective annual rate of interest earned by the assets of the HI trust fund during the 12 months ending on December 31, 2012 was 4.6 percent. Interest on special issues is paid semiannually on June 30 and December 31. The interest rate on public-debt obligations issued for purchase by the trust fund in June 2012 was 1.375 percent, payable semiannually.

Table V.H10 shows a comparison of the total assets of the SMI trust fund, Parts B and D combined, and their distribution at the end of fiscal years 2011 and 2012. At the end of 2012, assets totaled $71.8 billion: $69.3 billion in the form of U.S. Government obligations and an undisbursed balance of $2.5 billion.

Table V.H10.—Assets of the SMI Trust Fund, by Type, at the End of Fiscal Years 2011 and 2012[1]

	September 30, 2011	September 30, 2012
Investments in public-debt obligations sold only to the trust funds (special issues):		
Certificates of indebtedness:		
1.250-percent, 2013	—	3,905,872,000.00
Bonds:		
2.500-percent, 2014	563,904,000.00	—
2.500-percent, 2015-2026	11,508,113,000.00	11,508,113,000.00
2.875-percent, 2014	488,228,000.00	—
2.875-percent, 2015-2025	9,623,531,000.00	9,623,531,000.00
3.250-percent, 2014	337,422,000.00	—
3.250-percent, 2015-2024	7,289,830,000.00	7,289,830,000.00
4.000-percent, 2014	882,474,000.00	—
4.000-percent, 2015-2023	13,522,056,000.00	13,522,056,000.00
5.000-percent, 2017-2022	14,896,093,000.00	14,896,093,000.00
5.125-percent, 2015-2017	1,669,336,000.00	1,669,336,000.00
5.250-percent, 2016	297,753,000.00	297,753,000.00
5.625-percent, 2016	1,822,107,000.00	1,822,107,000.00
5.875-percent, 2013	972,590,000.00	—
6.000-percent, 2013	470,259,000.00	—
6.000-percent, 2014	2,991,887,000.00	1,715,335,000.00
6.500-percent, 2013	36,288,000.00	—
6.500-percent, 2014-2015	3,074,382,000.00	3,074,382,000.00
Total investments	$70,446,253,000.00	$69,324,408,000.00
Undisbursed balance	2,380,328,755.79	2,458,929,972.36
Total assets	$72,826,581,755.79	$71,783,337,972.36

[1]Certificates of indebtedness and bonds are carried at par value, which is the same as book value.

The effective annual rate of interest earned by the assets of the SMI trust fund for the 12 months ending on December 31, 2012 was 3.5 percent. Interest on special issues is paid semiannually on June 30 and December 31. The interest rate on special issues purchased by the account in June 2012 was 1.375 percent, payable semiannually.

I. GLOSSARY

Accountable care organizations (ACOs). Groups of clinicians, hospitals, and other health care providers that choose to come together to deliver coordinated, high-quality care to the Medicare patients they serve.

Actuarial balance. The difference between the summarized income rate and the summarized cost rate over a given valuation period.

Actuarial deficit. A negative actuarial balance.

Actuarial rates. One-half of the Part B expected monthly benefit and administrative costs for each aged enrollee adjusted for interest earned on the Part B account assets attributable to aged enrollees and a contingency margin (for the aged actuarial rate), and one-half of the expected monthly benefit and administrative costs for each disabled enrollee adjusted for interest earned on the Part B account assets attributable to disabled enrollees and a contingency margin (for the disabled actuarial rate), for the duration the rate is in effect.

Actuarial status. A measure of the adequacy of the financing as determined by the difference between assets and liabilities at the end of the periods for which financing was established.

Administrative expenses. Expenses incurred by the Department of Health and Human Services and the Department of the Treasury in administering HI and SMI and the provisions of the Internal Revenue Code relating to the collection of contributions. Such administrative expenses, which are paid from the HI and SMI trust funds, include expenditures for contractors to determine costs of, and make payments to, providers, as well as salaries and expenses of the Centers for Medicare & Medicaid Services.

Aged enrollee. An individual, aged 65 or over, who is enrolled in HI or SMI.

Allowed charge. Individual charge determined by a carrier for a covered Part B medical service or supply.

Annual out-of-pocket threshold. The amount of out-of-pocket expenses that must be paid for prescription drugs before significantly reduced Part D beneficiary cost sharing is effective. Amounts paid by a third-party insurer are not included in testing this threshold, but amounts paid by State or Federal assistance programs are included.

Assets. Treasury notes and bonds guaranteed by the Federal Government, and cash held by the trust funds for investment purposes.

Assumptions. Values relating to future trends in certain key factors that affect the balance in the trust funds. Demographic assumptions include fertility, mortality, net immigration, marriage, divorce, retirement patterns, disability incidence and termination rates, and changes in the labor force. Economic assumptions include unemployment, average earnings, inflation, interest rates, and productivity. Three sets of economic assumptions are presented in the Trustees Report:

(1) The low-cost alternative, with relatively rapid economic growth, low inflation, and favorable (from the standpoint of program financing) demographic conditions;
(2) The intermediate assumptions, which represent the Trustees' best estimates of likely future economic and demographic conditions; and
(3) The high-cost alternative, with slow economic growth, more rapid inflation, and financially disadvantageous demographic conditions.

See also "Hospital assumptions."

Average market yield. A computation that is made on all marketable interest-bearing obligations of the United States. It is computed on the basis of market quotations as of the end of the calendar month immediately preceding the date of such issue.

Baby boom. The period from the end of World War II through the mid-1960s marked by unusually high birth rates.

Base estimate. The updated estimate of the most recent historical year.

Beneficiary. A person enrolled in HI or SMI. See also "Aged enrollee" and "Disabled enrollee."

Benefit payments. The amounts disbursed for covered services after the deductible and coinsurance amounts have been deducted.

Benefit period. An alternate name for "spell of illness."

Board of Trustees. A Board established by the Social Security Act to oversee the financial operations of the Federal Hospital Insurance

Trust Fund and the Federal Supplementary Medical Insurance Trust Fund. The Board is composed of six members, four of whom serve automatically by virtue of their positions in the Federal Government: the Secretary of the Treasury, who is the Managing Trustee; the Secretary of Labor; the Secretary of Health and Human Services; and the Commissioner of Social Security. Two other members are public representatives who are appointed by the President and confirmed by the Senate. Charles P. Blahous III and Robert D. Reischauer began serving on September 17, 2010. The Administrator of the Centers for Medicare & Medicaid Services (CMS) serves as Secretary of the Board of Trustees.

Bond. A certificate of ownership of a specified portion of a debt due by the Federal Government to holders, bearing a fixed rate of interest.

Callable. Subject to redemption upon notice, as is a bond.

Carrier. A private or public organization under contract to CMS to administer the Part B benefits under Medicare. Also referred to as "contractors," these organizations determine coverage and benefit amounts payable and make payments to physicians, suppliers, and beneficiaries.

Case mix index. A relative weight that captures the average complexity of certain Medicare services.

Cash basis. The costs of the service when payment was made rather than when the service was performed.

Certificate of indebtedness. A short-term certificate of ownership (12 months or less) of a specified portion of a debt due by the Federal Government to individual holders, bearing a fixed rate of interest.

Closed-group population. Includes all persons currently participating in the program as either taxpayers or beneficiaries, or both. See also "Open-group population."

Coinsurance. Portion of the costs for covered services paid by the beneficiary after meeting the annual deductible. See also "Hospital coinsurance" and "SNF coinsurance."

Consumer Price Index (CPI). A measure of the average change in prices over time in a fixed group of goods and services. In this report, all references to the CPI relate to the CPI for Urban Wage Earners and Clerical Workers (CPI-W).

Contingency. Funds included in the SMI Part B trust fund account to serve as a cushion in case actual expenditures are higher than those projected at the time financing was established. Since the financing is set prospectively, actual experience may be different from the estimates used in setting the financing.

Contingency margin. An amount included in the actuarial rates to provide for changes in the contingency level in the SMI Part B trust fund account. Positive margins increase the contingency level, and negative margins decrease it.

Contribution base. See "Maximum tax base."

Contributions. See "Payroll taxes."

Cost rate. The ratio of HI cost (or outgo or expenditures) on an incurred basis during a given year to the taxable payroll for the year. In this context, the outgo is defined to exclude benefit payments and administrative costs for those uninsured persons for whom payments are reimbursed from the general fund of the Treasury, and for voluntary enrollees, who pay a premium to be enrolled.

Covered earnings. Earnings in employment covered by HI.

Covered employment. All employment and self-employment creditable for Social Security purposes. Almost every kind of employment and self-employment is covered under HI. In a few employment situations—for example, religious orders under a vow of poverty, foreign affiliates of American employers, or State and local governments—coverage must be elected by the employer. However, effective July 1991, coverage is mandatory for State and local employees who are not participating in a public employee retirement system. All new State and local employees have been covered since April 1986. In a few situations—for instance, ministers or self-employed members of certain religious groups—workers can opt out of coverage. Covered employment for HI includes all Federal employees (whereas covered employment for OASDI includes some, but not all, Federal employees).

Covered Part D drugs. Prescription drugs covered under the Medicaid program plus insulin-related supplies and smoking cessation agents. Drugs covered in Parts A and B of Medicare will continue to be covered there, rather than in Part D.

Covered services. Services for which HI or SMI pays, as defined and limited by statute. Covered HI services are provided by hospitals (inpatient care), skilled nursing facilities, home health agencies, and hospices. Covered SMI Part B services include most physician services, care in outpatient departments of hospitals, diagnostic tests, durable medical equipment, ambulance services, and other health services that are not covered by HI. See "Covered Part D drugs" for SMI Part D.

Covered worker. A person who has earnings creditable for Social Security purposes on the basis of services for wages in covered employment and/or on the basis of income from covered self-employment. The number of HI covered workers is slightly larger than the number of OASDI covered workers because of different coverage status for Federal employment. See "Covered employment."

Creditable prescription drug coverage. Prescription drug coverage that meets or exceeds the actuarial value of Part D coverage provided through a group health plan or otherwise.

Dedicated financing sources. The sum of HI payroll taxes, HI share of income taxes on Social Security benefits, Part D State transfers, and beneficiary premiums. This amount is used in the test of excess general revenue Medicare funding.

Deductible. The annual amount payable by the beneficiary for covered services before Medicare makes reimbursement. See also "Inpatient hospital deductible."

Deemed wage credit. See "Non-contributory or deemed wage credits."

Demographic assumptions. See "Assumptions."

Diagnosis-related groups (DRGs). A classification system that groups patients according to diagnosis, type of treatment, age, and other relevant criteria. Under the inpatient hospital prospective payment system, hospitals are paid a set fee for treating patients in a single DRG category, regardless of the actual cost of care for the individual.

Direct subsidy. The amount paid to the prescription drug plans representing the difference between the plan's risk-adjusted bid and the beneficiary premium for basic coverage.

Disability. For Social Security purposes, the inability to engage in substantial gainful activity by reason of any medically determinable physical or mental impairment that can be expected to result in death or to last for a continuous period of not less than 12 months. Special rules apply for workers aged 55 or older whose disability is based on blindness. The law generally requires that a person be disabled continuously for 5 months before he or she can qualify for a disabled-worker cash benefit. An additional 24 months is necessary to qualify for benefits under Medicare.

Disability Insurance (DI). See "Old-Age, Survivors, and Disability Insurance (OASDI)."

Disabled enrollee. An individual under age 65 who has been entitled to disability benefits under Title II of the Social Security Act or the Railroad Retirement system for at least 2 years and who is enrolled in HI or SMI.

DRG Coding. The DRG categories used by hospitals on discharge billing. See also "Diagnosis-related groups (DRGs)."

Durable medical equipment (DME). Items such as iron lungs, oxygen tents, hospital beds, wheelchairs, and seat lift mechanisms that are used in the patient's home and are either purchased or rented.

Earnings. Unless otherwise qualified, all wages from employment and net earnings from self-employment, whether or not taxable or covered.

Economic assumptions. See "Assumptions."

Economic stabilization program. A legislative program during the early 1970s that limited price increases.

Employer subsidy. The amount paid to the sponsors of qualifying employment-based retiree prescription drug plans. This amount subsidizes a portion of actual drug expenditures between specified coverage limits and is determined without regard to actual employer plan payments.

End-stage renal disease (ESRD). Permanent kidney failure.

Extended care services. In the context of this report, an alternate name for "skilled nursing facility services."

Fallback prescription drug plan. Prescription drug coverage provided by plans bearing no risk. One fallback plan will be approved in regions that do not have a choice of at least two at-risk plans.

Federal Insurance Contributions Act (FICA). Provision authorizing taxes on the wages of employed persons to provide for OASDI and HI. The tax is paid in equal amounts by covered workers and their employers.

Financial interchange. Provisions of the Railroad Retirement Act providing for transfers between the trust funds and the Social Security Equivalent Benefit Account of the Railroad Retirement program in order to place each trust fund in the same position as if railroad employment had always been covered under Social Security.

Fiscal year. The accounting year of the U.S. Government. Since 1976, each fiscal year has begun October 1 of the prior calendar year and ended the following September 30. For example, fiscal year 2013 began October 1, 2012 and will end September 30, 2013.

Fixed capital assets. The net worth of facilities and other resources.

Frequency distribution. An exhaustive list of possible outcomes for a variable, and the associated probability of each outcome. The sum of the probabilities of all possible outcomes from a frequency distribution is 100 percent.

General fund of the Treasury. Funds held by the U.S. Treasury, other than revenue collected for a specific trust fund (such as HI or SMI) and maintained in a separate account for that purpose. The majority of this fund is derived from individual and business income taxes.

General revenue. Income to the HI and SMI trust funds from the general fund of the Treasury. Only a very small percentage of total HI trust fund income each year is attributable to general revenue.

Gramm-Rudman-Hollings Act. The Balanced Budget and Emergency Deficit Control Act of 1985.

Gross Domestic Product (GDP). The total dollar value of all goods and services produced in a year in the United States, regardless of who supplies the labor or property.

High-cost alternative. See "Assumptions."

Home health agency (HHA). A public agency or private organization that is primarily engaged in providing the following services in the home: skilled nursing services, other therapeutic services (such as physical, occupational, or speech therapy), and home health aide services.

Hospice. A provider of care for the terminally ill; delivered services generally include home health care, nursing care, physician services, medical supplies, and short-term inpatient hospital care.

Hospital assumptions. These include differentials between hospital labor and non-labor indices compared with general economy labor and non-labor indices; rates of admission incidence; the trend toward treating less complicated cases in outpatient settings; and continued improvement in DRG coding.

Hospital coinsurance. For the 61st through 90th day of hospitalization in a benefit period, a daily amount for which the beneficiary is responsible, equal to one-fourth of the inpatient hospital deductible; for lifetime reserve days, a daily amount for which the beneficiary is responsible, equal to one-half of the inpatient hospital deductible (see "Lifetime reserve days").

Hospital input price index. An alternate name for "hospital market basket."

Hospital Insurance (HI). The Medicare trust fund that covers specified inpatient hospital services, posthospital skilled nursing care, home health services, and hospice care for aged and disabled individuals who meet the eligibility requirements. Also known as Medicare Part A.

Hospital market basket. The cost of the mix of goods and services (including personnel costs but excluding nonoperating costs) comprising routine, ancillary, and special care unit inpatient hospital services.

Income rate. The ratio of income from tax revenues on an incurred basis (payroll tax contributions and income from the taxation of OASDI benefits) to the HI taxable payroll for the year.

Incurred basis. The costs based on when the service was performed rather than when the payment was made.

Infinite horizon. The period extending into the indefinite future.

Independent laboratory. A free-standing clinical laboratory meeting conditions for participation in the Medicare program and billing through a carrier.

Initial coverage limit. The amount up to which the coinsurance applies under the standard prescription drug benefit.

Inpatient hospital deductible. An amount of money that is deducted from the amount payable by Medicare Part A for inpatient hospital services furnished to a beneficiary during a spell of illness.

Inpatient hospital services. These services include bed and board, nursing services, diagnostic or therapeutic services, and medical or surgical services.

Interest. A payment for the use of money during a specified period.

Intermediary. A private or public organization that is under contract to CMS to determine costs of, and make payments to, providers for HI and certain SMI Part B services.

Intermediate assumptions. See "Assumptions."

Late enrollment penalty. Additional beneficiary premium amounts for those who either do not enroll in Part D at the first opportunity or fail to maintain other creditable coverage for more than 63 days.

Lifetime reserve days. Under HI, each beneficiary has 60 lifetime reserve days that he or she may opt to use when regular inpatient hospital benefits are exhausted. The beneficiary pays one-half of the inpatient hospital deductible for each lifetime reserve day used.

Long range. The next 75 years.

Low-cost alternative. See "Assumptions."

Low-income beneficiaries. Individuals meeting income and assets tests who are eligible for prescription drug coverage subsidies to help finance premiums and out-of-pocket payments.

Managed care. See "Private Health Plans."

Market basket. See "Hospital market basket."

Maximum tax base. Annual dollar amount above which earnings in employment covered under HI are not taxable. Beginning in 1994, the maximum tax base was eliminated under HI.

Maximum taxable amount of annual earnings. See "Maximum tax base."

Medicare. A nationwide, federally administered health insurance program authorized in 1965 under Title XVIII of the Social Security Act to cover the cost of hospitalization, medical care, and some related services for most people age 65 and over. In 1972, lawmakers extended coverage to people receiving Social Security Disability Insurance payments for 2 years and people with end-stage renal disease. (For beneficiaries whose primary or secondary diagnosis is Amyotrophic Lateral Sclerosis, the 2-year waiting period is waived.) In 2010, people exposed to environmental health hazards within areas under a corresponding emergency declaration became Medicare-eligible. In 2006, prescription drug coverage was added as well. Medicare consists of two separate but coordinated trust funds: Hospital Insurance (HI, or Part A) and Supplementary Medical Insurance (SMI). The SMI trust fund is composed of two separate accounts: the Part B account and the Part D account. Almost all persons who are aged 65 and over or disabled and who are entitled to HI are eligible to enroll in Part B and Part D on a voluntary basis by paying monthly premiums.

Medicare Advantage (formerly called Medicare+Choice). An expanded set of options, established by the Medicare Modernization Act, for the delivery of health care under Medicare. Most Medicare beneficiaries can choose to receive benefits through the original fee-for-service program or through one of the following Medicare Advantage plans: (i) coordinated care plans (such as Health Maintenance Organizations, Provider Sponsored Organizations, and Preferred Provider Organizations); (ii) Medical Savings Account (MSA)/High Deductible plans; (iii) Private Fee-for-Service plans; or (iv) special needs plans.

Medicare Advantage Prescription Drug Plan (MA-PDP). Prescription drug coverage provided by Medicare Advantage plans.

Medicare Advantage ratebook. A set of statutory capitation payment rates, by county, originally used directly to establish payments to private health insurance plans contracting with Medicare. Under current law, the ratebook amounts are used as "benchmarks," against which plan costs are compared in the calculation of plan payments.

Medicare Economic Index (MEI). An index often used in the calculation of the increases in the prevailing charge levels that help to determine allowed charges for physician services. In 1992 and later, this index is considered in connection with the update factor for the physician fee schedule.

Medicare Payment Advisory Commission (MedPAC). A commission established by Congress in the Balanced Budget Act of 1997 to replace the Prospective Payment Assessment Commission and the Physician Payment Review Commission. MedPAC is directed to provide the Congress with advice and recommendations on policies affecting the Medicare program.

Medicare Prescription Drug Account. The separate account within the SMI trust fund to manage revenues and expenditures of the Part D drug benefit.

Medicare Severity-Diagnosis Related Groups (MS-DRGs). A refinement of the Diagnosis Related Group classification system that groups patients according to diagnosis, type of treatment, age, and other relevant criteria. Under the inpatient hospital prospective payment system, hospitals are paid a set fee for treating patients in a single MS-DRG category, regardless of the actual cost of care for the individual.

Military service wage credits. Credits recognizing that military personnel receive other cash payments and wages in kind (such as food and shelter) in addition to their basic pay. Noncontributory wage credits of $160 were provided for each month of active military service from September 16, 1940 through December 31, 1956. For years after 1956, the basic pay of military personnel is covered under the Social Security program on a contributory basis. In addition to contributory credits for basic pay, noncontributory wage credits of $300 were granted for each calendar quarter in which a person received pay for military service from January 1957 through December 1977. Deemed wage credits of $100 were granted for each $300 of military wages, up to a maximum of $1,200 per calendar year, from January 1978 through December 2001. See also "Quinquennial military service determinations and adjustments."

National average monthly bid. The weighted average of all Part D drug bids including all of the bids from PDPs and the drug portion of bids from MA-PDPs.

Noncontributory or deemed wage credits. Wages and wages in kind that were not subject to the HI tax but are deemed as having been. Deemed wage credits exist for the purposes of (i) determining HI eligibility for individuals who might not be eligible for HI coverage without payment of a premium were it not for the deemed wage credits; and (ii) calculating reimbursement due the HI trust fund from the general fund of the Treasury. The first purpose applies in the case of providing coverage to persons during the transitional periods when HI began and when it was expanded to cover Federal employees; both purposes apply in the cases of military service wage credits and deemed wage credits granted for the internment of persons of Japanese ancestry during World War II.

Old-Age, Survivors, and Disability Insurance (OASDI). The Social Security programs that pay for (i) monthly cash benefits to retired-worker (old-age) beneficiaries, their spouses and children, and survivors of deceased insured workers (OASI); and (ii) monthly cash benefits to disabled-worker beneficiaries and their spouses and children, and for providing rehabilitation services to the disabled (DI).

Open-group population. Includes all persons who will ever participate in the program as either taxpayers or beneficiaries, or both. See also "Closed-group population."

Outpatient hospital. Part of the hospital providing services covered by SMI Part B, including services in an emergency room or outpatient clinic, ambulatory surgical procedures, medical supplies such as splints, laboratory tests billed by the hospital, etc.

Part A. The Medicare Hospital Insurance trust fund.

Part A premium. A monthly premium paid by or on behalf of individuals who wish for and are entitled to voluntary enrollment in Medicare HI. These individuals are those who are aged 65 and older, are uninsured for Social Security or Railroad Retirement, and do not otherwise meet the requirements for entitlement to Part A. Disabled individuals who have exhausted other entitlement are also qualified. These individuals are those not now entitled but who have been entitled under section 226(b) of the Act, who continue to have the disabling impairment upon which their entitlement was based, and whose entitlement ended solely because the individuals had earnings that exceeded the substantial gainful activity amount (as defined in section 223(d)(4) of the Act).

Part B. The account within the Medicare Supplementary Medical Insurance trust fund that pays for a portion of the costs of physician services, outpatient hospital services, and other related medical and health services for voluntarily enrolled aged and disabled individuals.

Part B premium. The monthly amount paid by those individuals who have voluntarily enrolled in Part B. Most enrollees pay the standard premium amount, which currently represents approximately 25 percent of the average program costs for an aged beneficiary. Beneficiaries with high income are also required to pay an income-related monthly adjustment amount starting in 2007, and those who enroll late are required to pay a penalty. In addition, beneficiaries who are affected by the hold-harmless provision pay a lower premium. See section V.E for more details about the Part B premium.

Part C. See "Private Health Plans."

Part D. The account within the Medicare Supplementary Medical Insurance trust fund that pays private plans to provide prescription drug coverage.

Pay-as-you-go financing. A financing scheme in which taxes are scheduled to produce just as much income as required to pay current benefits, with trust fund assets built up only to the extent needed to prevent depletion of the fund by random fluctuations.

Payroll taxes. Taxes levied on the gross wages of employees and net earnings of self-employed workers.

PDP regions. Regional areas that are fully serviced by prescription drug plans.

Peer Review Organization (PRO). A group of practicing physicians and other health care professionals paid by the Federal Government to review the care given to Medicare patients. Starting in 2002, these organizations are called Quality Improvement Organizations.

Percentile. A number that corresponds to one of the equal divisions of the range of a variable in a given sample and that characterizes a value of the variable as not exceeded by a specified percentage of all the values in the sample. For example, a score higher than 97 percent of those attained is said to be in the 97th percentile.

Prescription Drug Plans (PDPs). Stand-alone prescription drug plans offered to beneficiaries in traditional fee-for-service Medicare and to beneficiaries in Medicare Advantage plans that do not offer a prescription drug benefit.

Present value. The present value of a future stream of payments is the lump-sum amount that, if invested today, together with interest earnings would be just enough to meet each of the payments as it fell due. At the time of the last payment, the invested fund would be exactly zero.

Private Health Plans. Plans offered by private companies that contract with Medicare to provide coverage for Part A and Part B services. Medicare Advantage plans, cost plans, and Program of All-Inclusive Care for the Elderly (PACE) plans are all private health plans.

Projection error. Degree of variation between estimated and actual amounts.

Prospective payment system (PPS). A method of reimbursement in which Medicare payment is made based on a predetermined, fixed amount. The payment amount for a particular service is derived based on the classification system of that service (for example, DRGs for inpatient hospital services).

Provider. Any organization, institution, or individual who provides health care services to Medicare beneficiaries. Hospitals (inpatient services), skilled nursing facilities, home health agencies, and hospices are the providers of services covered under Medicare Part A. Physicians, ambulatory surgical centers, and outpatient clinics are some of the providers of services covered under Medicare Part B.

Quality Improvement Organization (QIO). See "Peer Review Organization."

Quinquennial military service determination and adjustments. Prior to the Social Security Amendments of 1983, quinquennial determinations (that is, estimates made once every 5 years) were made of the costs arising from the granting of deemed wage credits for military service prior to 1957; annual reimbursements were made from the general fund of the Treasury to the HI trust fund for these costs. The Social Security Amendments of 1983 provided for (i) a lump-sum transfer in 1983 for (a) the costs arising from the pre-1957 wage credits, and (b) amounts equivalent to the HI taxes that would have been paid on the deemed wage credits for military service for 1966 through 1983, inclusive, if such credits had been counted as covered earnings; (ii) quinquennial adjustments to the pre-1957 portion of the 1983 lump-sum transfer; (iii) general fund transfers equivalent to HI taxes on military deemed wage credits for 1984 and later, to be credited to the fund on July 1 of each year; and (iv) adjustments as deemed necessary to any previously transferred amounts representing HI taxes on military deemed wage credits.

Railroad Retirement. A Federal insurance program similar to Social Security designed for workers in the railroad industry. The provisions of the Railroad Retirement Act provide for a system of coordination and financial interchange between the Railroad Retirement program and the Social Security program.

Ratebook. See "Medicare Advantage ratebook."

Real-wage differential. The difference between the percentage increases, before rounding, in (i) the average annual wage in covered employment, and (ii) the average annual CPI.

Reasonable-cost basis. The calculation to determine the reasonable cost incurred by individual providers when furnishing covered services to beneficiaries. The reasonable cost is based on the actual cost of providing such services, including direct and indirect costs of providers, and excluding any costs that are unnecessary in the efficient delivery of services covered by a health insurance program.

Reinsurance subsidy. Payments to the prescription drug plans in the amount of 80 percent of drug expenses that exceed the annual out-of-pocket threshold.

Residual factors. Factors other than price, including volume of services, intensity of services, and age/sex changes.

Risk corridor. Triggers that are set to protect Part D prescription drug plans from unexpected losses and that allow the government to share in unexpected gains.

Self-employment. Operation of a trade or business by an individual or by a partnership in which an individual is a member.

Self-Employment Contributions Act (SECA). Provision authorizing taxes on the net income of most self-employed persons to provide for OASDI and HI.

Sequester. The reduction of funds to be used for benefits or administrative costs from a Federal account, based on the legislated requirements.

Short range. The next 10 years.

Skilled nursing facility (SNF). An institution that is primarily engaged in providing skilled nursing care and related services for residents who require medical or nursing care, or that is engaged in the rehabilitation of injured, disabled, or sick persons.

SNF coinsurance. For the 21st through 100th day of extended care services in a benefit period, a daily amount for which the beneficiary is responsible, equal to one-eighth of the inpatient hospital deductible.

Social Security Act. Public Law 74-271, enacted on August 14, 1935, with subsequent amendments. The Social Security Act consists of 20 titles, four of which have been repealed. The HI and SMI trust funds are authorized by Title XVIII of the Social Security Act.

Special public-debt obligation. Securities of the U.S. Government issued exclusively to the OASI, DI, HI, and SMI trust funds and other Federal trust funds. Sections 1817(c) and 1841(a) of the Social Security Act provide that the public-debt obligations issued for purchase by the HI and SMI trust funds, respectively, shall have maturities fixed with due regard for the needs of the funds. The usual practice in the past has been to spread the holdings of special issues, as of every June 30, so that the amounts maturing in each of the next 15 years are approximately equal. Special public-debt obligations are redeemable at par at any time.

Spell of illness. A period of consecutive days, beginning with the first day on which a beneficiary is furnished inpatient hospital or extended care services, and ending with the close of the first period of 60 consecutive days thereafter in which the beneficiary is in neither a hospital nor a skilled nursing facility.

Standard prescription drug coverage. Part D prescription drug coverage that includes a deductible, coinsurance up to an initial coverage limit, and protection against high out-of-pocket expenditures by having reduced coinsurance provisions for individuals exceeding the out-of-pocket threshold.

Stochastic model. An analysis involving a random variable. For example, a stochastic model may include a frequency distribution for one assumption. From the frequency distribution, possible outcomes for the assumption are selected randomly for use in an illustration.

Summarized cost rate. The ratio of the present value of expenditures to the present value of the taxable payroll for the years in a given period. In this context, the expenditures are on an incurred basis and exclude costs for those uninsured persons for whom payments are reimbursed from the general fund of the Treasury, and for voluntary enrollees, who pay a premium in order to be enrolled. The summarized cost rate includes the cost of reaching and maintaining a "target" trust fund level, known as a contingency fund ratio. Because a trust fund level of about 1 year's expenditures is considered to be an adequate reserve for unforeseen contingencies, the targeted contingency fund ratio used in determining summarized cost rates is 100 percent of annual expenditures. Accordingly, the summarized cost rate is equal to the ratio of (i) the sum of the present value of the outgo during the period, plus the present value of the targeted ending trust fund level, plus the beginning trust fund level, to (ii) the present value of the taxable payroll during the period.

Summarized income rate. The ratio of (i) the present value of the tax revenues incurred during a given period (from both payroll taxes and taxation of OASDI benefits), to (ii) the present value of the taxable payroll for the years in the period.

Supplemental prescription drug coverage. Coverage in excess of the standard prescription drug coverage.

Supplementary Medical Insurance (SMI). The Medicare trust fund composed of the Part B account, the Part D account, and the Transitional Assistance Account. The Part B account pays for a portion of the costs of physician services, outpatient hospital services, and other related medical and health services for voluntarily enrolled aged and disabled individuals. The Part D account pays private plans to provide prescription drug coverage, beginning in 2006. The Transitional Assistance Account paid for transitional assistance under the prescription drug card program in 2004 and 2005.

Sustainable growth rate. A system for establishing goals for the rate of growth in Medicare Part B expenditures for physician services.

Tax rate. The percentage of taxable earnings, up to the maximum tax base, that is paid for the HI tax. Currently, the percentages are 1.45 for employees and employers, each. The self-employed pay 2.9 percent.

Taxable earnings. Taxable wages and/or self-employment income under the prevailing annual maximum taxable limit.

Taxable payroll. A weighted average of taxable wages and taxable self-employment income. When multiplied by the combined employee-employer tax rate, it yields the total amount of taxes incurred by employees, employers, and the self-employed for work during the period.

Taxable self-employment income. Net earnings from self-employment—generally above $400 and below the annual maximum taxable amount for a calendar or other taxable year—less any taxable wages in the same taxable year.

Taxable wages. Wages paid for services rendered in covered employment up to the annual maximum taxable amount.

Taxation of benefits. Beginning in 1994, up to 85 percent of an individual's or a couple's OASDI benefits is potentially subject to Federal income taxation under certain circumstances. The revenue derived from taxation of benefits in excess of 50 percent, up to 85 percent, is allocated to the HI trust fund.

Taxes. See "Payroll taxes."

Term insurance. A type of insurance that is in force for a specified period of time.

Test of Long-Range Close Actuarial Balance. The conditions required to meet this test are as follows: (i) the trust fund satisfies the short-range test of financial adequacy; and (ii) the trust fund ratios stay above zero throughout the 75-year projection period, such that benefits would be payable in a timely manner throughout the period. This test is applied to HI trust fund projections made under the intermediate assumptions.

Test of Short-Range Financial Adequacy. The conditions required to meet this test are as follows: (i) If the trust fund ratio for a fund exceeds 100 percent at the beginning of the projection period, then it must be projected to remain at or above 100 percent throughout the 10-year projection period; (ii) alternatively, if the fund ratio is initially less than 100 percent, it must be projected to reach a level of at least 100 percent within 5 years (and not be depleted at any time during this period), and then remain at or above 100 percent throughout the rest of the 10-year period. This test is applied to HI trust fund projections made under the intermediate assumptions.

Transitional assistance. An interim benefit for 2004 and 2005 that provided up to $600 per year to assist low-income beneficiaries who had no drug insurance coverage with prescription drug purchases. This benefit also paid the enrollment fee in the Medicare Prescription Drug Discount Card program.

Transitional Assistance Account. The separate account within the SMI trust fund that managed revenues and expenditures for the transitional assistance drug benefit in 2004 and 2005.

Trust fund. Separate accounts in the U.S. Treasury, mandated by Congress, whose assets may be used only for a specified purpose. For the HI and SMI trust funds, monies not withdrawn for current benefit payments and administrative expenses are invested in interest-bearing Federal securities, as required by law; the interest earned is also deposited in the trust funds.

Trust fund ratio. A short-range measure of the adequacy of the HI and SMI trust fund level; defined as the assets at the beginning of the year expressed as a percentage of the outgo during the year.

Unit input intensity allowance. The amount added to, or subtracted from, the hospital input price index to yield the prospective payment system update factor.

Valuation period. A period of years that is considered as a unit for purposes of calculating the status of a trust fund.

Voluntary enrollees. Certain individuals, aged 65 or older or disabled, who are not otherwise entitled to Medicare and who opt to obtain coverage under Part A by paying a monthly premium.

Year of depletion. The first year in which a trust fund is unable to pay full benefits when due because the assets of the fund are depleted.

TABLES

FIGURES

J. STATEMENT OF ACTUARIAL OPINION

It is my opinion that (1) the techniques and methodology used herein to evaluate the financial status of the Federal Hospital Insurance Trust Fund and the Federal Supplementary Medical Insurance Trust Fund are based upon sound principles of actuarial practice and are generally accepted within the actuarial profession; and (2) with the important caveats noted below, the principal assumptions used and the resulting actuarial estimates are, individually and in the aggregate, reasonable for the purpose of evaluating the financial status of the trust funds under current law, taking into consideration the past experience and future expectations for the population, the economy, and the program.

In past reports, and again this year, the Board of Trustees has emphasized the strong likelihood that actual Part B expenditures will exceed the projections under current law due to further legislative action to avoid substantial reductions in the Medicare physician fee schedule. While the Part B projections in this report are reasonable in their portrayal of future costs under current law, they are not reasonable as an indication of actual future costs. Current law would require a physician fee reduction of an estimated 24.7 percent on January 1, 2014—an implausible expectation.

Further, while the Affordable Care Act makes important changes to the Medicare program and substantially improves its financial outlook, there is a strong likelihood that certain of these changes will not be viable in the long range. Specifically, the annual price updates for most categories of non-physician health services will be adjusted downward each year by the growth in economy-wide productivity. The best available evidence indicates that most health care providers cannot improve their productivity to this degree for a prolonged period as a result of the labor-intensive nature of these services.

Without unprecedented changes in health care delivery systems and payment mechanisms, the prices paid by Medicare for health services are very likely to fall increasingly short of the costs of providing these services. By the end of the long-range projection period, Medicare prices for hospital, skilled nursing facility, home health, hospice, ambulatory surgical center, diagnostic laboratory, and many other services would be less than half of their level without consideration of the productivity price reductions. Medicare prices would be considerably below the current relative level of Medicaid prices, which have already led to access problems for Medicaid enrollees, and

273

far below the levels paid by private health insurance. Well before that point, Congress would have to intervene to prevent the withdrawal of providers from the Medicare market and the severe problems with beneficiary access to care that would result. Overriding the productivity adjustments, as Congress has done repeatedly in the case of physician payment rates, would lead to substantially higher costs for Medicare in the long range than those projected under current law.

For these reasons, the financial projections shown in this report for Medicare do not represent a reasonable expectation for actual program operations in either the short range (as a result of the unsustainable reductions in physician payment rates) or the long range (because of the strong likelihood that the statutory reductions in price updates for most categories of Medicare provider services will not be viable). I encourage readers to review the "illustrative alternative" projections that are based on more sustainable assumptions for physician and other Medicare price updates. These projections are summarized in appendix V.C of this report, and additional details are available at http://www.cms.gov/Research-Statistics-Data-and-Systems/Statistics-Trends-and-Reports/Reports TrustFunds/Downloads/2013TRAlternativeScenario.pdf.

In 2010, the Board of Trustees convened an independent panel of expert actuaries and economists to consider these issues further and to make recommendations to the Board regarding the most appropriate long-range growth assumptions for Medicare projections. In their final report,[110] the Panel made recommendations for refining the long-range cost growth assumptions for Medicare projections as well as suggesting a number of improvements to the detailed short-range assumptions. The Office of the Actuary concurred with all of the Panel's findings and recommendations and has worked with the Trustees to implement as many of them as possible starting in this report.

Paul Spitalnic
Associate, Society of Actuaries
Member, American Academy of Actuaries
Acting Chief Actuary, Centers for Medicare & Medicaid Services

---

[110]The *"Review of Assumptions and Methods of the Medicare Trustees' Financial Projections"* can be found at http://aspe.hhs.gov/health/reports/2013/MedicareTech/ TechnicalPanelReport2010-2011.pdf.